Audit the Audit

Huishu Wu • Chuan Zhang

Audit the Audit

Redefining the Concept of Audit in the Context of Personal Data Protection

Springer

Huishu Wu
Faculty of Law
University of Montreal
Montreal, QC, Canada

Chuan Zhang
School of Cyberspace Science and Technology
Beijing Institute of Technology
Beijing, Beijing, China

ISBN 978-981-95-2472-3 ISBN 978-981-95-2473-0 (eBook)
https://doi.org/10.1007/978-981-95-2473-0

This Springer imprint is published by the registered company Springer Nature Singapore Pte Ltd.
The registered company address is: 152 Beach Road, #21-01/04 Gateway East, Singapore 189721, Singapore

Preface

With the thrill of digital technology, we are facing a world of a "digital unconscious," where the protection of personal data has long been criticized as a "rituals of protection." Consequently, the regulatory focus shifts to a "data processor-based" approach, wherein data controllers must manifest their compliance for personal data protection purposes, as many data protection laws require.

Audits have long been criticized as "a ritual of verification," originating from the financial sector. Within the personal data protection context, it seems to use complex tools to prescribe a more complicated target. Instead of using a literal interpretation, a functional approach proposes to the notion of an audit. This book arguably states that the audit is, in fact, a control system rather than a "guarantee" method to deliver accountability or transparency. The failure of an audit should be described as a systematic failure instead of collapsing as a precertification tool. This book proposes that compliance audits for personal data protection should be interpreted as a control system that entails the management and legal control.

Saint Laurent, QC, Canada

Huishu Wu

Contents

Acknowledgement

Firstly, I would like to express my sincere gratitude to my supervisor Professor Vincent Gautrais for his academic advice, support and encouragement for this book. His guidance on my research and career is priceless. Besides, I want to thank all the lecturers I have met at the University of Montreal for their contribution to the accumulation of my professional knowledge, our lovely secretaries for their hard work, and our adorable librarians for their affability. And for my dear family members, my father, my mother and my love, your supports always behind me to path my way. I would like also take this opportunities to thank the co-author of this book, Prof. Zhang Chuan for his valuable inputs from technical perspective.

To think, to read and to write makes me fly. I would like to use this opportunities to share my journey of control study and to fly with you, my dear reader.

Huishu Wu

Competing Interests The authors have no competing interests to declare that are relevant to the content of this manuscript.

Abbreviations

AAA	American Accounting Association
ADLM	Abstract Data Lifecycle Model
AICPA	American Institute of Certified Public Accountants
APEC	Asia-Pacific Economic Cooperation
Article 29 of Working Party	A group made up of a representative from the data protection authority of each EU Member State, the European Data Protection Supervisor and the EC.
ASB	Accounting Standards Board
CEN	European Committee for Standardization
CNIL	Commission Nationale de Informatique et des libertes
COBIT	Control Objectives for Information and Related technologies
COSO	Committee of Sponsoring Organizations
CSL	Cybersecurity Law of People's Republic of China
CCPA	California Consumer Privacy Act
DA	Data Subjects
DC	Data Controllers
Directive 95/46/EC	Directive 95/46/EC on the Protection of Individuals regarding the Processing of Personal Data and on the Free Movement of Such Data
DP	Data Processor
DPL	Data protection Laws
DPO	Data Protection Officer
DPBD	Data Protection by Design
DPIA	Data Protection Impact Assessment
DSL	Data Security Law of People's Republic of China
DPA	United Kingdom Data Protection Act
FTC	Federal Trade Commission of United States of America
GAAP	Generally Accepted Accounting Principles

GAAS	Generally Accepted Accounting Standards
GDPR	General Data Protection Regulation
HOP	Standard Operation Protocols
HIPAA	United States Health Insurance Portability and Accountability Act
IAPP	International Association of Privacy Professionals
IAS	International Accreditation Services
IAS	International Accounting standards
IASB	International Accounting Standards Board
ICO	Information Commissioner's Office
IIA	Institute of Internal Auditors
ISO	International Organization for standardization
ITAC	Information Technology Application Control
ITGC	Information Technology General Control
LGPD	Lei Geral de Protecgao de Dados
MCS	Management Control System
NIST	National Institute of Standards and Technology
OECD	Organization for Economic Co-operation and Development
OECD Guidelines	OECD Guidelines on the Protection of Privacy and Trans-border Flows of Personal Data
PDCA	Personal Data Compliance Audit
PDET	Personal Data Enhancing Technologies
PDMS	Personal Data Management System
PDPA	Singapore Personal Data Protection Act
PET	`Privacy Enhancing Technologies
PIA	Privacy Impact Assessment
PIPEDA	Personal Information Protection and Electronic Document Act of Canada
PIPL	Personal Information Protection Law of People's Republic of China
SA	Supervisory Authorities
TET	Transparency Enhancing Technologies
TLA	Swedish Tort Liability Act
UEEA	Uniform Electronic Evidence Act of Canada

Part I
Overview

Chapter 1
Introduction

1.1 Background of Audit

The word audit has become a common term in the business world, and it refers to a process of control to ascertain accountability and reliability. The term "audit" comes from the Latin word "audire," which means "to hear."[1] In the early days, an auditor was a person who listened to the accounts read aloud to check their accuracy. Over time, the concept of audit has evolved, and it is now used to refer to a wide range of activities that go beyond financial records.[2] Audit has always served as a function for individuals or society to monitor conduct or performance to obtain more trustworthy information. As it noted, audit was recognized in late of the nineteenth century. Followed by a large-scale production, joint stock form originated from organizations. Shareholders of the companies naturally be interested in acknowledging accountant's information in support their financial position. As for the consequence, independent person who takes account to check the accuracy of the accountant is needed for shareholders and board of directors.[3] As noted by Lee, he divided the evolution of audit practices into five stages: Prior to 1840; 1840–1920s; 1920s–1960s; 19602–1990s; and 1990s until now.[4] Prior to 1840, although development of audit is not well documented, it was defined as checking activities happened in ancient China, Egypt and Greece.[5] During the period of the 1840s–1920s of

[1] David Flint, Philosophy and principles of auditing: an introduction (Macmillan Education, 1988) at 12.

[2] American Accounting Association & Committee on Basic Auditing Concepts, A statement of basic auditing concepts (Sarasota, Fla.: American Accounting Association, 1973) at 23.

[3] Lee Teck-Heang & Azham Md Ali, "The evolution of auditing: An analysis of the historical development." (Researchgate, 2008) at 3.

[4] *Ibid* at 5.

[5] J S Mackay et al, *A history of accounting and accountants*, (Edinburgh: T.C. & E.C. Jack, 1905) at 74.

H. Wu, C. Zhang, *Audit the Audit*, https://doi.org/10.1007/978-981-95-2473-0_1

Industrial Revolution, regulated by Joint Stock Companies Act, auditors were required to perform complete checking of transactions and the preparation of correct accounts and financial statements, no little attention was paid to the internal control of the company.[6] During the 1920s–1960s, the audit focused on providing credibility to the financial statements. Sampling technically was adopted due to large number of transactions and auditors can't verify all transactions. Auditors started to rely on internal control of the company to facilitate the use of such a research approach.[7] Starting in 1990s, audits expanded beyond the basic financial statement and attest function. The ability of audit to detect fraud is being challenged by high levels of litigation and criticism against the auditors for fraud awareness, risk attention and independence.[8]

Following the development of societal expectations, one critical feature of auditing is independence. Auditors are expected to maintain independence from the organizations they audit to guarantee unbiased and objective findings. This concept is particularly crucial in financial audits, where auditors are tasked with offering an impartial opinion on the accuracy and reliability of financial statements. Another essential feature of auditing is transparency. Auditors are expected to present clear and concise reports on their findings that stakeholders can easily comprehend. This commitment to transparency promotes accountability and ensures that stakeholders are well-informed about the organization's performance and compliance status. Transparency in auditing encompasses various activities aimed at ensuring compliance with regulations, standards, and best practices. Auditing plays a vital role in organizational governance, fostering transparency, accountability, and good governance practices. The concept of independence is pivotal in the audit process, ensuring that auditors deliver unbiased and objective opinions regarding the organization's performance and compliance status.

1.1.1 Meaning of Audit

Many auditors such as Abdel-Qader stated that the aim of the audit has always been a dynamic rather than a static one.[9] The obscurity of auditing processes existed not only because of the information asymmetry needed to maintain auditor confidentiality but also due to the risk of undue responsibility that auditors have to overcome.[10]

---

6 Lyrics World, "Principles of External Auditing Fourth Edition"(7 July 2021), See online: <https://www.academia.edu/39309560/Principles_of_External_Auditing_Fourth_Edition> at 32.

7 *Ibid* at 223.

8 Philomena Leung et al, Modern auditing and assurance services (Milton, Qld: John Wiley & Sons, 2015) at 27.

9 Bere Gebre, "The historical background of auditing". See online: <https://www.academia.edu/30621275/The historical background of auditing at 7.(Visited at 11 July 2020).

10 Michael Power, *The Audit Society: Rituals of Verification*, (Oxford: Oxford University Press, 1999) at 65.

As a result, auditors rely heavily on internal statements from actors and thus the difference between internal and external audits is increasingly vague, which has indeed impaired the effectiveness of the audit process.[11] However, "ambiguity" is not a methodological problem but a substantive fact,[12] and the deficiency of an audit cannot conceal what it could achieve possibility. It is a question of how to make audits work instead of whether to regard them as a fiction or myth, especially in the private sector. Although the definition of auditing makes it hard to be precise, not any practice can be called an audit.[13]

1.1.1.1 Meaning of Audit in Financial Sector

[History of financial auditing] To fill normative gap, the law requires proper internal controls from actors to enhance the possibility of compliance.[14] Moreover, dubiousness concerning the validation of the internal control process can be generated, which makes it essential for the process of internal controls to be externally verifiable or certifiable; the proposal of audits as a benchmark has garnered much interest, but the audit system itself has also been criticized regarding its own effectiveness.[15] Despite these difficulties, the truth is that financial auditing still remains strong. Like any verification approach that aimed to restore the public's trust, the validity of such approach needs to be "audited." Starting from the late 1980s, audits were increasingly required in different contexts, the obscurity of auditing processes existed not only because of the information asymmetry needed to maintain for auditor's confidentiality but also due to the risk of undue responsibility which auditors have to overcome.[16] The history of financial auditing is longer than many other fields, the work of auditing has a strong influence on business of accountants as well as financial institutions.[17] The commencement of modern financial auditing system started from the nineteenth century where the power of control separated from the ownership of companies.[18] It is as Flint argued:

> When the economic resources of one party are entrusted to another, human nature is assumed to be weak, untrustworthy and in need check. In short, the need for principals to monitor agents give rise to auditing. Because of the remoteness and complexity of the

---

[11] *Ibid* at 67.

[12] Anthony Steele, *Audit Risk and Audit Evidence: The Bayesian Approach to Statistical Auditing* (London: Academic Pr, 1992).

[13] Power, *supra* note 10 at 64.

[14] *Id.*, at 65.

[15] *Ibid* at 67.

[16] Charles P Kindleberger & Robert Z Aliber, *Manias, Panics and Crashes: A History of Financial Crises, Sixth Edition* (Palgrave Macmillan, 2011) at 214.

[17] Mark Stevens, *The Big Eight*, 1st collier books ed ed (New York: Scribner, 1984).

[18] Power, *supra* note 10 at 17.

subject matter of auditing, principals are unable to do this monitoring themselves and require the services of an auditor.[19]

In other words, the conation to developing a financial audit process is to build greater trust between principal and agent. But to be more precise, how could we interpret such trust? At the end of the nineteenth century, financial auditing gradually owned its formal nature of practice in Britain. And the bible of such codified guidance revealed different aspects that financial audit process shall contain.[20] One of important idea from Dicksee entails that detection of fraud seems to have been a primary objective. The early stage of financial auditing require to test some transactions in order to find evidence that "assets have not been misappropriated (Fraud). Starting from the twentieth century, company managers began to take the responsibility of detecting fraud, "provision of opinion" became the primary task for auditing body.[21] Since the announcement the Company Act of the UK, 'true and fair' statement of financial statements became a compulsory requirement for every limited company.[22] For the sake of giving opinion through audit process, auditor was authorized to give his or her independence opinion on financial statements produced by accountants. The financial auditor was also required to join professional organizations or associations to maintain their independent position or to sustain their qualification.

[Changing the purpose of audit] The change from "detecting fraud" to "giving an objective opinion" manifested modern dimension of financial auditing, where the auditor was finding that instead of checking the arithmetical accuracy of every transaction, he could verify these factors on a test basis if he first evaluated the strength of internal control.[23] It is therefore suggested that from the 1930s, large companies which had established systems of internal control became operational partners in the financial audit process.[24] It is turning point where "system audit approach" separate audit system into "internal audit" and "external audit." At this point, the systems itself became "auditable object" instead of "financial statements."[25]

---

[19] David Flint, *Philosophy and principles of auditing: an introduction* (Macmillan Education, 1988) at 13.

[20] Lawrence Robert Dicksee & Stanley William Rowland, *Auditing: A Practical Manual for Auditors* (Gee, 1933) at 126.

[21] There existed another understanding of primary objective changing, Chandler pointed out that the existence of financial statement verification as early as 1840, the detection of fraud subsequently became important as an issue , and was registered in texts such as Dicksee, as a consequence of the wave of corporate collapses in the late nineteenth century and was then never fully revised out of these texts to correspond to changes in practitioner sentiment. In the USA, there is similar issue: 1912 edition of Montgomery states that the primary objective of auditing is to ascertain the financial condition and earnings of an enterprise for various parties. Only after 1940 is the confusion over audit objectives finally resolved and fraud detection is generally agreed not to be a primary objective.

[22] Power, *supra* note 10 at 18.

[23] Steele, *supra* note 12 at 32.

[24] T A Lee & Robert H Parker, *Evolution of Corporate Financial Reporting*, 1st ed (Routledge, 2014).

[25] Power, *supra* note 10 at 20.

It also arose a problem of definition for the scope of the internal control system and for the effectiveness of external audit.[26] One of interesting commission generated from audit guidance is the "expectation gap" between "detecting fraud" and "opinion on financial statements."[27] In other words, within a reasonable statement, whether the responsibility of financial auditor implies the expectation of detecting fraud is widely discussed by both practitioners as well as scholars.[28] Critique about "audit failure" always contains the argument about failure of delivering a clear opinion on misrepresentation of financial statements. Moreover, it is always logically possible that a 'good' audit was performed even though the company failed to detect fraud activities.[29] For instance, Deloitte was fined the Beijing office of 30.8 million for failing to adequately audit a Chinese state-owned asset management company.[30] It was found that Huarong had internal control and risk control failures and serious distortion of accounting information to varying degrees from 2014 to 2019. Deloitte did not pay sufficient attention to the substance of many economic operations of Huarong. They did not penetrate to audit the true state of underlying assets, ignored approval compliance for significant investment matters, and did not properly express audit opinions on identified unusual transactions. Furthermore, they failed to objectively evaluate the condition of corporate assets, accurately assess the reasonableness of expected credit loss model parameters, and maintain professional skepticism during the provision of audit services. There were lapses in effectively performing the necessary audit procedures, resulting in the failure to obtain sufficient and appropriate audit evidence and serious audit deficiencies.[31] For this case, there has an expectation gap between the function of audit and the what it practically achieve.

---

[26] David Hay, "Internal Control: How it Evolved in Four English-speaking Countries" (Accounting Historians Journal, 1993) at 102. See online: <http://www.jstor.org/stable/40698098>.(Visited at 2 August 2022).

[27] Stauart Manson& Mahbub Zaman, "Auditor communication in an evolving environment: Going beyond SAS 600 Auditor's reports on financial statement". (British Accounting Review, 2001 33:2). See online: <https://www.sciencedirect.com/science/article/pii/S089083890190157X> at 132. (Visited at 4 June 2021)

[28] Baldwin Robert, "Why Rules Don't Work" (The Modern Law Review 331,1990) at 13.

[29] Kevin Keasey & Mike Wright, "Issues In Corporate Accountability and Governance: An Editorial" (Accounting & Business Research 23:91, 1993), See online: <http://www.tandfonline.com/doi/abs/10.1080/00014788.1993.9729897> at 303.(Visited at 1 July 2021)

[30] The Journal Record, "Deloitte was fined for audit failings". See Online: China fines Deloitte $30.8M over audit failings | The Journal Record. (Visited at 1 April 2023)

[31] The Journal Record, "Administrative Penalties for Deloitte China by Ministry of Finance of the People Republic of China". See online: China fines Deloitte $30.8M over audit failings | The Journal Record. (Visited at 1 April 2023).

1.1.1.2 Meaning of Audit in Personal Data Protection

[Meaning of personal data protection] In the 1970s, as the definition of personal information was being established, scholars explored distinctions between "private" and "public" information.[32] Ultimately, a consensus emerged, defining personal data for the context of data protection law as 'any information related to a data subject who is or can be identified.[33] As defined by GDPR, personal data refers to "any information relating to an identified or identifiable natural person (data subject)."[34] The notion of "identifiability" is the core concept in constructing the definition of personal data, and it is widely used in other transnational policies as well as national data protection laws. For instance, the OECD guidelines define personal information as:

> Any information relating to an identified or identifiable individual.[35]

In Canada, Personal Information Protection and Electronic Documents Act of Canada (hereafter PIPEDA) defines personal information as:

> Information about an identifiable individual.[36]

Given this literal interpretation, since the emergence of Web 2.0, there are large volumes of information that can be regarded as personal information.[37] Such as address book information, identity information, phone numbers, photographs, bank account information (property information), biometric information, work-related information, cookies, and text message information; for example, when downloading social apps such as Facebook on one's phone, one will find them to be giant "data catchers" that request all kinds of access to information. The situation has become more serious in the big data era in which "gathering large amounts of data

---

[32] Eloïse Gratton, *Understanding Personal Information: Managing Privacy Risks* (Markham, Ont, 2013) at 21.

[33] Chairman Sir Norman Lindop, Report of the Committee on Data Protection: Presented to Parliament by the Secretary of State for the Home Department by Command of Her Majesty (London, UK: H.M.S.O., 1978) at 11–12, para. 2.12.

[34] GDPR, Article 4 (1): For the purpose of this regulation, personal data mean any information relating to an identified or identifiable natural persona; an identifiable natural persona is one who can be identified. directly or indirectly, in particular, by reference to an identifier such as a name, an identification number, location data, an online identifier or to one or more factors specific to the physical, physiological, genetic, mental, economic, cultural or social identity of the natural person.

[35] The OECD was created in 1960 and brings together the governments of countries around the world committed to democracy and the market economy. OECD, *Guidelines on the Protection of Privacy and Transborder Flows of Personal Data at* Article 1(b).

[36] Personal Information Protection and Electronic Documents Act, S.C. 2000, c. 5, Schedule 1 [PIPEDA].

[37] Vincent Gautrais, "Circulation des renseignements personnels et web 2.0". See online: <https://www.gautrais.com/publications/circulation-des-renseignements-personnels-et-web-2-0/>.(Visited at 8 January 2019).

is far more important than developing highly sophisticated algorithms."[38] A, the efficiency of this interpretation for personal information is challenged due to the development of information technology.[39] In other words, the protection of personal information shall be interpreted in the context of data protection laws and regulations. As Nicola Lugaresi noted:

> The protection of privacy is often adjusted to meet the needs of personal data protection, and personal data protection law is a facet of privacy protection.[40]

These two concepts cannot be replaced by each other because "privacy has many hues and covers both more and less than the notion of personal data."[41] This is one of the significant considerations of the Charter of Fundamental Rights of the European Union in separating "respect for private and family life" from the right of the "protection of personal data."[42]

[Purpose of personal data audit] To some extent, the answer to this question could be transferred to another issue to discussion, it is exactly as Bennett argued:

> How to install good data protection governance into the complex organization, which has many other pressures, incentives and interests?[43]

Comparing with the evolution of audit in the financial sector, it's crucial to identify the genuine incentives that drive organizations to safeguard personal data. In essence, we seek an explanation for why audits are essential in the data protection process for organizations. The separation of executive power from company ownership led to the imperative for financial accounts to undergo audits. In the realm of personal data, a distinction naturally exists between the right to personal data and the right to process data by processors. Put differently, processors do not own the personal data of users; instead, they possess the right to process it with the users' consent. Unfortunately, the conceptual exploration of the fulfillment need for accountability is often overlooked and appears to be lacking in the discourse

---

[38] Mireille Hildebrandt, *Smart Technologies and the End(s) of Law: Novel Entanglements of Law and Technology* (Cheltenham, UK Northampton, MA, USA: Edward Elgar Pub, 2016) at 7.

[39] Gratton, *supra* note 32.

[40] Nicola Lugaresi, "Principles and Regulations about Online Privacy: Implementation Divide and Misunderstanding in the European Union TPRC 2002". See online at: < http://papers.ssrn.com/sol3/papers.cfm?abstract id=333440 (Visited at19 January 2019). Also see Vincent Gautrais, Ed., Droit du commerce electronicque (Montreal: Editions Themis, 2002) at 19.

[41] Pierre Trudel, *Privacy Protection on the Internet: Risk Management and Networked Normativity* (Springer Netherlands, 2009) at 319.

[42] Giacomo Di Federico, *The EU Charter of Fundamental Rights: From Declaration to Binding Instrument* (Springer Science & Business Media, 2010) at 12. Article 7 of the Charter of Fundamental Rights of the European Union (2012/C 326/02) states the following: "Everyone has the right to respect for his or her private and family life, home and communications."

[43] Colin J Bennett, "The Accountability Approach to Privacy and Data Protection: Assumptions and Caveats" in Daniel Guagnin et al, eds, *Managing Privacy through Accountability* (London: Palgrave Macmillan UK, 2012) at 41.

surrounding data protection.[44] Since 2009, Madrid Resolution indicated eight pro-active measures to promote fulfillment of accountability, including privacy officers, employee training, ePIAs, and code of practice which includes external and transparent audits.[45] But it did not clarify what kinds of form that an efficient audit should be like, or what could be defined as an auditor?[46] Should we consider audit as a modality to actuate data protection measures or cogitate it as a way to demonstrate commitment to accountability? An undetailed list of general principle for protecting personal data given by Article 29 working party includes:

> Implementation and supervision of verification procedures to ensure that all the measures not only exist on paper but that they are implemented and work in practice (internal and external audits, etc.).[47]

It appears that integrating these principles into practical implementation is the preferred approach.[48] This book envisaged that third-party accountability agents and privacy supervisory authorities are essential for measuring the degree to which organizations fulfill their accountability in terms of the definitions, fundamentals, and essential elements adopted by the project. But short of that, validation procedures such as audits will be necessary.[49]

[Ritual of consent] Similarly speaking with the financial sector, there has a real trust gap between data owners and data processors. As Daniel Solove said:

> What has failed is not privacy but 'privacy self-management'[50]

Technologies are developing while their outputs are also evolving; we have witnessed furtherance of outputs from voice signal to voice, data and internet signal, basic internet actions such as web surfing is supported with 2G on cell phones. However, the development of 3G facilitated people to interact with internet-based applications more intensively. "Web applications" are no longer so popular for social media usage; mobile Internet has become one of the most fundamental entrances to the market for many Internet companies that claim they are paving the way from "Web" to "App" for using the Internet. This is not only due to the

---

[44] Charles Raab, "The Meaning of 'Accountability' in the Information Privacy Context". (ResearchGate 2012) at 15.

[45] Ibid at 16.

[46] The Madrid Resolution, "International standards on the Protection of Personal Data and Privacy". See Madrid, International Conference Paper of Data Protection and Privacy Commissioners, 2009.

[47] Article 29 Data Protection Working Party, Opinion 3/2010 on the principle of Accountability. WP 173, Brussels: European Commission, 2010 at Paragraph 41.

[48] As a way to demonstrate or to measure accountability, in terms of the nine fundamental types of activity that an accountable organization should undertake. The project focused on policies; executive oversight; staffing and delegation; education and awareness; ongoing risk assessment and mitigation; program risk assessment oversight and validation; event management and compliant handling; internal enforcement; redress.

[49] Raab, *supra* note 44 at 29.

[50] The idea is that it is possible or desirable for every individual to monitor and manage a shifting collection of privacy settings of which they may only be dimly aware.

widespread use of smartphones but also because of how the distinct features of the "app," compared with the application of the "web" in terms of interactive experiences, displays functions of the app as concisely as possible. App settings, often by default, request the authority to collect all information at once; users do not easily recognize the real meaning of pressing the "consent button." The purpose of consent is to ensure a certain degree of control concerning personal information of the user, but practically it became a discretionary tool entitling internet companies to circulate personal information, whether or not processing action is justified hinges quite simply and exclusively on whether it has the consent of the user.

We are faced with an ugly situation where personal information managers using contractual rules in order to protect themselves.[51] An audit for personal data protection involves an independent examination of an organization's policies, procedures, and systems related to the collection, processing, storage, and sharing of personal data. The purpose of the audit is to assess the effectiveness of the organization's data protection measures, identify gaps or weaknesses in those measures, and provide recommendations for improvement. The stated privacy policies failed to become an effective norm to regulate the processors. As Bennett put it:

> It is difficult to see how accountability of practice can be satisfactorily claimed without regular auditing, internal in some circumstances, but external and independent in others.[52]

Practically speaking, some of validation of data protection compliance based on words instead of practice.[53] For instance, acknowledgement and consent from data subjects are one of the fundamental origins of grounds for processing personal information,[54] while we are still facing cognitive problems wherein people are reluctant to read privacy policies, or it is hard for ordinary people to determine what is the "necessary and adequate" information for various purposes (acknowledgement processes are difficult for us).[55] The reality is that personal information is going through a lifecycle process, and it makes us wonder if it is enough for the concept of individual interest to serve as the starting point for analyzing the regime of personal data protection.[56] Consequently, consent from users is becoming increasingly meaningless because people have no idea of the substance of their agreements. As Thomas Olsen put it:

---

[51] This example is discussed in Gautrais, "Web 2.0" , *supra* note 37 at 178.

[52] Bennett, *supra* note 43 at 41.

[53] Graham Greenleaf, *Asian Data Privacy Laws: Trade & Human Rights Perspectives* (OUP Oxford, 2014) at 45.

[54] Rosemary Jay, *Guide to the General Data Protection Regulation: A Companion to Data Protection Law and Practice*, 4th revised edition edition ed (London: Sweet & Maxwell, 2017) at 12.

[55] They can leave individual's privacy badly exposed, as individuals are forced to make overly complicated decisions based on limited information, while data processors can perhaps too easily point to the formality of notice and consent and thereby abrogate much of their responsibility.

[56] Bart van der Sloot & Sascha van Schendel, "Ten Questions for Future Regulation of Big Data: A Comparative and Empirical Legal Study" (2016) .See online: <http://www.jipitec.eu/issues/jipitec-7-2-2016/4438> at 124.(Visited at 24 July 2018).

> Providing the user with a lot of information regarding the processing of personal data may paradoxically be a burden for the user because it encourages or requires the user to stop and reflect on the relevance of the information.[57]

The purpose of consent is to ensure a certain degree of control concerning personal information of the user, but practically it became a discretionary tool entitling internet companies to circulate personal information, whether or not processing action is justified hinges quite simply and exclusively on whether it has the consent of the user. We are faced with an ugly situation where personal information managers using contractual rules in order to protect themselves.[58] Data processor has a strong incentive position to explore the value of personal data, and individuals who have the right to protect their personal data, but it is hard for users to see whether the processor satisfied the requirement of accountable compliance.

[Call for accountability] Despite the application of different approaches, both the United States and the European Union chose accountability as a legal tool to manage risk as well as achieve corporate social responsibility. From a legal perspective, accountability enables actors to hold responsible for their behaviors.[59] At another level, irrespective,[60] it seems to be a consensus that the process must involve being called to "account" by some authority for one's actions,[61] the involvement of an external body is, therefore, indispensable.[62] Recently, there is a trend in the literature considering adding processor-based regulation on the data processing side.[63] Such regulation is not new, there are many domains for individuals to comprehend without expert knowledge, and that has important negative externalities such as food, drug and car safety sector. A key sentiment as Viktor Mayer-Schönberger noted:

---

57 *Ibid* at 125.

58 See Gautrais "Web 2.0", *supra* note 37 at 178.

59 Deven R Desai& Joshua A Kroll, *Trust But Verify: A Guide to Algorithms and the Law*, SSRN Scholarly Paper ID 2959472 (Rochester, NY: Social Science Research Network, 2017) at 9.

60 Bennett, *supra* note 43 at 2.

61 Rosemary Jay, *Guide to the General Data Protection Regulation: A Companion to Data Protection Law and Practice*, 4th Revised edition ed (London: Sweet & Maxwell, 2017) at 84.

62 See Van der Sloot & van Schendel, "Ten Questions for Future Regulation of Big Data". *supra* note 56 at 124.

63 For example, James Nehf, "Protecting Privacy with Heightened Notice and Choice" (Research handbook on electronic commerce law, 2016); Fred H. Cate & Viktor Mayer-Schönberger, "Notice and consent in a world of Big Data". (International data privacy law, 2013): Suggesting that notice and choice have become an ineffective mechanism of privacy protection in need to be replaced by a use-based approach. For more critiques on the currently prevailing mechanism of notice and choice, for example, see Kirsten E. Martin, "Transaction costs, privacy, and trust: The laudable goals and ultimate failure of notice and choice to respect privacy online"(First Monday, 2013); Robert H. Sloan & Richard Warner, "Beyond Notice and Choice, Privacy, Norms, and Consent" (Suffolk University Journal of High Tech, 2014): Agreeing with the critique of notice and choice; Alessandro Mantelero, "The Future of Consumer Data Protection in the E.U. Rethinking the "Notice and Consent" Paradigm in the New Era of Predictive Analytics" (COMPUTER L. & SECURITY REV ,2014) :Suggesting that notice and consent no longer is effective and is in need of at least partial replacement.

> All of the discussion is that those new approaches must shift responsibility away from data subjects towards data users, and towards a focus on accountability for responsible data stewardship, rather than mere compliance while ensuring that expectations and protection of privacy are preserved.[64]

This research tries to express the attempt to face the problem by cultivating an effective regulatory environment (audit environment) to verify the accountability of internal controls (data protection by design) for the purpose of managing risk associated with personal data protection.[65] From normative perspective, some regimes such as the EU has growing incentive to protect the personal data, organizations also have strong need of legal compliance for protecting data. Compared with the 1995 European data protection directive,[66] General Data Protection Regulations (hereafter GDPR) introduced "right to explanation" which spark discourse profoundly.[67] Besides, it sweeps new enforcement power to Europe's data protection authorities.[68] The sweeping new enforcement powers given to European data protection authorities(DPAs) by Chapters 6 and 8 of the powers of the regulation are unlike the 1995 Data Protection Directive that it replaced, the GDPR's new investigatory, advisory, corrective, and punitive powers granted by chapters 6 and 8 render DPAs de facto interpretive authorities of the regulation's controversial right to explanation.

Article 28 of GDPR entailed that:

> Makes available to the controller all information necessary to demonstrate compliance with the obligations laid down in this Article and allow for and contribute to audits, including inspections, conducted by the controller or another auditor mandated by the controller.[69]

---

[64] Fred H Cate & Viktor Mayer-Schönberger, "Notice and consent in a world of Big Data"(2013) 3:2 International Data Privacy Law. See online: <https://academic.oup.com/idpl/article/3/2/67/709124> at 70.(Visited at 9 Jan, 2019).

[65] Simon Roberts, "After Government? On Representing Law without the State"(2005) 68:1 The Modern Law Review. See online: <https://www.jstor.org/stable/3699110> at 12. (Visited at 10 Jan, 2019).

[66] Directive 95/46/EC of the European Parliament and of the Council of 24 October 1995 on the protection of individuals with regard to the processing of personal data and on the free movement of such data at 281.

[67] "Right to explanation" refer to Section2, Article 13,14,15 and 22 of GDPR, where information need to be provided when processing personal data. The original claim of this concept is Goodman's and Flaxman's conference paper "European Union Regulations on Algorithmic Decision-making and a Right of Explanation". After that, Wachter criticized it interpret GPDR too broad and the concept shall be replaced as "right to be informed", See Sandra Wachter, Brent Mittelstadt & Luciano Floridi, "Why a Right to Explanation of Automated Decision-Making Does Not Exist in the General Data Protection Regulation" (2017) 7:2 International Data Privacy Law 76–99. See online: <https://doi.org/10.1093/idpl/ipx005> at 84.

[68] Bryan Casey, Ashkon Farhangi& Roland Vogl, *Rethinking Explainable Machines: The GDPR's "Right to Explanation" Debate and the Rise of Algorithmic Audits in Enterprise*, SSRN Scholarly Paper ID 3143325 (Rochester, NY: Social Science Research Network, 2018) at 8.

[69] Article 28 of GDPR.

It gave a clear message about the demonstration obligation for data controller. Besides, Article 39 of GDPR provides the tasks that data protection officer (DPO) needs to follow, it entails:

> The DPO shall have at least to monitor compliance with this Regulation including the assignment of responsibilities, awareness raising and training of staff involved in processing operations, and the related audits.[70]

GDPR also includes:

> The protection of the rights and freedoms of natural persons with regard to the processing of personal data require that appropriate technical and organizational measures be taken to ensure that the requirement of this regulation is met. In order to be able to demonstrate compliance with this regulation, the controller should adopt internal policies and implement measures which meet in particular the principles of data protection by design and data protection by default." The strong power that DPAs given by GDPR derives from legal requirement which partially codified as 'data auditing' as well as 'data protection by design.[71]

1.2 Audit for Personal Data Protection

Audits for personal data protection provide organizations with a valuable tool for assessing their compliance with these regulations and ensuring that they are implementing adequate data protection measures. They also provide assurance to stakeholders, including customers, investors, and regulators, that the organization is taking data protection seriously and is taking steps to mitigate the risks associated with personal data.

1.2.1 Background of Personal Data Protection Audit

From social media platforms to online shopping websites, users constantly share personal information that companies use to tailor their services and advertising. However, with the rising number of data breaches and cyber-attacks, data protection has become a critical issue for individuals, businesses, and governments alike. Consequently, audits for personal data protection have become essential tools for assessing the adequacy of data protection measures and ensuring compliance with legal and regulatory requirements.

---

[70] Article 39 of GDPR.

[71] Recital 78 of GDPR.

1.2.1.1 Technical Background Personal Data Protection Audit

[Accountability of algorithms] To run an audit for more and more complex algorithmic systems, it is precisely as Selbst and Barca's argued:

> One must seek explanations of the process behind a model's development, not just explanations of the model itself.[72]

In a letter dated on May 25, 2001, relating a claim which Federal Trade Commission (hereafter FTC) received from Junkbusters and Electronic Privacy Information Center that:

> Notified Amazon.com of the conclusion of its Alexa Internet subsidiary for fraudulently collecting personal information and Web tracking data from customers in violation of Section 5 of the FTC Act.[73]

The FTC decided not to take formal action against the Amazon, Junkbuster sent another letter to the FTC, disputing that Amazon.com shall:

> Undergo an on-site audit by a competent and independent firm to determine whether its actual past conduct conformed with the various versions of its privacy policies.[74]

Specifically, Junkbusters questioned the Consumer Protection Bureau's reliance on Amazon's assertions without verifiable evidence of compliance with the revised privacy policy.[75] This book observes that there was indeed a public demand for a compliance agency to assist in protecting their data. Nearly two decades later, similar incidents occurred but with different outcomes. Facebook, during this period, faced a five-billion-dollar penalty from the FTC for violating consumer privacy. Additionally, the FTC imposed rules requiring the company to revamp its data governance approach to ensure accountability of Facebook executives for privacy decisions. Compliance officers were designated the duty to report quarterly privacy compliance certifications to the FTC.[76] Furthermore, an independent third-party assessor was granted the ability to evaluate the effectiveness of Facebook's privacy program.[77] Given that algorithms constitute the core of the system and cannot be held responsible due to their lack of legal personality, it falls upon the organizations

---

[72] Peter Rott, *Certification – Trust, Accountability, Liability* (Springer, 2019) at 117.

[73] Stephen F Jr Ambrose & Joseph W Gelb, *"Consumer Privacy Regulation and Litigation Survey"* (2001) 57:3 Bus Law.See online: <https://heinonline.org/HOL/P?h=hein.journals/busl57&i=1252> at 1241. (Visited at 12 March 2019).

[74] *Ibid* at 1243.

[75] *Ibid at 1244.*

[76] FTC News, "FTC settlement imposes historic penalty, and significant requirements to boost accountability and transparency". See online: https://www.ftc.gov/news-events/press-releases/2019/07/ftc-imposes-5-billion-penalty-sweeping-new-privacy-restrictions. (Visited at 2 March 2020).

[77] Ibid.

designing or deploying these algorithms to be accountable for their outcomes.[78] This has led to efforts to make software systems more explainable and intelligible.[79] Various methods, such as "Explaining the model; Explaining the outcome; Inspecting the black box; Creating a transparent box," are employed for algorithm audits to achieve explain ability in artificial intelligence systems.[80] Explaining the model always relied on the interpretation of logic for the whole system, while explaining of the outcome relied on the perception of ramifications. The different between the black box and transparent box could be deviated from whether the system use implicit predictors.[81]Although computer scientists have shown that there are much more powerful strategies that enable us to better understand the system such as:

> Disclosing commitments instead of sources of code or inputs and outputs.[82]

It is easier to verify the system using simpler steps, as this book discussed above, explainable or transparency of the algorithm cannot be equalized with the concept of algorithm accountability. Whereas transparency is that passive, accountability requires a more active and involved stance.[83] As Maranke Wieringa specified:

> Algorithmic accountability concerns a networked account for a social-technical algorithmic system, following the various stages of the system's lifecycle. In this accountability relationship, multiple actors have the obligation to explain and justify their use, design and or/ decisions of/concerning the system and the subsequent effects of that conduct.... The relationships between forum/fora and actors departs from a particular perspective on accountability.[84]

As a matter of fact, algorithmic auditing and data protection by design practices will likely become the new gold standard for enterprises deploying machine learning systems both inside and outside of the European Union.[85] From systemic point of view, to deliver algorithmic accountability, we need proper accountability

[78] Joanna J Bryson, Mihailis E Diamantis & Thomas D Grant, "Of, for, and by the people: the legal lacuna of synthetic persons" (2017) at 283.

[79] Riccardo Guidotti et al, "A Survey Of Methods For Explaining Black Box Models" (2018) arXiv:180201933 [cs]. See online: <http://arxiv.org/abs/1802.01933> at 12.

[80] Leighton Andrews, "Public administration, public leadership and the construction of public value in the age of the algorithm and 'big data'" (2019) at 312.

[81] Dennis Broeders et al, "Big Data and security policies: Towards a framework for regulating the phases of analytics and use of Big Data" (2017) 33:3 Computer Law & Security Review 309–323, See online: <http://www.sciencedirect.com/science/article/pii/S0267364917300675> at 318. (Visited at 1 April 2019).

[82] Joshua Kroll et al, "Accountable Algorithms" (2017) 165:3 University of Pennsylvania Law Review 633, See online: <https://scholarship.law.upenn.edu/penn_law_review/vol165/iss3/3> at 672.(Visited at 21 May 2019).

[83] Maranke Wieringa, *What to account for when accounting for algorithms: a systematic literature review on algorithmic accountability* (Barcelona, Spain: Association for Computing Machinery, 2020) at 4.

[84] Ibid at 10.

[85] Casey, Farhangi & Vogl, *supra* note 68.

arrangement organizes different actors both from social and technical sector. That is the reason we need processes such as audit to tell how it works and why. Audits are tools for interrogating complex processes, often to determine whether they comply with company policy, industry standards or regulations.[86] IEEE standard defined software audit as:

> An independent evaluation of conformance of software products and processes to applicable regulations, standards, guidelines, plans, specifications, and procedures.[87]

From a technical perspective, the concept of accountability referred as:

> Making sure that software produces evidence allowing oversight and verification of whether it is operating within agreed-upon rules.[88]

These rules always concern with non-discrimination, non-bias for using algorithms, and with protection of personal data. From a historical point of view, algorithm audit thrived for detecting bugs of the software or for detecting vulnerabilities.[89] Algorithm audit usually treat a decision process as a black box whose inputs and outputs are visible, but those inner procedures cannot be described.[90] Companies often paid to a third party to find defection of their system. This often refers as an external software audit. However, from internal perspective, software industries are not typically followed a "waterfall or verification-and validation approach."[91] The reason behind this, from one perspective, to build a large complex system such as artificial intelligence involved many stakeholders which may involve manifold interactions as well as large volume of data from users are used for data training. Additionally, an audit process for such system lacks regulatory motivation. However, Algorithm accountability has gained a lot of traction recently, due to the changed legislative and regulatory context of data practice, with the implementation of GDPR, several lawsuits and the integration with open government initiatives.[92] Also, the documentation process shall be proposed with the technical team of the project in each development stage to show proper evidence of how the system is followed the relevant guidelines and principles.

---

[86] Inioluwa Deborah Raji et al, "Closing the AI Accountability Gap: Defining an End-to-End Framework for Internal Algorithmic Auditing" (2020). See online: http://arxiv.org/abs/2001.00973 at 2.

[87] IEEE, "IEEE Standard for Software Reviews and Audits", Institute of Electrical and Electronics Engineers, IEEE Std 1028-2008 (2008) at 37.

[88] Andreas Haeberlen, "Pratical Accountability for distributed systems" (2007) Max Planck Institute for Software Systems at 13.

[89] Thomas Maillart et al, "Given enough eyeballs, all bugs are shallow? Revisiting Eric Raymond with bug bounty programs" (2017) 3:2 J Cybersecurity at 84.

[90] Kroll et al, *supra* note 82 at 660.

[91] Michael A Cusumano & Stanley A Smith, "Beyond the waterfall : software development at Microsoft" (1995), See online: <https://dspace.mit.edu/handle/1721.1/2593> at 12.

[92] Wieringa, *supra* note 84 at 115.

1.2.1.2 Legal Background of Personal Data Protection Audit

[Legislation for personal data protection] The legislation background for an audit of personal data protection varies depending on the country or region. Related requirement is proposed in varies legislations in different ways. For instance, The GDPR required organizations to conduct regular audits of their data processing activities, including the measures taken to protect personal data.[93] Compared with United States legislation, EU legislation of personal information protection was criticized as a more paternalistic regime. For instance, the GDPR required that data be:

> Collected for specified, explicit and legitimate purposes and not further processed in a manner that is incompatible with that purpose.[94]

California Consumer Privacy Act of the United States (hereafter CCPA) required organizations to conduct regular audits of their data processing activities and to implement appropriate measures to protect personal data.[95] PIPEDA required organizations to conduct regular audits of their data processing activities, including the measures taken to protect personal data.[96] Health Insurance Portability and Accountability Act of the United States (hereafter HIPAA) required healthcare organizations to conduct regular audits of their data processing activities, including the measures taken to protect personal data.[97] Personal Data Protection Act of

[93] Article 24 of GDPR: Responsibility of the controller to implement appropriate measures to ensure and demonstrate compliance with the GDPR. Article 28 of GPDR: Requirements for data processing agreements between controllers and processors, which may include provisions for audits by the controller. Article 32 of GDPR: Requirements for security of processing, which may include regular audits of security measures.

[94] "Right to explanation" refer to Section2, Article 13,14,15 and 22 of GDPR, where information need to be provided when processing personal data. The original claim of this concept is Goodman's and Flaxman's conference paper "European Union Regulations on Algorithmic Decision-making and a Right of Explanation". After that, Wachter criticized it interpret GPDR too broad and the concept shall be replaced as "right to be informed", See "Why a right to explanation of automated decision-making does not exist in General Data Protection Regulation."

[95] Section 1798.140(c)(1)(D) of CCPA: Right to request information on the categories of personal information collected by a business and the purposes for which the information is used. Section 1798.105: Requirement for businesses to implement and maintain reasonable security procedures and practices appropriate to the nature of the personal information they collect, including regular audits of such procedures and practices.

[96] Principle 4.1.4 of PIPEDA: Requirement for organizations to implement appropriate safeguards to protect personal information, including regular monitoring and testing of security measures. Principle 4.9: Requirement for organizations to make information about their privacy policies and practices available to individuals upon request, including information about the types of personal information the organization holds, how it is used, and any third parties with whom it is shared.

[97] § 164.308(a)(8) of HIPAA: Requirement for covered entities and business associates to periodically evaluate their security measures and maintain documentation of those evaluations. § 164.316(b)(2) of HIPAA: Requirement for covered entities and business associates to implement and maintain appropriate security measures to protect electronic protected health information, including regular assessments of those measures.

Singapore (hereafter PDPA) required organizations to conduct regular audits of their data processing activities, including the measures taken to protect personal data.[98] From practical perspective, In January 2019, the French data protection authority Commission Nationale de l'informatique et des libertés (hereafter CNIL) announced that it had fined Google 57 million euros (approximately £44 million or USD$65 million) for breaching the European Union's GDPR through its use of targeted advertising.[99] The CNIL issued the fine due to inefficient information provided by Google about how they used personal information about users, and the question was raised whether the user is the appropriate audience for these types of consent policies. As for this topic, it is apparently not the question of which norms provide the best protection for personal information; because norms co-existed between technological standards, management norms and legal rules.[100] Effective normativity always relies on the ability to incorporate different norms and principles of the Internet. The dilemma we face can be referred to the challenge of regulatory connection.[101] It is as Lyria Bennett Moses noted:

> The law should not race ahead by anticipating technological trajectories that may never come to pass. Rather, a useful goal should be to have mechanisms in place to ensure that law is designed around the socio-technical landscape of the present or, more realistically, the recent past.[102]

Along with formal normative tools, the growing number of informal norms enriched on internal control in order to regulate technology, such as mechanism of audit and risk assessment, certification, etc.[103] This trend calls for regulation to be redesigned to ensure that the incentive nature of technology can be understood.[104] As Michael Power noted:

---

[98] Section 24(1) of PDPA: Requirement for organizations to appoint one or more data protection officers to oversee compliance with the PDPA, including conducting regular audits of data protection policies and practices. Section 11: Requirement for organizations to make reasonable security arrangements to protect personal data, including regular reviews and assessments of such arrangements.

[99] McGuireWoods News, "CNIL vs. Google: 10 lessons from the largest data protection fine ever issued." See online: https://www.passwordprotectedlaw.com/2019/01/cnil-vs-google-largest-fine/ (Visited at Feb 19 2019).

[100] Pierre Trudel, *Web 2.0 Regulation: A Risk Management Process*, SSRN Scholarly Paper ID 1573980 (Rochester, NY: Social Science Research Network, 2009) at 16.

[101] Roger Brownsword, Rights, Regulation and the Technological Revolution (Oxford ; New York: Oxford University Press, 2011) at 117.

[102] Lyria Bennett Moses, "Agents of Change: How the Law Copes with Technological Change Special Issue: The Laws of Technology and the Technology of Law" (Griffith L Rev 2011). See online: <https://heinonline.org/HOL/P?h=hein.journals/griffith20&i=773> at 788.(Visited at 16 Aug 2021).

[103] Nikolas Rose & Peter Miller, "Political Power beyond the State: Problematics of Government" (1992) 43:2 Br J Sociol at 198.

[104] *Socially Responsible Investment in the 21st Century: Does it Make a Difference for Society?* (Emerald Group Publishing, 2014) at 12.

> The growing formalization of regulatory layers has generated interest in the internalization of control mechanisms and the validation of their internal by external audit.[105]

An audit explosion has been triggered by this formalization of regulatory layers, wherein record keeping and disclosure requirements became important as ways of connecting the different layers of encouraging a certain kind of organizational introspection.[106] Nevertheless, this approach is operated in a relatively autonomous way and is bereft of legal oversight.[107] The law required proper internal controls from actors to enhance the possibility of compliance. In the meantime, dubiousness about the validation of the internal control process can be generated. This makes it important for the process of internal controls to be externally verifiable or certifiable; the proposal of audits as a benchmark has garnered interest, but the audit system itself is also criticized for its own effectiveness.[108]

---

[105] Power, *supra* note 10 at 53.

[106] Peter N Grabosky, "Using Non-Governmental Resources to Foster Regulatory Compliance" (1995) 8:4 Governance 527–550, See online: <https://onlinelibrary.wiley.com/doi/abs/10.1111/j.1468-0491.1995.tb00226.x> at 531.(Visited at 01 Feb 2019).

[107] Vincent Gautrais, "Normativité et droit du technique", See online:<\https://www.gautrais.com/publications/normativite-et-droit-du-technique/> at 330.(Visited 04 Feb 2019).

[108] Power, *supra* note 10 at 67.

Part II
The Function of Audit

Chapter 2
Deconstructing the Audit

2.1 Deconstructing the Definition of Audit

For this part, this book delves into deconstructing the definition of audit, distinguishing it from concepts like verification, validation, certification, and assessment. It dissects these concepts further, emphasizing verification as a process of confirming and checking, especially in personal data protection contexts. It also distinguishes validation, often applied in software development, and certification, which involves a third party assuring conformity to specific requirements. Accreditation is introduced as proof of third-party competency for certification. The paper questions whether compliance or standards can be exchanged for monetary gain, emphasizing the misalignment between these concepts and the broader understanding of audits.

2.1.1 Deconstructing the Definition of an Audit as an Elusive Concept

Audit is always demanded where there is lack of trust and full of risk. Audit demanded under circumstances where resources are entrusted while trust is also lacking and must be restored. As a result, outsiders such as auditors have come into play to correct the flaws inherent in trust. While the word "Audit" is always blended with the concept of verification, validation, certification and accreditation. While As a matter of fact it is a misuse for these different concepts as an interchangeable word as audit.

H. Wu, C. Zhang, *Audit the Audit*, https://doi.org/10.1007/978-981-95-2473-0_2

[Definition of Trust] Hardin interpreted trust as follows:

> Trust is generally a three-part relation: A Trusts B to do X.[1]

Moreover, trust always implies the significance of someone's action being predictable. If someone wants to identify the predictability of doing X, it will involve a "scale" for measuring in what extent A can trust B. In other words, trust requires an element of cynicism. As Regan stated:

> Trust also requires an element of skepticism, of watchfulness or wariness, recognizing the reality that trust is not unassailable, that it does instead have a tenuous element.[2]

Trust is an interactive manner requiring understanding the expectation of doing X. Two elements, an objective component, and an intuitive component, are always identified regarding trust. From an objective perspective, both A and B need to know how to do X as well as the purpose for doing X. From an intuitive perspective, how both parties understand X, which is a psychological deed rather than a statement of fact.[3] For personal data protection, both elements are difficult to achieve. Algorithm systems are often complicated, and a lack of explain ability and visibility as to how these systems process personal data is apparent. From a subjective aspect, users are usually not experts in software systems; to understand how these systems they work is complicated for users to fathom, and once they provide their personal data to processors, it is virtually impossible to trace how the data are being used for specific purposes. Therefore, it is very difficult to build trust between a user and a data controller. Trust needs to be built both from social side and the technical side, and apparently, the burden of doing this cannot be placed on individuals. Rather, the designers and managers of these data systems need to show that personal data are well protected. The puzzle we are facing is that users need information to fulfill their expectations, but the information provided by the data controller may be other than information that users can trust.

[Audit for trust] An audit is a second order of trust or a relationship.[4] Shapiro interpreted this concept as follows:'

> One of the ironies of trust is that we frequently protect it and respond to its failures by bestowing even more trust…new strains of deviance and new procedural cures, one gets the feeling that the original agency agenda has become distorted along the way… By creating guardians of trust, we foster all kinds of ancillary certifications or guarantees of trustworthiness…that are readily manipulated yet are now essential to principals who have abdicated their distrust to these new guardians.[5]

---

[1] Russell Hardin, *Trust and trustworthiness* (New York, NY, US: Russell Sage Foundation, 2002) at 9.

[2] Priscilla M Regan, "Privacy and Trust in Socio-technical System of Accountability." (2010) at 10.

[3] *Ibid* at 11.

[4] Clifford D Shearing & Phillip C Stenning, *Private Policing* (SAGE Publications, 1987) at 199.

[5] Susan P Shapiro, "The Social Control of Impersonal Trust" (1987) 93:3 American Journal of Sociology 623–658, See online: <https://www.jstor.org/stable/2780293> at 649, 652.

In short, auditing is demanded under circumstances where resources are entrusted and trust is also lacking and must be restored by the audited activity.[6] As a result, outsiders such as auditors have come into play to correct the flaws inherent in trust by ensuring that the data controller is using the data as was ensured.[7] The identification of different kinds of risk mitigates the possibility of undermining trust. "With trust, there is always risk."[8] Risk entails the unspecific ty of having an expected outcome. Risk also entails an obligation to take precautions.[9] Beyond an institutional normative analysis, there is also a more precautionary approach, which involves having a regulatory enterprise for the purpose of "managing risk",[10] and it relies on how to interpret risk given multiple sociotechnical stakeholders.[11] Generally, risk is seen as a social object. Yvette Viret stated the following:

> Risk as a social object is defined as the perception of danger. Risk exists only in relation to an individual, social or professional group, community or society that perceives it … and deals with it through specific practices. Risk does not exist when there are not people or individuals who perceive or could be affected by it.[12]

Moreover, Risk does not exist in a vacuum.[13] In the context of protecting personal data, consequences are not easily predicted by users when data processors collect their data. People gave consent to sharing their information because they want to use the services provided by the data processor, and they agree to bear risk under the promise made by the data controller that he/she will protect their information. Superficially, the processor himself/herself has the best knowledge of the various substantial factors involved in processing, but how can he/she have a persistent incentive to protect user's personal data From the technical perspective, at the same time, a consistent technical risk we face is that unaccountable algorithms have taken center stage and are now used to make decisions for us, about us, or with us.[14] This technical risk also generates fear that algorithms may allow those who use such techniques to wield power in ways society prohibits or should disfavor, but which

---

[6] Power, *supra* note 10 in Chap. 1 at 134, 135.

[7] Deborah G Johnson & Priscilla M Regan, eds, *Transparency and Surveillance as Sociotechnical Accountability: A House of Mirrors*, 1 edition ed (New York: Routledge, 2014) at 5.

[8] Anthony Giddens, *The Consequences of Modernity*, 1 edition ed (Stanford, Calif: Stanford University Press, 1991) at 34–35.

[9] Trudel, *supra* note 41 in Chap. 1 at 330.

[10] Pierre Trudel, Privacy Protection on the Internet: Risk Management and Networked Normativity (Springer Netherlands, 2009) at 331.

[11] Andy Stirling, "Science, precaution, and the politics of technological risk: converging implications in evolutionary and social scientific perspectives" (2008) 112.8 at 108.

[12] Trudel, *supra* note 41 in Chap. 1 at 330. Yvette Veyret, "Les risques, dossier des images economiques du mondes, Fedes cited by Franck Verdun, La gestion des risques juridiques, (Paris: Editions d'organisation, 2006) at 11.

[13] *Ibid* at 331.

[14] Gry Hasselbalch, "The Ethics of Algorithms: from radical content to self-driving cars" See Center for Internet & Human Rights of European University Viadrina, (2018), See online: <https://cihr.eu/wp-content/uploads> (Visited on April 16, 2019).

society would not be able to detect.[15] As this work suggests, the risk of personal data originated in the social world and was aggregated with a technical background. Different stakeholders of personal data coexist, and the network supposes interconnected environments uniting stakeholders, regulators and the bodies playing a role in the governance of the Internet.[16] We must bear in mind that the scope and effectiveness of personal data protection on the Internet results from risk management decisions.[17] The core problem is to assess the risk associated with different application contexts properly. Various sets of regulation-producing norms compete with one another: technological, market, and legal standards are not always consistent. In some situations, legal references are absent from debates over what is seen as essentially management or technological issues. In other contexts, technology is bridled by law. The system of regulation is designed to re-establish a balance between risks and precautions. It has to encourage all stakeholders to minimize the risks flowing in from situations over which they have some control and to maximize the risk incurred by stakeholders who choose to behave in ways that are harmful or unduly increase risks to legitimate users. Privacy protection on the Internet belongs to this approach. However, an audit served as a risk management system is often confused with the concepts of verification, validation, certification, and assessment. As a matter of fact, it is a misuse of these different concepts to use "audit" interchangeably with them.

2.1.1.1 Deconstructing the Definition of an Audit as Verification

[Concept of Verification] Verification is defined as:

> The act of the process of verifying or the state of being verified.[18]

It often involves proving or checking that it exists or what is true or correct.[19] The word originated from the word "verify," borrowed from the old French term "verifier" of the early sixteenth century or the medieval Latin term "verificatio" and from the classical Latin term "verus". Therefore, the meaning of verification is:

> To check the truthfulness of something" and "to present something as being true.[20]

From social sciences perspective, interpreted by Daniel Little, verification refers to:

> The use of empirical data, observations, tests, or experiments to confirm the truth or rational justification of a hypothesis.[21]

---

[15] Desai & Kroll, *supra* note 59 in Chap. 1 at 4.

[16] *Manuel Castells, "La société en réseaux - Tome 1 : L'Ere de l'information",* (2019) at 21.

[17] Trudel, *supra* note 41 in Chap. 1 at 318.

[18] Merriam-Webster Dictionary, "Definition of verification". See online: https://www.merriam-webster.com/dictionary/verification#h1

[19] IDM, *Cambridge Advanced Learner's Dictionary with CD-ROM*, 4 edition ed (Cambridge: Cambridge University Press, 2013)at 4.

[20] Ibid.

[21] Michael Lewis-Beck, Alan E Bryman & Tim Futing Liao, *The SAGE Encyclopedia of Social Science Research Methods* (SAGE Publications, 2003) at 145.

We have realized that verification is the progress of checking and confirming. Scientific beliefs must be evaluated and supported by empirical data. Two fundamental concepts in discussing scientific methods: truth and justification (Warrant). A hypothesis is true if it corresponds to the way the world is. Justification has to do with the grounds we have for believing a given statement to be true.[22] A hypothesis is rationally warranted if a body of evidence and inference has been provided in support of it. One of the most important consequences of this extended and complex debate is the conclusion that theories cannot be verified, but they can be confirmed, warranted, or falsified.[23] For instance, there are two people, A and B; A tells you that "the sun will rise in the east," and B tells you that "the sun will rise in all directions." We cannot verify the conclusion of A because we are unable to obtain a finite observation to prove that the sun rises in the east. Apparently, the conclusion of A can be falsified because we can try to find evidence that the sun rises in other directions but cannot find a way to deny the conclusion of B. As for the result, verification usually takes the form of indirect inductive or hypothetico-deductive support for the hypothesis: based on evidence, the hypothesis is likely to be true.[24] In other words, the hypothesis itself cannot be verified, but its truthfulness or justification can be confirmed. "Within qualitative research, verification is often used for ensuring reliability and validity which refers to:

> The mechanisms used during the process of research to incrementally contribute to ensuring reliability and validity and, thus, the rigor of a study.[25]

This description of verification does not provide an absolute conclusion as to whether the research is rigorous or not. However, instead, it provides a conclusion on variable concepts, such as reliability or validity. Within the field of computer science, verification often serves as a quality assurance tool, referring to:

> The demonstration of consistency, completeness, and correctness of the software at each stage and between each stage of the development lifecycle.[26]

The verification process is often done along with every step of code construction to ensure that the function codes achieved meet the specification. It saves time in coding and helps stay within the budget because it is easier to find small bugs than errors during the application lifecycle.

[Meaning of verification for personal data protection] To be more specific, the purpose of the GDPR is to prevent the infringement of an individual's rights, such as human rights and the right to protect personal data from the freedom of

[22] *Ibid.*

[23] *Ibid.*

[24] *Ibid.*

[25] Janice M Morse et al., "Verification Strategies for Establishing Reliability and Validity in Qualitative Research": (2016) International Journal of Qualitative Methods, See online: <https://journals.sagepub.com/doi/10.1177/160940690200100202> at 2 (Visited at March 23, 2020).

[26] Adrion Richards, "Validation, Verification, and Testing of Computer Software" Computer Science and Technology (NBS Special Publication 500–75) at 5.

natural persons. Generally, the purpose of data protection laws, as Gratton discussed, is to:

> Address or avoid the risk of harm to individuals triggered by organizations handing their personal information.[27]

In addition, as the Charter requires:

> Compliance with these rules shall be subject to control by an independent authority.[28]

This obviously implies that the compliance process needs to be verified by a third party. As the GDPR requires that:

> The controller shall be responsible for and be able to demonstrate compliance with paragraph 1.[29]

As this book discusses, the general definition of verification can be divided into three parts: First, the material provided for verification; Second, the checking and confirming processes; Third, the conclusion. Thus, verification for personal data protection can be defined as follows: The use of relevant data or evidence given by the data controller to prove that the data processor did not infringe the rights of individuals as well as mitigate the risk of harm to individuals associated with processing personal data and to demonstrate the compliance of rules for data protection. At the same time, it should be noted that the protection of personal data subject to sociotechnical background also raises the question of who should be responsible for verifying this evidence. What kind of evidence needs to be provided? In other words, we should still ask the following questions: Who conducts this verification? Who is being verified? How is the verification process carried out?

[Difference between Verification and Validation] Verification has often appeared alongside another similar appellation, "validation." The definition of "validation" is as follows:

> An activity that ensures that an end-product stakeholder's true needs and expectations are met.[30]

Verification often takes place when software projects are not completed, while validation often starts at the end of a project to ensure that people receive their desired application. For software engineering, verification and validation (V&V) processes are used to "determine whether the development products of a given activity conform to the requirements of that activity and whether the products satisfy its intended uses and user needs. V&V processes include the analysis, evaluation, review, inspection, assessment, and testing of products" (Fig. 2.1).[31]

---

[27] Gratton, *supra* note 32 in Chap. 1 at 5.

[28] Ibid.

[29] GDPR at Article 5 (2).

[30] Note 16 at 610.

[31] IEEE, "IEEE Standard 1012–2012 Standard for System and Software Verification and Validation".

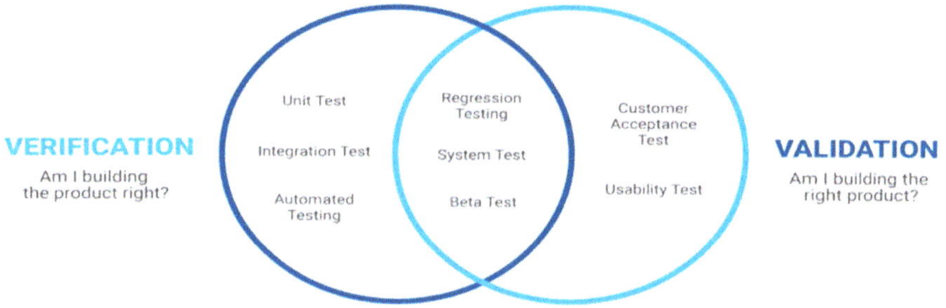

Fig. 2.1 Difference between verification and validation (Plutora blog, "Verification and Validation, do you know the difference"? See online: https://www.plutora.com/blog/verification-vs-validation (Visited on March 25, 2020))

Table 2.1 Certification, testing, and proof of correctness

Certification	Acceptance of software by an authorized agent typically occurs after the software has been validated or its validity has been demonstrated to the agent
Testing	Examining the behavior of a program involves executing the program on sample data sets
Proof of correctness	Use of technical logic to infer that an assertion assumed true at program entry implies that an assertion holds at program exit.

After comparing the concept of verification from both social and technical backgrounds, it can be noted that, verification can be defined as a process of checking, conforming or proving the truthfulness of a theory or of a hypothesis for a specific purpose from a very broad interpretation. However, this is unlikely, as verification is distinguished in the technical field from the concept of validation. The broad definition is unable to illustrate every specific stage of the process to prove or justify its purpose, and the concept of verification is often confused with the concept of certification, testing, and proof of correctness.[32] As a matter of fact, a problem exists as to how to understand verification. To be more precise, shall we define verification as a proving and checking process, or shall we define verification as a status for the purpose of compliance or as a result of proving verifiability? Verification has a specific meaning, in addition to a general meaning, in a specific context (Table 2.1).

2.1.1.2 Deconstruct the Definition of Audit as Certification

[Concept of Certification] The definition provided by the International Standards Organization is as follows:

[32] Richards, *supra* note 32 at 6.

> Certification is a procedure by which a third party gives written assurance that a product, process or service conforms to specified requirements…it is distinct from the other systems of proof of conformity, such as supplier declarations and laboratory test reports.[33]

There are many different tools that can be defined in this way, such as "trust marks, certifications, seals, accreditations." All these processes exist only where there is a "verifiable assertion." In other words, the objective assessment carried out by third parties is indispensable when these verification processes are involved. From this point of view, it is difficult to distinguish between the audits from these processes. This book highlight the distinct features of audits have in the personal data protection context. The first notion that appears in regimes of personal data protection is "certification," a word borrowed from the medieval Latin term "certificatio," which referred to "the act of certifying," as well as from the Christian Latin term "certificatus."[34] According to Cambridge English Dictionary, certification is defined as "the process of earning an official document or the act of providing an official document as proof that something has happened or been done."[35] In other words, it can be referred to as the act of certifying someone or something, the result of having been certified, or an official document. However, the definitions of certification vary in the extant literature. Certification is based on the results of tests, inspections and audits and gives confidence to customers on account of the systematic intervention of a competent third party. Another interpretation given by the World Bank is as follows:

> Product certification involves written documentation that a product meets detailed technical specifications. Governments and consumers are increasingly demanding such certifications of goods in international commerce. Certification involves testing a product against either a voluntary, de facto, or regulatory standard and is often carried out in organizations that are independent of any link to the manufacturer or purchaser. After testing, a certificate is issued that attests to the fact that a product meets a set standard.[36]

In most of the scientific literature, the definition of certification can be classified into two approaches: some envisage it as a conformity assessment process, while others deem it as an attestation of conformity.[37] Certification schemes contain standards, processes to check compliance initially and over time and marks to

---

[33] Conroy Michael, "Can Advocacy-Led Certification Systems Transform GlobalCorporate Practices? Evidence and Some Theory" (Political Economy Research Institute, 2001) at 4.

[34] Oxford Dictionaries, ed., *Oxford Dictionary of English*, third edition ed (New York, NY: Oxford University Press, 2010).

[35] IDM, *supra* note 25.

[36] Michael, *supra* note 40 at 4.

[37] Eric Lachaud, "Why the certification process defined in the General Data Protection Regulation cannot be successful" (2016) 32:6 Computer Law & Security Review 814–826, See online: <http://www.sciencedirect.com/science/article/pii/S0267364916301157> at 815. As Eijlander believed, "Certification is a method of (conformity) assessment". See "A study commissioned by the Ministry of Economic Affairs." Instituut, Centrumvoor Wetgevingsvraagstukken, Universiteit van Tilburg, (2003) at 12. Additionally, see "Third party attestation related to products, processes, systems or persons" in ISO/IEC 17000:2004: General Vocabulary: "Certification includes all activities under which an independent, expert and reliable institution adopts and writes that there is a

reward compliance.[38] Although diverse connotations can be discovered in different disciplines, similarly, certification is a market-driven process designed to encourage compliance with standards by providing the customer with confidence.[39] In other words, certification is always a profit process in practice. One substantial element of certification is that it severely relies on the recognition and confidence of users or consumers, it endeavors to eliminate information asymmetry among goods, lowering consumer search costs by "informing the consumer that a good that bears a specific mark has the same quality and characteristics as other products that bear that same mark."[40] In other words, certification adopts voluntary self-regulatory measures to promote consumer trust and confidence in e-commerce.[41] It indeed pushes the issue of trust back from producers to certified entities. However, do consumers or users understand the information that certification aims to express?

[Object-oriented Process] Certification is defined as an "object-oriented" process that is static and implies a nexus between concrete products and specific standards within the IT sector. In other words, the degree of stability of a product or standard needs to be known for the certification process, which often focuses on specific products and services.[42] For instance, the "Wi-Fi" mark, owned by the Wi-Fi alliance, is widely used worldwide.[43] As a result, a product with the "WI-FI CERTIFIED" mark (Fig. 2.2), which is registered by the alliance, is known as complying with a series of IEEE 802.11 networking standards.

Regarding certification for personal data protection, the consequences stemming from this process demonstrate that the services or a specific product provided by a company comply with data protection laws and regulations at a specific point in time. This process eagerly protects the rights of users through its the method of consumer protection. However, data protection compliance, which is largely influenced by the operational environment, scourges the stability required for certification, and the addition of factors such as the installation of hardware and software also needs to be considered as a whole when the certification scheme is processed.[44] This, As a matter of fact, acts as an obstacle to the standardization of different prod-

---

justified confidence that a clearly defined object (product, process, system or the competence of a person) meets predetermined requirements".

[38] Michael, *supra* note 40 at 64.

[39] World Standards Services Network, "General Info on Standardization. Additionally, see: The World Bank Group International Trade & Development, "Standards and International Trade: Introductory Lecture: Basic Concepts: Product Standards." (2019) at 12.

[40] William P Kratzake, "*Normative Economic Analysis of Trademark Law*," (1991),Social Science Research Network191 at 207.

[41] Rowena Rodrigues et al., "The future of privacy certification in Europe: an exploration of options under article 42 of the GDPR" (2016) 30:3 Int Rev. Law Comput Technol 248–270 at 252. Also See Rodrigues, Wright and Wadhwa, *"Developing a Privacy Seal Scheme"*(2013) International Data privacy law 3(2) at 96.

[42] Peter Rott, "*Certification – Trust, Accountability, Liability*" (Springer, 2019) at 119.

[43] Jorge L Contreras: "*Trademarks, Certification Marks and Technical Standards*", (Social Science Research Network, 2018) at 24.

[44] Rott, *supra* note 49 at 115.

Fig. 2.2 WiFi mark

ucts operational environments. To find a solution, technology-specific requirements need to be proposed because a general requirement of data protection compliance may be too vague for a valid certification process. In addition, the ambiguity of the roles that certification enacts in DPAs has challenged the reliability of such an approach. The word "accreditation" was borrowed from the classical French term "accreditation," which is divisible into accreditors, meaning those who "give credence to" and "believe."[45] It conveys the perception of the fact of being officially recognized, accepted or approved of or the act of officially recognizing, accepting, or approving of something.[46] Many certification bodies serving as independent third parties often need to prove their competence and be formally accredited by accreditation bodies, which are often known as "accredited certification bodies." This accreditation is As a matter of fact proof of the competency or authority of these third parties. Well-known accreditation entities, such as International Accreditation Services (IAS), have conducted accreditation processes according to the International Organization for Standardization (ISO). For personal data protection, accreditation is often used to justify the legitimacy of the certification body. For instance, the GDPR noted the following:

> The accreditation of certification bodies as referred to in paragraphs 1 and 2 of this Article shall take place on the basis of the criteria approved by the supervisory authority, which is competent pursuant to Article 55 or 56 or by the Board pursuant to Article 63…those requirements shall complement those envisaged in Regulation (EC) No. 765/2008 and the technical rules that describe the methods and procedures of certification bodies.[47]

National supervisory authorities have the power to regulate certification bodies. In 2015, the UK Information Commissioner's Office (ICO) adopted a coregulatory approach for privacy seals to ensure that "any ICO privacy seal scheme is viable, promotes high standards and complements existing priorities."[48] In addition, accreditation can also be conducted by the national accreditation body in accordance with EN-ISO/IEC 17065/2012 (ISO 2012).[49] Alternatively, based Article 70.1 of the GDPR, the European Data Protection Board (EDPB) can "carry out the

[45] IDM, *supra* note 25.

[46] *Ibid.*

[47] Article 43 of GDPR.

[48] Rodrigues et al., "The future of privacy certification in Europe", *supra* note 9 in Chap. 1 at 11.

[49] "Conformity assessment-requirements for bodies certifying products, processes and services." See International Organization for Standardization. See online: http://www.iso.org/iso/catalogue_detail.htm?csnumber=46568 (Visited on May 5, 2020).

accreditation of certification bodies and their periodic review pursuant to Article 43."[50] Generally, accreditation has seemed to harmonize the standard for certification across the EU in a self-regulatory context.

[Certification and Trademark] From a legal point of view, certification is usually qualified as a "special trademark" that "protects the rights of the third parties that have been authorized to use it."[51] As a matter of fact, certification marks evolved from trademarks. A trademark is a word, name, symbol or other device that is used to identify the source of a particular product or service, and the ability to be allowed to use this mark is affected by its distinctiveness.[52] Trademarks must be used in commerce if there is a need for proof of valid. The value of trademarks originated through the recognition of users, and their own experiences determined the meaning attached to trademarks.[53] This is why firms invest enormous amounts of money in trademarks. As Burgunder stated:

> Brand image…a complex constellation of associations and images that comprise a consumer's knowledge of the brand and his/her attitudes towards it. It may include knowledge on the source of the product, awareness of other product characteristics, beliefs about the value of the object, and judgments about the suitability of the brand.[54]

For instance, UK firms invest 33 billion pounds per year in trademarks, which equates to 12 percent of all intangible investment in the UK economy.[55] To allow consumers to have positive feedback on their products, companies endeavor to build a well-known trademark that embodies strong reputations and features powerful connections between producers and individual consumers.[56] This trademark is summarized by the Westminster Business School as follows:

> A brand is a reputational asset that has been developed over time to embrace a set of values and attributes, resulting in a powerfully held set of beliefs by consumers and a range of other stakeholders.[57]

---

[50] Article 70.1 of the GDPR: European Data Protection Board, on its own initiative or, where relevant, at the request of European the Commission, shall carry out the accreditation of certification bodies and their periodic review pursuant to Article 43 and maintain a public register of accredited bodies pursuant to Article 43.6 and of the accredited controllers or processors established in third countries pursuant to Article 42.7. The board may specify the requirements for the accreditation of certification bodies under Article 43. See Rodrigues et al., "The future of privacy certification in Europe", *supra* note 9 in Chap. 1 at 12.

[51] Jeffrey Belson, *Certification Marks* (Sweet & Maxwell, 2002) at 20."

[52] "A certification mark is statutorily defined as an indication that the goods and services in connection with which the mark is used are certified by the proprietor in respect to origin, material, mode of manufacture of goods or performance of service, quality, accuracy or other characteristics." See Jorge L Contreras, Contreras, *supra* note 50 at 3.

[53] Contreras, *supra* note 50 at 14.

[54] Lee B Burgunder, "An Economic Approach to Trademark Genericism" (1985) 23:3 American Business Law Journal 391–416. See online: <https://onlinelibrary.wiley.com/doi/abs/10.1111/j.1744-1714.1985.tb00480.x> at 402.

[55] Deven R Desai, "Brands, Competition Law and IP."(Cambridge University Press, 2015) at 50.

[56] *Ibid* at 48.

[57] Urwin Peter, "Valuing brands in the UK economy" (2008) Westminster Business for British Brands Group, See online: <https://westminsterresearch.westminster.ac.uk/item/918qv/valuing-brands-in-the-uk-economy> at 9.

In other words, by nature, brand building by companies to highlight the importance of a "consumer-centric" approach requires "ongoing, profound consumer insights in order to satisfy ever-evolving needs and wants better than competitors."[58] Trademarks heavily rely on market mechanisms, which emphasize the interaction between users and producers. In any market context, trademarks play an informational and identificatory role, which is also the objective of trademark law.[59] The opposite is also true: There will be no investment in a word or symbol that cannot convey product information. In other words, the "monopolistic competition" conferred to the trademark enables producers to execute their exclusive rights to use the trademark for the sake of distinguishing their product from those of their competitors.[60] Trademarks and certification marks are both essential to the standardization ecosystem, as stated by Conroy:

> Certification is not only an assessment, it's a complete ecosystem.[61]

This ecosystem composes a series of stakeholders that interact with each other, designating certification as a process or a result.[62] Certification marks differs from certification and can be defined as a species of trademarks, although dissimilar from trademarks in their intention to indicate to consumers the source of a particular product, and are intended to identify the particular characteristics of a product to consumers, typically when those characteristics are not easily discernable from an inspection of the product.[63] Nelson, Darby and Karni distinguished three types of products on the market: "search goods, experience goods and credence goods."[64] Search goods involve the situation where no information asymmetries exist because all parties related to the deal have complete information about the goods, which is easily acquired; experience goods involve situations in which buyers cannot easily acquire the information of goods before they buy them but can do so after purchase; credence goods involve the situation in which buyers cannot easily acquire the information of goods even after buying them.[65] As for consequences, "adverse selection," as introduced by Akerlof in 1970, may occur, where buyers are not

58 Ibid at 49.

59 Kratzke, *supra* note 47 at 209.

60 R F Harrod, "The Theory of Monopolistic Competition. by Edward Chamberlin" (1933) 43:172 Econ J 661–666. See online: <https://academic.oup.com/ej/article/43/172/661/5267382> at 664.

61 Michael, *supra* note 40 at 64.

62 Lachaud, *supra* note 44 at 816.

63 Contreras, *supra* note 50 at 5.

64 Phillip Nelson, "Information and Consumer Behavior" (1970) 78:2 Journal of Political Economy. See online: <https://www.jstor.org/stable/1830691> at 326. Also see Michael Darby & Edi Karni, "Free Competition and the Optimal Amount of Fraud" (1973) 16:1 Journal of Law and Economics 67–88. See online: <https://econpapers.repec.org/article/ucpjlawec/v_3a16_3ay_3a1973_3ai_3a1_3ap_3a67-88.htm> at 67. (Visited at 12 March 2020)

65 Peter Rott, *Certification – Trust, Accountability, Liability* (Springer, 2019) at 12.

willing to offer a higher price than the average price for more valuable goods.[66] Based on the theory of Akerlof, Viscusi proposed a model for market-based certification for quality and believed that it is not worthwhile for low-quality producers to have certification because consumers will decide which high-quality certified goods they can buy at a specific price.[67] However, economic analyses cannot fully interpret the role of a reputation in the certification market to solve the problem of information asymmetry.[68] Certifications or seals enable Internet companies to demonstrate accountability for data protection or compliance with laws and regulations.[69] Regarding the topic of this book, it should be noted that the GDPR has endorsed two elements associated with the certification process.[70] The purpose of the introduction of a certification approach by European legislators it was to help them implement the principles of accountability and transparency. Theoretically, certification cannot be issued without a successful assessment, but practically, this is not always true. As a matter of fact, some certification is issued following a self-assessment or even a self-declaration of conformity without the required assessment.[71] Currently, there are several data protection certification schemes in operation, such as ESPB Privacy Online Certification, EuroPrisSe, GIgya's Social Privacy Certification, Privo Privacy Certified, and Trustify-me Privacy Certification Seal.[72] These schemes are provided by either private or public bodies and adhere to different kinds of standards and rules. However, all these privacy certification programs fall short of achieving the purpose of personal data protection regulations in different ways.[73] To be more specific, there are several arguments for the efficiency of such an approach, for instance, the problem of conflicts of interest in which certification issuers are too close to their clients regarding earning a commercial profit,[74] invalid guarantees regarding

[66] GEORGE A Akerlof, "The Market for Lemons: Quality unspecific and the market mechanism". in PETER Diamond & Michael Rothschild, eds, *Unspecific Econ* (Academic Press, 1978) at 235.

[67] Rott, *supra* note 49 at 13.

[68] W Kip Viscusi, "A Note on 'Lemons' Markets with Quality Certification" (1978) 9:1 at 279.

[69] IAPP, "Certifications, Seals and Marks under the GDPR and Their Roles as Accountability Tools and Cross-Border Data Transfer Mechanisms" at 3. See online: https://iapp.org/media/pdf/resource_center/cipl_gdpr_certifications_discussion_paper_12_april_2017.pdf (Visited on May 3, 2020).

[70] Lachaud, *supra* note 44 at 807. Additionally, See the joint statement on the final adoption of new EU rules for personal data protection of the 14 April 2016. Also See Data protection reform-Parliament approves new rules fit for the digital era-Press release-Policy Cooperation.

[71] See Lachaud, *supra* note 44 at 816. Additionally, See: Michael E Conroy, *Branded, How the "Certification Revolution" is Transforming Global Corporations*(New Society Publishers, 2007) at 12: Certification scheme involves: Set of requirements, Assessment Process. Certification can be issued by self-assessment or 1/3 party.

[72] Alessandro Mantelero, *The Future of Consumer Data Protection in the E.U. Rethinking the "Notice and Consent" Paradigm in the New Era of Predictive Analytics*. (Social Science Research Network, 2014) at 13.

[73] David Wright & Paul De Hert, *Enforcing Privacy: Regulatory, Legal and Technological Approaches* (Springer, 2016) at Part 1.4.

[74] Rhee, Joseph, and Brain Ross, "Terror Group Gets 'A' Rating From Better Business Bureau?" See Online: https://abcnews.go.com/Blotter/business-bureau-best-ratings-money-buy/story?id=12123843 (Visited on April 27–28, 2020).

the data protections of ambiguous evaluation and verification processes, a lack of enforcement for violating certification requirements,[75] and confusion among users as to what is being certified.[76] An important settlement involving these concerns occurred in the U.S. In which TRUSTe agreed to settle with the US Federal Trade Commission (FTC) concerning its deception regarding its certification practices.[77] The FTC ordered the following:

> TRUSTe should directly or indirectly not misrepresent, in any manner, expressly or by implication (a) the steps it takes to evaluate, certify, review, or recertify a company's privacy practices; (b) the frequency with which it conducts any such evaluation, certification, review, or recertification of a company's privacy practices; (c) its corporate status and its independence; and (d) the extent to which the person or entity is a member of, adheres to, complies with, is certified by, is endorsed by, or otherwise participates in any privacy program sponsored by TRUSTe.[78]

This presented an awkward situation where a trust scheme need to have more confidence for regulators and users. Private standard setting has become increasingly interconnected with public regulation since the WTO was established in 1995. Trademarks are an indispensable part of this regulatory regime; they contribute to harmonizing of private standards, sustainable global production and development-oriented trade. Significant international standard-setting and harmonizing organizations, such as the International Organization for Standardization (ISO), play an important role in mediating various stakeholders and standards.[79] The question that needs to be asked is as follows: "Can a standard or compliance be exchanged for money?"

An interchangeable concept in certification is a privacy seal, which is a certification mark or a guarantee issued by a certifying entity verifying an organization's adherence to specified privacy standards that aim to promote consumer trust and confidence in ecommerce.[80] A privacy seal emphasizes the role of the 'mark,' which attracts the attention of the data subject (Fig. 2.3). It is a visual signal that highlights that the website or services delivered conform with privacy protection requirements, and it acts as a brand label guaranteeing that the data controller adheres to specific

[75] Lee In, *Electronic Business: Concepts, Methodologies, Tools, and Applications: Concepts, Methodologies, Tools, and Applications* (IGI Global, 2008) at 10.

[76] Connolly, "*Trustmark Schemes Struggle to Protect Privacy.*"(2008) See online: http://www.galexia.com/public/research/assets/trustmarks_struggle_20080926/ (Visited on April 27–28, 2020).

[77] Wright & Hert, *supra* note 80 at 280.

[78] Federal Trade Commission, "In the Matter of True Ultimate Standards Everywhere, Inc., a corporation. Agreement containing consent order". See online: https://www.ftc.gov/news-events/press-releases/2015/03/ftc-approves-final-order-truste-privacy-case (Visited on April 28, 2020).

[79] Rott, *supra* note 49. Also see, Margaret Chon, "Marks and more(s): certification in global value chains" (2014) Trademark Prot Territ Chall Glob Econ at 315. See Online: <https://www.elgaronline.com/view/edcoll/9781781953907/9781781953907.00013.xml> (Visited on May 10, 2020).

[80] Rowena Rodrigues, David Wright & Kush Wadhwa, "Developing a privacy seal scheme (that works)" (2013) 3:2 Int Data Priv Law at 112.

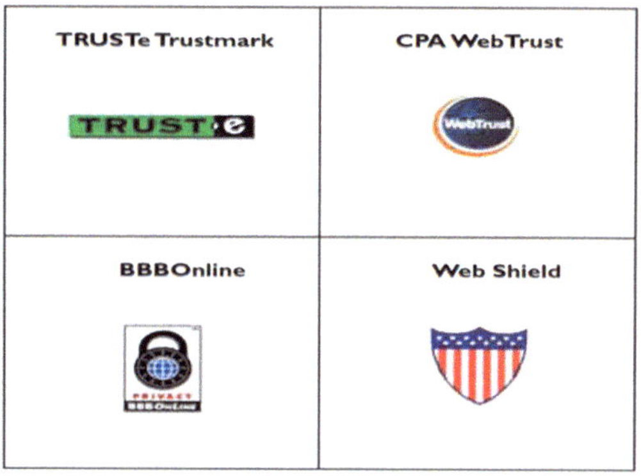

Fig. 2.3 The Four Main Web Assurance Seals

principles. However, do consumers understand the role of privacy seals?[81] Most users understand that privacy seals are related to promoting trust online, but they are generally unaware of what a site must do to acquire a seal or even what a genuine seal actually looks like.[82] Moreover, some users simply were not aware of the existence of privacy seals. According to Moore:

> Most of the respondents do not fully understand the form or function of privacy seals.[83]

2.1.1.3 Deconstructing the Definition of Audit as Evaluation

[Definition of evaluation] Since the 1990s, numerous pieces of literature have delved into the practical distinctions between evaluation and audit, with a series of articles written by Rist, Leeuw, and Wisler.[84] The origins of program evaluation could be traced to the Age of reform in England, where studies of educational achievement conducted in the year 1879 brought contemporary recommendations for "incentives" to teachers in the form of "payment by results." A recent definition of evaluation given by Chelimsky referred to as:

> The application of systematic research methods to the assessment of program design, implementation and effectiveness.[85]

---

[81] Trevor Moores, "Do consumers understand the role of privacy seals in e-commerce?" (2005) 48:3 Commun ACM 86–91. See online: <https://doi.org/10.1145/1047671.1047674> at 86 (Visited at 26 Feb 2021).

[82] *Ibid* at 88.

[83] *Ibid* at 91.

[84] Ray C Rist, "Management Accountability: The Signals sent by Auditing and Evaluation" (1989) 9:3 Journal of Public Policy 355–369, See online: <https://www.cambridge.org/core/journals/journal-of-public-policy/article/abs/management-accountability-the-signals-sent-by-auditing-and-evaluation/43D61F356063BDDD9B0F062E85FF3281#> at 360.

[85] Eleanor Chelimsky, "Comparing and Contrasting Auditing and Evaluation: Some Notes on Their Relationship" (1985) 9:4 Eval Rev. 483–503, See online: <https://doi.org/10.1177/0193841X8500900406> at 488.

For evaluation, terms also include various methods such as qualitative and quantitative, experimental, theory-based, empowerments, etc. Chelimsky provides a good general definition of evaluation:

> Evaluation is careful retrospective assessment of the merit, worth and value of administration, output and outcome of government interventions, which is intended to play a role in future, practical action situations.[86]

[Audit and evaluation] To clarify the difference between audit and evaluation, it may be helpful to build a basis for analyze these two concepts from learning and accountability. Audit is more characterized by the concept of accountability whereas evaluation more focus on learning. In other words, audit is not sought to inform policy or program design. The term "audit" is used to represent a range of activates, and audit is being conducted through different contexts. Following the explanation of Barzelay, the traditional audit can be distinguished from a performance audit and a regulatory audit.[87] A Performance audit defines itself with different perspectives of performance within an organization which could distinguish two types: substantive performance as well as procedures performance audits.[88] A modern development stipulated the growth of performance audits to assess the effectiveness and efficiency as well as economy of the audited body. Usually, this type of audit is discrete and focuses on evaluation-type methods such as surveys, data analysis, and focus group. Unlike an audit, some of them are conducted through accountability. As a matter of fact, in different contexts, the terms of the work for evaluation are determined by the management team of the organization. Most of the time, evaluation is to help identify appropriate policies and how it can be more effective. In other words, the role and profession of evaluation are very different from audit. As Mayne noted:

> While audit may be able to evolve to better meet a secondary purpose of fostering improvements in public programs and their management, their primary purpose and corresponding institutional setting would seem to ensure that most external performance auditing and evaluation will continue to have different roles to play.[89]

Mayne identified three purposes of evaluation to increase knowledge about the evaluation target, to improve delivery to public and to justify and reconsider the rationale for the policy or program.[90] From the perspective of methods used between evaluation and audit, Leeuw and Divorski noted that they are quite different. For

---

[86] *Ibid* at 485.

[87] Michael Barzelay, "Central Audit Institutions and Performance Auditing: A Comparative Analysis of Organizational Strategies in the OECD" (1997) 10:3 Governance 235–260, See online: <https://onlinelibrary.wiley.com/doi/abs/10.1111/0952-1895.411997041> at 246.

[88] OECD: *Performance auditing and the modernisation of government*, Public Management Service (Paris: OECD, 1996) at 132.

[89] John Mayne, "Ensuring quality for evaluation: Lessons from auditors" (2005) 20 Canadian Journal of Program Evaluation 37–64 at 55.

[90] John Mayne, "Audit and evaluation in public management: Challenges, reforms, and different roles" (2006) 21 Canadian Journal of Program Evaluation 11–45 at 20.

instance, the experimental and quasi-experimental designs have been applied infrequently in performance audits.[91] From perspective of institutional settings, Pollitt and Summa pointed that audit usually focused on corrective action and accountability of the organization. At the same time, evaluation does not have an institutional base. Iingts aim is to help the entity to improve.[92] Schwartz often criticized evaluation as is not providing definitive conclusions and is not robust. As a matter of fact, keeping audit and evaluation separate is the best model in most organizations.[93] External audit may not be suitable for evaluation, and evaluation shall not focus on organizational systems and procedures.[94]

In summary, there are some distinguishing differences between audit and evaluation. First, audit always asked normative questions, whereas evaluation always addresses descriptive and cause-and-effect questions. Second, the audit always assumed that the agreement on "established criteria" could always be found, while evaluations use criteria-referenced designes more rarely. It always focuses on the relationship between the changes that have been found. The third is that an audit does not produce what might happen in the absence of the program while evaluation does. However, from practical perspective, both audit and evaluation face challenges in playing their roles. For instance, they have also faced the challenge of credibility where quality assurance practices in evaluation and audit are often highlighted in different standardizations and white papers (Fig. 2.4).[95]

[Definition of Assessment in connection with personal data protection] Assessment, as defined by Oxford Languages, is:

> The evaluation or estimation of nature, quality, or ability of someone or something. It is the action or instance of making a judgment about something.[96]

It is a process by which information needs to be acquired relative to some goal or objective. It is meant to help define the current situation and reveal new insights for providing direction for improvement efforts. Compared with evaluation, assessment is usually based on a process instead of a project. As noted by Federal Trade Commission, Privacy Impact Assessment is referred as:

---

[91] Stan Divorski, "Differences in the approaches of auditors and evaluators to the examination of government policies and programs" (1996) 1996:71 New Directions for Evaluation 7–14, See online: <https://onlinelibrary.wiley.com/doi/abs/10.1002/ev.1039> at 13 (Visited at 12 January 2022).

[92] Christopher Pollitt & Hilkka Summa, "Performance audit and evaluation: Similar tools, different relationships?" (1996) 1996:71 New Directions for Evaluation 29–50. See online: <https://onlinelibrary.wiley.com/doi/10.1002/ev.1041> at 39 (Visited 12 January, 2022).

[93] Robert Schwartz & John Mayne, *Does Quality Matter? Who Cares about the Quality of Evaluative Information?* (Routledge, 2018) at 301.

[94] Marie-Louise Bemelmans-Videc, *Dilemmas for Evaluation and for Audit* (New York: Routledge, 2017) at 12.

[95] Chelimsky, "Comparing and Contrasting Auditing and Evaluation", *supra* note 92 at 501.

[96] Dictionaries, *supra* note 41.

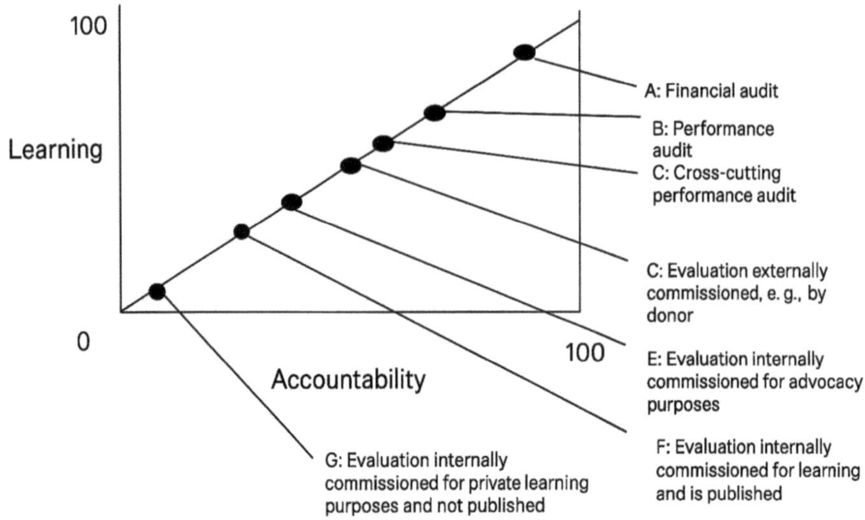

Fig. 2.4 Accountability curve

> An analysis of how personally identifiable information is collected, used, shared and maintained.[97]

The purpose of a PIA is to demonstrate that program managers and system owners at the FTC have consciously incorporated privacy protections throughout the development lifecycle of a system or program. Data protection impact assessment defined by information commissioner's office of United Kingdom as:

> A process to help you identify and minimize the data protection risks of a project.[98]

Although GDPR does not give a clear definition of data protection impact assessment, it gives a clear content scope as:

> A systematic description of the envisaged processing operations and the purposes of the processing, including, where applicable, the legitimate interest pursued by the controller; an assessment of the necessity and proportionality of the processing operations in relation to the purposes; an assessment of the risks to the rights and freedoms of data subjects referred to in paragraph 1; and; The measures envisaged to address the risks, including safeguards, security measures and mechanisms to ensure the protection of personal data and to demonstrate compliance with this Regulation taking into account the rights and legitimate interests of data subjects and other persons concerned.[99]

---

[97] "Federal Trade Commission Privacy Impact Assessments". See FTC website, See online: https://www.ftc.gov/policy-notices/privacy-policy/privacy-impact-assessments (Visited at December 19, 2022)

[98] Data protection risk assessment: See online: https://ico.org.uk/for-organisations/uk-gdpr-guidance-and-resources/accountability-and-governance/guide-to-accountability-and-governance/accountability-and-governance/data-protection-impact-assessments/ (Visited at 11 January, 2024)

[99] "Guide to the General Data Protection Regulation (GDPR)"(1 November 2018), See online: <https://ico.org.uk/for-organisations/guide-to-the-general-data-protection-regulation-gdpr/> (Visted at 11January, 2024)

From Chinese legislation perspective, Article 56 of PIPL explains the substance of personal data protection assessment as:

> (a) Whether the purpose of processing personal information, the manner of processing, etc. is legal, legitimate and necessary.
> (b) The impact on the rights and interests of individuals and security risks.
> (c) whether the protection measures taken are legal, effective and appropriate to the degree of risk.[100]

Compared with the definition and content of data protection impact assessment within different jurisdictions, this book found that, usually, the size and scope of an impact assessment depend on factors such as the importance of the information being processed, the extent to which personal information is collected, used or disclosed, the budget for the impact assessment, and the time required to perform the impact assessment. The more extensive the scale of the information is, the more comprehensive the impact assessment should be. Conversely, if the scope of impact of a processing is relatively limited, only an abbreviated personal information protection impact assessment may be required. An impact assessment is a resource-intensive exercise, and personal information processors should consider the impact assessment's objectives, scale and scope in a manner commensurate with the risks identified. If the risk is not significant, then the size and scope of the impact assessment may be limited. The impact assessment should be more detailed. The size and scope of the assessment can be updated and supplemented at any time as the treatment process evolves and the issues become clearer.

[Applicable condition of DPIA] Article 35 systematically corresponds to Articles 24, 25, and 36 of the General Data Protection Regulation (GDPR). Article 35 of GDPR states:

> Where a type of processing in particular using new technologies, and taking into account the nature, scope, context and purposes of the processing, is likely to result in a high risk to the rights and freedoms of natural persons, the controller shall, prior to the processing, carry out an assessment of the impact of the envisaged processing operations on the protection of personal data. A single assessment may address a set of similar processing operations that present similar high risks.[101]

The article then stipulated the applicable conditions as:

> A systematic and extensive evaluation of personal aspects relating to natural persons which is based on automated processing, including profiling, and on which decisions are based that produce legal effects concerning the natural person or similarly significantly affect the natural person; Processing on a large scale of special categories of data referred to in Article 9(1), or of personal data relating to criminal convictions and offences referred to in Article 10 or a systematic monitoring of a publicly accessible area on a large scale.[102]

---

[100] Ibid at article 56.

[101] "Guideline of GDPR", *Supra* note 106 at 14.

[102] *Ibid.*

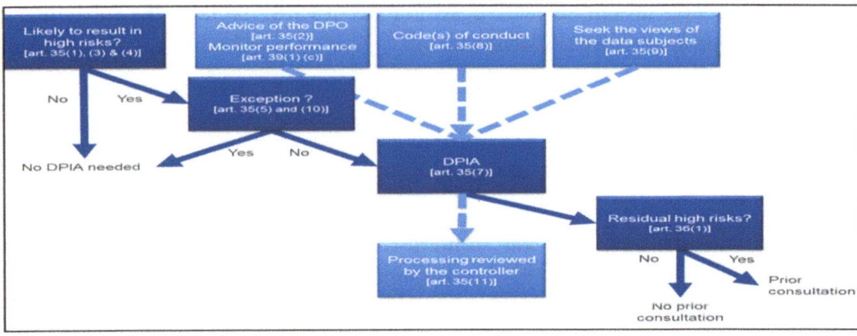

Fig. 2.5 The basic principles related to the DPIA in the GDPR

Article 24 outlines general provisions addressing the risks associated with data processing. It mandates that data controllers implement appropriate technical and organizational measures to ensure compliance with the GDPR. Article 25 focuses on the principles of design and default data protection, emphasizing the necessity of specific actions during the planning and actual data processing. It clarifies the requirement for a data protection impact assessment before processing personal data. This assessment ensures the consideration of the rights and freedoms of individuals during data processing. Risks should be eliminated or mitigated through technical, procedural, and other design aspects. Additionally, Article 36 stipulates that if the data protection impact assessment reveals a higher risk associated with data processing, and data controller takes no additional measures, the controller must seek the opinion of the data protection supervisory authority before initiating the data processing (Fig. 2.5).[103]

Compared with GDPR, Article 55 of PIPL stated that:

> In any of the following cases, the personal information processor shall conduct a prior impact assessment of personal information protection and record the handling.
> (i) Handling of sensitive personal information.
> (ii) The use of personal information for automated decision-making.
> (iii) Entrusting the handling of personal information, providing personal information to other personal information processors, and disclosing personal information.
> (iv) Providing personal information outside the country.
> (v) Other personal information processing activities that have a significant impact on the rights and interests of individuals.[104]

Before personal information protection law of China published, the national standard association of China announced: "Information Security Technology Personal Information Security Impact Assessment Guide" (GB/T 39335-2020), published in

[103] "Guidelines on Data Protection Impact Assessment (DPIA)" See official website of European Union. See online: https://ec.europa.eu/newsroom/article29/items/611236 (Visited at 27 January, 2024)

[104] Article 55 of Personal Information Protection Law of People's Republic of China (Visited at 18 December, 2022).

November 2020 and effective on June 1, 2021, happens to provide a solid and scientific basis for the implementation of Article 55 and 56 of the Personal Information Protection Law.[105] Attributed to the National Technical Standards Committee for Information Security (TC260), the standard was developed over two years ago and fully draws on the latest legal provisions, institutional design, standard texts and practical practices of the United States, Europe and other countries and regions, such as China's Personal Information Protection Law (Draft), ISO/IEC 29134:2017 "Privacy Impact Assessment Guidelines," the EU Data Protection Board (EDPB)'s Data Protection Impact Assessment Guidelines (WP248), the French National Commission on Freedom of Information (CNIL)'s Privacy Impact Assessment Guidelines and Tools, and the U.S. National Institute of Standards and Technology (NIST)'s standard document on Privacy Impact Assessment, etc.

In sum, GDPR and PIPL both set up risk assessment mechanisms for high risk scenarios; besides some similarities contexts such as automated decision-making and large volumes of personal data being processed, PIPL is more specific for explaining what kind of context could be or shall be defined as high risk with the supporting technical standards. Besides, the PIPL also included consideration from a data localization perspective, such as cross-border data transfer.

2.2 Deconstructing the Effectiveness of the Audit

For this part, the paper explores historical theories of auditing, shifting from policing financial honesty to broader social control mechanisms for accountability. It navigates the concept of accountability within data protection laws, particularly in relation to GDPR, highlighting the evolving nature of accountability and its contextual application. The discussion emphasizes the challenges in measuring accountability and the liability issues faced by data controllers. The paper then focuses on goal of audit in transparency, emphasizing its role in offering visibility and understanding within the GDPR's framework. It highlights the challenges in providing technical methods for algorithmic and data transparency, especially in complex systems. In sum, this book found that audit could deliver many things, while it is a more "control" system other than guarantee the result of accountability.

2.2.1 Deconstructing Audit for Accountability

[Audit Theory] As discussed above, the word "audit" always appears in the context of having normative requirements. There is, of course, a danger that some practitioners will believe that they do not need a philosophy or set of unifying theories that

---

[105] National Standardization Management Committee: See online: https://openstd.samr.gov.cn/bzgk/gb/newGbInfo?hcno=9EA84C0C3C2DBD3997B23F8E6C8ECA35 (Visited at 19 December, 2022).

explain what they do or should do.[106] These people believe that auditing is a series of practical procedures and techniques without the need for clarification, so it is difficult to organize the audit process as "theory."[107] As a matter of fact, the theory of audits is demanding for a series of reasons, stated by Mautz and Sharaf as follows:

> Through a serious and substantial investigation into the possibility and nature of auditing theory, the hope is that it will provide us with solutions or, at least, clues to identify solutions to problems that we now find difficult.[108]

The definition given by Mautz and Sharaf explain why audits exist in the first place and the purpose of conducting an audit. As a starting point for understanding audits, one sentiment is that auditing is a "rule-governed" practice.[109] Auditing is an institutional practice that follows the rules promulgated by institutions.[110] Thus, to understand the meaning of an audit is to understand how the rules are settled and which rules should be promulgated. For instance, in the United States, financial auditors should follow the rules and standards of the American Institute of Certified Public Accountants (hereafter AICPA). Internal auditors adhere to the guidelines of their professional organization, the Institute of Internal Auditors (hereafterIIA).[111] To set a standard, it is very important to agree on the desires that the standard setter is going to use in making standard-setting decisions.[112] In other words, the identification of the objectives of rulemaking is essential, as is the objective of the audit, because the nature of the audit sets out appropriate practice standards.[113] As Dennis noted, rather than analyzing what the concept of an audit ought to be, it is better to conduct "normative theorizing," the meaning of which is as follows:

> The outcome of these activities constitutes a normative theory of practice.[114]

There are four types of theories that can be identified in terms of their purpose: policeman theory, lending credibility theory, the theory of inspired confidence, and agency theory (Fig. 2.6).[115]

Policeman theory regards the auditing process as detecting and preventing fraud. Taking financial audits as an example, the detection of fraud seemed to be the

---

[106] Iain Gray & Stuart Manson, *The Audit Process: Principles, Practice and Cases*, 5 edition ed (Andover: Cengage Learning EMEA, 2011) at 31.

[107] Robert Kuhn Mautz & Hussein Amer Sharaf, *The philosophy of auditing* (American Accounting Association, 1961) at 1.

[108] *Ibid.* Additionally, see Yliopiston julkaisuja Vaasan, *A Theoretical Examination of the Role of Auditing and the Relevance of Audit Reports* (Opetusjulkaisuja 61 Business administration 28 Accounting and Finance, 2010) at 7.

[109] Brian P West, *Professionalism and Accounting Rules* (Routledge, 2003) at 66.

[110] Dennis, *supra* note 6 at 21.

[111] Robert R Moeller, *IT Audit, Control, and Security*, 1 edition ed (Wiley, 2010) at 3.

[112] Dennis, *supra* note 6 at 22.

[113] *Ibid* at 137.

[114] *Ibid* at 33.

[115] Rick Hayes, *Principles of Auditing, 3rd edition*, (Harlow, England London New York: Trans-Atlantic Pubns Inc., 2014) at 14.

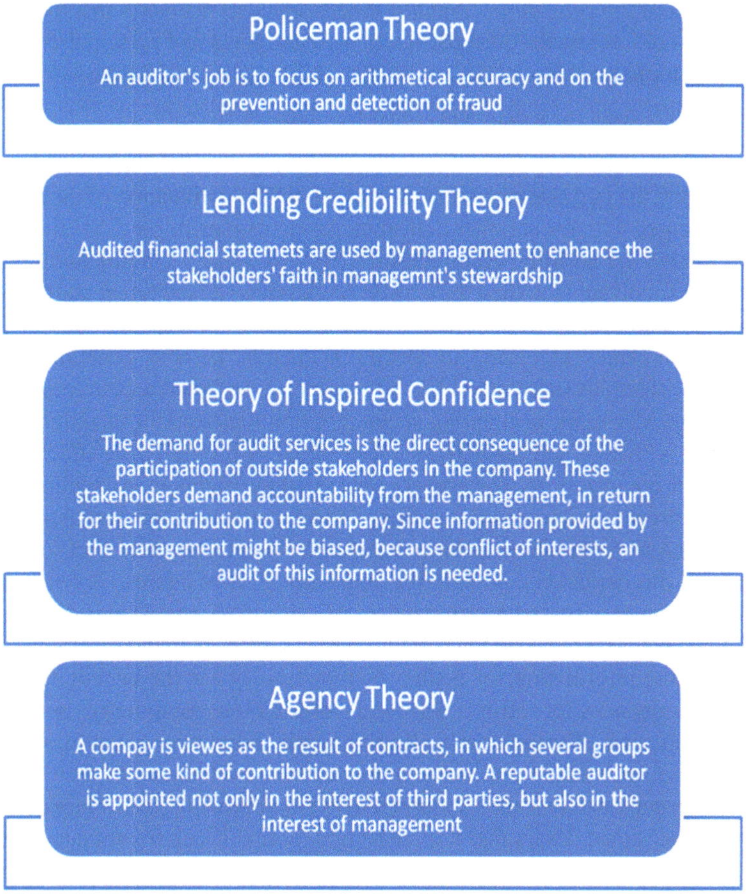

Fig. 2.6 Audit Theories

primary objective of auditing in the early twentieth century until after 1941 when the provision of an opinion on the financial statement finally became the primary role of audits.[116] Given this presumption, untrustworthiness appears when there are economic resources transmitted from one party to another.[117] Lending credibility theory suggests that the purpose of conducting audits is to add credibility. For instance, the objective of financial audits can be summarized as increasing the credibility of financial statements. The theory of inspired confidence suggests that the accountability provided by third parties is demanding due to the need for the

[116] T A Lee, *Company auditing* (Wokingham, Berkshire, England: Van Nostrand Reinhold (UK), 1986) at 11.

[117] Power, *supra* note 10 in Chap. 1 at 16.

management of the company.[118] Agency theory suggests that audit institutions serve as managers of interest for third parties as well as agents and principals.[119]

As Kim Ittonen noted:

> The most prominent and widely used audit theory is agency theory.[120]

Meanwhile, the extent of the aforementioned four types of theories overlaps. As a matter of fact, the purpose of audits changes from "the verification of the honesty of persons charged with fiscal rather than managerial responsibilities" to "a social control mechanism for securing accountability."[121] If we were to classify audit practices based on the audit subject, then they could be classified as statement audits, compliance audits, and operational audits.[122] Statement audits process the statements prepared by companies according to specific standards, such as generally accepted accounting principles (hereafterGAAP) or generally accepted accounting standards (hereafterGAAS), in the accounting sector.[123] Compliance audits examine company compliance with laws and regulations. Operational audits verify the effectiveness or efficiency of organizations.[124] Another way to explain audits is to examine the conditions that create the demand for auditing. The American Accounting Association's (hereafter AAA) Committee on basic auditing concepts has identified four criteria that created this demand: a. potential or actual conflicts of interest, b. consequences of errors, c. complexity, and d. remoteness.[125] Conflicts of interest may exist between a principal and users for different reasons, such as the principal deliberately preparing misleading information for his/her own interest or for the benefit of the company. Consequences of errors represent information asymmetry between the principal and users. Through the auditing process, users may obtain more reliable and complete information and make more accurate evaluations of their decisions. Complexity demonstrates the complexity of the subject or the context in which audits are performed. Users find it increasingly more difficult to evaluate the disclosure of information provided by the principal. Remoteness refers to user-facing difficulty in gaining full access to evidence to provide proof of the information in their statements, such as financial records.[126]

---

[118] Theodore Limperg, "Theory of Inspired Confidence" (Univeristy of Amsterdam, 2016)at 131.

[119] Ross L Watts & Jerold L Zimmerman, "Positive Accounting Theory: A Ten Year Perspective" (1990) 65:1 Account Rev. at 141.

[120] Vaasan, *supra* note 115 at 5.

[121] Prem Sikka, "Philosophy and principles of auditing: An introduction D. Flint Macmillan (Basingstoke, 1988). 191 pp. E9.95 (pbk); E30 (hbk)" (1989) 21 Br Account Rev. at 201.

[122] Ray Whittington & Kurt Pany, *Principles of Auditing & Other Assurance Services*, 20th edition edition ed (New York, NY: McGraw-Hill Education, 2015) at 11.

[123] A C Littleton, *Accounting evolution to 1900,* (New York, N.Y.: American Institute Pub. Co., Inc., 1933) at 99.

[124] Business Bliss Consultant FZE: Concepts and Theories of Auditing. See online: https://ukdiss.com/examples/theory-of-auditing.php?vref=1 (Visited at 4 April, 2020).

[125] American Accounting Association & Committee on Basic Auditing Concepts, *supra* note 2 in Chap. 1.

[126] Vaasan, *supra* note 115 at 32.

2.2.1.1 Deconstruct the Concept of Accountability

The concept of accountability finds its origins in ancient Sumerian civilization, where kings were held responsible for the actions of their officials. In the modern era, accountability has been refined and applied across various fields. Although a multifarious sentiment of accountability is more prevalent than the signification of liability, accountability indeed presupposes responsibility. Technological advancements and the ever-increasing reliance on digital technologies have given rise to new challenges in safeguarding personal data. The issue of data privacy and protection is not new and has been a topic of discussion for many years. However, the term "accountability" in the context of personal data protection is relatively new and has gained significant importance in recent times. In the next section, we will explore the historical background leading to the definition of accountability in the context of personal data protection.

[Etymological meaning] The concept of accountability originated from common law tradition responding to an idea of responsibility.[127] In general terms, the definition of accountability refers to an obligation or willingness to accept responsibility or to account for one's actions.[128] From an etymological point of view, the term originated from the "Anglo-Saxon" world, "accountability" formed within English appellation "accountable," referring as "responsible and answerable."[129] However, within European jurisdiction, the term could not be easily be understood and translated because of different legal tradition with common law. Consequently, the risk of varying interpretation of the term, and thereby lack of harmonization, is substantial.[130] As a matter of fact, the term "accountability "could be divided into two parts. The first clings to "account," and the second is the "ability." From the perspective of mathematics, "account" entails senses "relating to counting, enumerating or calculating numerically."[131] With the suffix-able, the purpose of the term not only conveys the ability to justify a series of input and output, but also, it implies the competence that input and output shall be produced in a specific way which could be calculated or measured.[132] For sake of having a comprehensive acquaintance of accountability, along with etymology study, it is imperative to explicate the concept with variable context. As mentioned by Deborah G. Johnson:

[127] Melvin J Dubnick, *Seeking Salvation for Accountability* (2002) at 3.

[128] Noah Webster, New International dictionary of the English language, second ed. (Springfield: Merriam, 1949) at 214.

[129] Bryan A Garner, *Black's Law Dictionary*, eighth edition edition ed (St. Paul, MN: West Group, 2004) at 20.

[130] *Supra* note 5 in Chap. 1 at 13

[131] Dictionaries, *supra* note 41 at 21.

[132] Emilie Mouchard, *L'accountability ou le principe de responsabilité en matière de protection des renseignements personnels* University of Montreal, 2018) [unpublished] at 33. Also see Felix Gaffiot, Dictionary Latin-Francais, (Paris, 1934) at 29.

> Accountability practice is embedded in many, if not all, domains of life and are importantly connected to our sense of what we are entitled to expect from others (individuals and organizations) and what they can require or expect of us.[133]

[Accountability in context] The understanding of the term must be analyzed through its historical pathway. For instance, the first utilized principle of accountability from ancient Egypt for seed control.[134] The sixth king of Babylon, Hammurabi, is credited as the pioneer who implemented the principle into modern procedures to monitor and control his kingdom.[135] The first juridical appearance of accountability could be found in the thirteenth century at England.[136] In modern times, the principle of accountability is applied in various fields, including political accountability, financial accountability, educational accountability, and more. The meaning of accountability and its elements shaped through the ages. As a matter of fact, accountability is the representation of society which encompasses different meaning.[137] As this book noticed, the concept has been deployed on various contexts with distinctive signification through history. The word often received a context or discipline-specific connotation. Various context entails different responsibilities that reliable subject needs to take for state of affairs and the whole society. In the context of personal data protection for this book, responsibilities refer to accountability, which shall be interpreted as the liability of responsible people to protect personal data in accordance with specific rules and standards.[138] It also implies that the responsible person to implement proper measure to answer the requirements of legal guidance.[139] For instance, the first document to introduce the principle of accountability regarding to personal data protection is OECD Guidelines on the Protection of Privacy and Trans-border Flows of Personal Data. (HereafterOECD Guideline).[140] The principle plays a critical role for ensuring the effective implementation of other principles within this guideline:

---

133 Johnson & Regan, *supra* note 13 at 144.

134 Mahmoud Ezzamel, "Accounting control and accountability: preliminary evidence from ancient egypt" (1997).8:6 Critical Perspectives on Accounting 563–601, See online: <http://www.sciencedirect.com/science/article/pii/S1045235497901234> at 563 (Visited at 12 March, 2022).

135 Erwin J Urch, "The law code of hammurabi" (1929) 15:7 Am Bar Assoc J at 440.

136 Bryce Dale Lyon, *Constitutional and Legal History of Medieval England*, second ed (New York: Norton, 1980) at 467.

137 Dubnick, *supra* note 134 at 3.

138 International Standards on the Protection of Personal Data and Privacy-The Madrid Resolution, Madrid: International Conference of Data Protection and Privacy Commissioners, 2009. "Responsible person" refers as any natural person or organization, public or private which, alone or jointly with others, decides on the processing of personal data.

139 Hunton&Williams LLP, "The Centre for Information Policy Leadership, "Demonstrating and Measuring Accountability- A Discussion Document". Accountability Phase-The Paris Project at 2.

140 Organization for Economic Co-operation and Development (OECD), "Recommendation of the Council concerning Guidelines governing the protection of privacy and trans-border flows of personal data".

> A data controller should be accountable for complying with measures which give effect to the principles stated above.[141]

Then in 2000, the Personal Information Protection and Electronic Documents Act (hereafter PIPEDA) was released to protect personal information by Canadian legislation.[142] Similar with OECD guideline. The Principle of accountability was also adopted to ensure effective implementation of other principles of the legislation and organizations shall take responsible measure in order compliance the requirements of PIPEDA,[143] it also introduces a new dimension of personal information protection as "internal accountability." It stated:

> One or more individuals who shall be accountable for the organization's compliance with data principles.[144]

It also emphasized the responsibility of the Data Protection Officer (hereafter DPO) to oversight the internal compliance of the rule within the organization. Besides, The DPO also has a duty to contact with external parties.[145] In 2005, Asian Pacific Economic Cooperation (hereafter APEC) privacy framework was published,[146] which has also taken into account of accountability as main principle which gave it a broader interpretation.[147] Along with the framework, APEC Privacy Pathfinder also involved with practical perspective for personal data protection.[148] Notably, it clearly demonstrated that the data controller has the responsibility to support the compliance verification.[149] In 2010, to add principle of accountability in revised

---

[141] Ibid at paragraph14.

[142] Schedule 1 at Canadian Personal Information Protection and Electronic Document Act (S.C.2000. c5).

[143] Schedule 1 of PIPEDA: This enumeration of measures serves to provide an indication of what responsible organizations are expected to do in order to ensure compliance with the other principles of Schedule 1. It does not change the meaning of the accountability principle as such, but rather defines a number of its implications. The following subsections will elaborate how subsequent articulations of the principle of accountability continue in this direction and almost go so far as to assimilate the principle of accountability with the obligation of controllers to implement policies and practices that 'give effect' to data protection requirements.

[144] Ibid at Chap. 4.1.

[145] Joseph Alhadeff, Brendan Van Alsenoy & Jos Dumortier,"The Accountability Principle in Data Protection Regulation: Origin, Development and Future Directions" in Daniel Guagnin et al., eds, *Manage Privacy Account* (London: Palgrave Macmillan UK, 2012) at 49.

[146] Electronic Commerce Steering Group (ECSG), "APEC Privacy Framework" at 12.

[147] Ibid at Principle IX, Paragraph 26: When personal information is to be transferred domestically or internationally the personal information controller should either obtain the consent of the individual or exercise due diligence and take reasonable steps to ensure that the recipient person or organization will protect information consistent with these principles.

[148] Electronic Commerce Steering Group (ECSG), "APEC data privacy pathfinder projects implementation work plan" 2008/SOM1/ECSG/024, 2008″: Pathfinder Project is an APEC project in which more than half but not all APEC economics participate, Sixteen of the APEC economics are participating in the Privacy Pathfinder Project.

[149] Ibid at p1: In terms of compliance verification, it indeed provides some flexibility in two perspectives, on the one hand, the ability to use multiple mechanisms to implement accountability

data protection directive of the EU, the Article 29 working party decided to announce an opinion.[150] The opinion clearly dedicated that the data controller has responsibility to put data protection requirement into practice.[151] In 2016. General Data Protection Regulation (hereafter GDPR) introduced "accountability" as principle to which the data controller shall take the responsibility to adhere and required a "clear and consistent" evaluation of risk associated with particular data processing.[152] In 2017, although the Cybersecurity Law of People's Republic of China (hereafter-CSL) did not specify accountability as a main principle but it included many relevant articles, such as the requirement of appointing a data protection officer introduced in Article 21 and the establishment of the principle of "Transparency" in Article 41 for processing personal data as well as legitimacy ground for network operators to process personal data.[153]

[Answerable meaning of accountability] Responsibility and accountability are two sides of the same coin, and both essential elements of good governance.[154] Needless to say, accountability means more than responsibility. As the Definition given by Andreas Schadler:

> A is accountable to be B when A is obliged to inform B about A's (past or future) actions and decisions.[155]

---

allows organizations a range of possible solutions to meet their compliance requirements. It also allows economics without omnibus privacy privacy laws more ways to develop credible and effective privacy frameworks. This approach also helps broaden the coverage of compliance for individuals by combining mechanisms of compliance to cover what may be gaps or limitations of any single approach. The process is predicated on the requirement that participating governments are able to provide an appropriate regulatory and policy framework to assure that framework requirements are applied, overseen, and enforced. The mechanisms related to this aspect of the CBPR are still in development.

[150] Article 29 Data Protection Working Party, "Opinion3/2010 on the principle of accountability. "It proposed that the Commission consider "accountability-based" mechanism and the introduction of an accountability principle in the revised directive in its opinion on the future of privacy.

[151] Article 29 Data Protection Working Party, "Opinion3/2010 on the principle of accountability."

[152] *Supra* note 106 at 171. Also see Article 5.2 of Regulation (EU) 2016/679 of the European Parliament and of the Council of 27 April 2016 on the protection of natural persons with regard to the processing of personal data and on the free movement of such data, and repealing Directive 95/46/EC.

[153] If a data protection officer failed to his or her duty with due diligence, then he or she may be accused of criminal liabilities in respect to his or her as a Data Protection Officer (English to verify). In Article 21 of China Cybersecurity Law,it stated: Network operators shall, according to the requirements of the rules for graded protection of cybersecurity, fulfil the following security protection obligation, so as to ensure that the network is free from interference, damage or unauthorized access, and prevent network data form being divulged, stolen or falsified. Article 41 of CSL stated that network operators shall make public the rules for collecting and using personal data, and expressly notify the purpose, methods and scope of such collection and use.

[154] Raab, *supra* note 44 in Chap. 1.

[155] Andreas Schedler, Larry Diamond & Marc F Plattner, *The Self Restraining State: Power and Accountability in New Democracies*, first printing ed (Boulder, Colo.: Lynne Rienner Pub, 1999) at 17.

However, the reality is that the presumption burden of responsibility has become an easy formula to legitimize political power, and it has also become a means to evade prospective accountability. If I am the one responsible, I can make decisions based on how I feel I should. I need not inform anybody about those decisions before I make them, nor do I have to respond to anybody except to my personal conscience. In essence, while accountability forces power to enter a dialogue, the notion of responsibility permits it to remain silent.[156] Keith Hoskin has also highlighted this by putting a three-step definition of accountability:

> First it aims to engage an individual with an authority; secondly, it seeks to evaluate an action against the rules issued by a given community. And finally, at a third time, there is a moral dimension which cannot be reduced to mere responsibility.[157]

"Accountability" is not equal to "Responsiveness."[158] Compared with it, accountability has a more positive meaning of "demonstration" than the passive meaning of "rescript." For instance, to be a responsible seller, it should respond to inquiries from consumers to establish a reputation of accountability. This means that consumers can trust the product because the seller has the ability to manage risks if something goes wrong. On the contrary, the "answerable'" perspective of accountability is to demonstrate that the product will not go wrong because we have already taken precautionary measures.[159] Accountability does not wait for a system failure; instead, it demands that organizations be ready to demonstrate, upon request by the proper authorities, that they are securing and protecting data in accordance with essential elements. Accountability for personal data protection involves not only complying with data protection laws and regulations but also demonstrating the effective implementation of data protection practices. This necessitates a proactive approach to data protection, encompassing clear policies and procedures, appropriate technical and organizational measures, staff training, awareness raising, and transparent communication with data subjects.

2.2.1.2 Deconstruct the Function of Audit for Accountability

While omnifarious conceptual frameworks have been used to identify the true definition of an audit, this book tries to benchmark some notable features of an audit. Flint stated seven postulates to describe audits as follows:

> 1. There is a relationship of accountability or a situation of public accountability. 2. Accountability cannot be demonstrated without an audit. 3. An audit requires independence and freedom. 4. The subject matter of audits is susceptible to verification by evidence. 5. Auditors are skilled judges who are able to measure and compare actual performance

---

[156] Schedler, Diamond & Plattner, *supra* note 46 in Chap. 1 at 17.

[157] Keith Hoskin, "The 'awful idea of accountability': inscribing people into the measurement of objects" (1996) at 21.

[158] Ibid at 3.

[159] Raab, *supra* note 44 in Chap. 1 at 26.

> against standards of accountability. 6. The meaning, significance, and intention of statements to be audited must be clear. 7. An audit produces an economic or social benefit.[160]

Power interpreted audits as follows:

> The limits of the term due to the word not being used simply and descriptively to refer to particular practices but normatively in the context of demands and aspirations for accountability and control.[161]

From this point of view, an "audit" can be regarded as a normative tool for delivering accountability. Likewise, it should be defined as a tool for delivering forbearance. While As a matter of fact, accountability is a flexible and ever-expanding word.

[Flexibility of accountability] Accountability is often used, yet the concept is not easily understood. When we hear a word, we acknowledge that it means something important, but that is about as far as it goes. Subsequently, because they need to grasp the concept of accountability, they need to learn know how to achieve it. As it noted, accountability has been called a "non-contestable" concept which is invariably viewed as a "good thing."[162] Accountability closely linked with the exercise of power and the legitimacy of policies, and those pursing them. As Gregory suggested:

> Issues of accountability are as much moral and ethical as they are technical in nature, and impinge firmly upon the trust need to underpin a democratically healthy relationship between politicians, bureaucrats and citizens.[163]

On the other hand, accountability is an "ever-expanding" concept that, even if it is widely utilized in different contexts, it failed to reach an unequivocal meaning for what it is. The literature on accountability is usually disconnected, most scholars chose to define their own interpretation of the term.[164] As a matter of fact, the expectations shaped by multiple accountabilities" could be based on laws (legal accountability), professional (professional accountability), and political demands (political accountability).[165] A common understanding connected for "multiple accountability" is that they appertained multiple relationships between "actors" and "principal." To be more specific, most of the definitions referred to a specific social relationship or mechanism that involved an obligation to explain one's responsibility.[166] For private sector, researchers have focus on a variety of corporate governance

[160] Vaasan, *supra* note 115 at 32.

[161] Power, *supra* note 10 in Chap. 1 at 6.

[162] Wolf Adam, "Symposium on Accountability in Public administration: Reconciling Democracy, Efficiency and Ethics" (2016) Volume 66, issue 1 International Review of Administrative Sciences at 18.

[163] R Gregory, "Accountability in modern government in 'accountability in modern government' in Handbook of Public Administration." See: https://sk.sagepub.com/reference/hdbk_pubadmin/n45.xml (2 Jan, 2023).

[164] Robert Behn, "Rethinking democratic accountability" (2001) Brookings Institution Press at 23.

[165] DUbnick Melvin, "Accountability in the public sector: lessons from the challenger tragedy" 47(3):227 Public Adm Rev. at 38.

[166] Patricia Day, *Accountabilities:* Five public sectors, (London: Tavistock, 1987) at 15.

mechanisms such as accountability, whereas accountability has been interpreted as to be responsible for shareholders and for the board.[167]

[Accountability and Verification] Two dimensions of accountability have been identified—internal accountability and external accountability—coexisting and interacting in complex ways.[168] From an internal perspective, accountability always refers to 'professionalism and personal morality or conscience of public servants and others in the exercise of their functions.[169] Externally, accountability always involves verification—an investigation by an independent party of actions—and an explanation of these actions requiring professional actors. As a matter of fact, the key concept related to accountability is stewardship. Thus, accountability is intrinsically linked to stewardship.[170] Thus, accountability is intrinsically linked to stewardship. Stewardship involves two parties: a steward, that is, the party to whom the stewardship or responsibility is given and who is obliged to present an account of its execution, and the principal or account. That is, the party entrusting the responsibility to the steward and to whom the account is present. There is, however, a third party in this relationship: the code based on which the relationship is struck and by which it is maintained and adjudicated. Codes may be explicit or, more often, implicit. Moreover, accountability always implies a process of transparent interaction in which the body seeks answers and possible ratification. Irrespectively, to effectively enforce accountability, there seems to be a consensus that the process must involve being called "to account" by some authority for one's actions, and the involvement of an external body is, therefore, indispensable.[171] The meaning of accountability implies that it consists of a process of verification, but As a matter of fact, this verification process is only one facet of accountability. In the context of personal data protection, despite the application of different approaches from the various above-mentioned jurisdictions, they all chose accountability as a tool for managing the risk associated with personal data, and the principles signified different responsibilities that the responsible person needed to take on.[172] First,

[167] McConnell Dahya, "The cadbury committee, corporate performance, and top managment turnover" (2002) Joural of finanace: Vol. 57 No.1 at 471.

[168] Richard Mulgan, "'Accountability': An Ever-Expanding Concept?" (2000) 78:3 Public Administration 555–573. See online: <https://onlinelibrary.wiley.com/doi/abs/10.1111/1467-9299.00218> at 560 (Visited at 28 February, 2023).

[169] Raab, *supra* note 44 in Chap. 1 at 18.

[170] James B Christoph, "Administrative Politics in British Government. By Andrew Gray and William I. Jenkins." (1986) 80:4 American Political Science Review at 1370. See online: <https://www.cambridge.org/core/journals/american-political-science-review/aricle/administrative-politics-in-british-government-by-gray-andrew-and-jenkins-william-i-sussex-wheatsheaf-books-and-new-york-st-martins-press-1985-pp-x-259-2600/EBD1CF7D1F69F0F88DFCF54D91645DB2> at 138 (Visited at 28 Febuary, 2023).

[171] Colin J Bennett, "The Accountability Approach to Privacy and Data Protection: Assumptions and Caveats" in Daniel Guagnin et al., eds, *Manag Priv Account* (London: Palgrave Macmillan UK, 2012) 33 at 2.

[172] Emilie Mouchard, *supra* note 139.

accountability "enables actors to hold individuals responsible for their behaviors".[173] Second, actors are responsible for fulfilling legal requirements (legal compliance). Third, to guarantee that these requirements can be fulfilled effectively, the principle serves as a tool requiring actors to take responsibility to demonstrate their compliance.[174] As a matter of fact, the responsibilities related to accountability for personal data protection can be classified into two categories: external responsibility and internal responsibility.[175] The external perspective is related to the legal and social obligations that the responsible person.[176] Internal responsibility is related to the hierarchical obligation of professionals to take reasonable measures for protecting personal data.[177]

[Accountability as result-oriented concept] The general accounting office observes:

> Accountability is an important yet elusive concept whose meaning and characteristics differ depend up on contest.[178]

The degree and nature of accountability are dictated by the delimitations of an actor's authority. This idea connects with one understanding of responsibility, defined as task or function. Responsibility presupposes the capacity to execute tasks (authority), implying that these duties or tasks have been formally delegated to the person in charge. In other words, there is no responsibility without authority, or, no responsibility and accountability without discretion[179] According to explanation of Stone, a non-exhaustive account would be like accountability as constituency or "political" relations, for example, accountability to ministers, Parliament, but also to voters and the public in general. Accountability is a judicial and quasi-judicial review of administrative action, branded as legal accountability, imposed formally by-laws or rules created by the legislature, the judiciary, or a regulatory agency such as a procurement office or civil service commission; Bureaucratic or administrative accountability imposed formally through the hierarchy within organizations—particularly bureaucratic organizations. It entails internal, but also mixed internal/external supervision like accountability to ombudsmen, supreme audit institutions, inspectorates in various policy fields, ad hoc civil service evaluation committees and the like market accountability:

> Responsiveness of service provided to a body of 'sovereign' consumers.[180]

---

173 Desai & Kroll, *supra* note 59 in Chap. 1 at 9.

174 Carla Ilten et al., *Managing Privacy through Accountability*, 2012 edition ed., D. Guagnin & L. Hempel, eds. (Houndmills, Basingstoke ; New York, NY: Palgrave Macmillan, 2012) at 46.

175 Andreas Schedler, "Conceptualizing Accountability" (1999). See online: <https://works.bepress.com/andreas_schedler/22/> at 19 (Visited at 22 February, 2023).

176 John Roberts, "The possibilities of accountability" (1991) 16:4 Account Organ Soc at 362.

177 Ibid.

178 Behn, *supra* note 171 at 3.

179 *Ibid* at 27.

180 Burt Perrin, *Making accountability work: Dilemmas for evaluation and for audit* at 13.

This may also imply accountability to citizens not as actors in constituency relations but as intended beneficiaries of services, whether or not provided directly by government. Professional accountability involves being accountable to professional associations and their codes and ethics committees. This type of accountability may be imposed, sometimes formally, more often by the members of the organization itself, through their expertise and standards (which may be established by professional organizations or through education and training).[181] In the modern context, it has to navigate a diversity of accountability relations, often referred to as "the problem of many eyes."[182] As it highlighted, the accountability seemed a context-based concept where Behn devoted specifically to the meaning of it:

> I am not sure that I can offer a good definition. And I am not sure that any of these accountability holders...know exactly what it means to 'hold someone accountable.[183]

Many discussions about the concept of accountability focus on how it needs to evolve to keep up to date with transmuting in a more appropriate way at the operational level. These appear to be two basic approaches to operationalizing accountability:

> Compliance-based approach following the rules that have been laid out, including more recently 'meeting the numbers' or targets specified in advance. A principled approach-more broadly, doing the right thing or acting responsibly.[184]

However, these definitions usually leave it rather open as to whom and for what one is expected to be accountable and about how one can appropriately answer for a responsibility or power that has been conferred. The question is, how to make accountability accountable? Just like the relationship between responsibility and accountability, outputs cannot be equalized as an outcome that has a value judgment of attribution. As for the results, the misuse of indicators for accountability often occurs, such as distorted or inaccurate data or goal displacement. As this book notes, accountability is always tied to performance in terms of target achievement at the operational level. The outcomes could be too difficult to measure. There was minimal attention in most countries to outcomes, some to outputs, but with attention still primarily placed on the development of better ways to control inputs. Accountability should be referred to as a static position rather than a dynamic status. This leads to a situation where 'for accountability' is vague, and it's not clear how this information would be used. Here, we face a situation where 'for accountability' should be interpreted as 'process-oriented,' whereas 'accountability' refers to 'result-oriented.' To interpret accountability based on a 'result-oriented' approach, Maria L. Bemelmans-Videc proposed an interpretation framework based on the following principles:

---

[181] *Ibid.*

[182] Bovens, *The quest for responsibility, accountability and citizenship in comlex organisations* (Cambridge University Press, 1998) at 13.

[183] Behn, *supra* note 171 at 3.

[184] Perrin, *supra* note 187 at 221.

> Acting responsibly being trustworthy, being true to the mandate, demonstrating responsibility in taking decisions; Addressing the overall need or rationale for why the program is in place; Doing the best possible job given the circumstances, resources and constraints, consistent with the overall mandate.[185]

To interpret what Bemelans-Videc has provided, more consideration and discussion about the concept of accountability and how it needs to evolve to keep up with changes in approaches to management could pave the way for more operational levels. In other words, explaining accountability itself can only be done at the principle level to leave room for flexibility. On the other hand, the principles set should be based on a result-oriented approach for how one can answer for a responsibility or power that has been conferred. In practical terms, accountability means punishment. Accountability can serve both as an end in itself and as a means to a greater goal. A major purpose (some would say its prime function) is the legitimization of the exercise of authority, including the most appropriate use of public resources. In this sense, accountability can be viewed as an end in itself, providing greater confidence or assurance in what government is doing and how. A new vision of accountability should encompass the following three essential characteristics.:

> A primary orientation on results rather than the process"; "A focus on continuous and responsive learning"; "A dynamic rather than a static approach that reflects the complexities and unspecific ties inherent in most public policy areas.[186]

The new vision of accountability also acknowledges the importance of a reciprocal approach to accountability, with accountability outwards to stakeholder groups including citizens as well as upwards to those with authority and power, partly to provide for the credibility of accountability efforts and also because this is basic to most democratic models.

[Accountable for more than they can control] The accountability principles entail holding people accountable only for what they can control. If they have no effect on an outcome, it serves no purpose to hold them accountable for that outcome. However, it has been noted that management levels are often held accountable for many things they cannot control.[187] The main reason for this circumstance can be divided into two categories: The first is caused by the difficulty of distinguishing uncontrollable and controllable effects on performance levels. The other is caused by the fact that organizations want the management level to respond to changes in those uncontrollable factors.[188] To hold a controller liable, users must succeed in demonstrating three elements: (1) the performance of an unlawful act (i.e., an unlawful processing operation or other act incompatible with the national provisions adopted pursuant to the directive); (2) the existence of damages; and (3) a causal relationship between the unlawful act and the damages incurred. In addi-

---

[185] *Ibid* at 53.

[186] *Ibid* at 66.

[187] Kenneth A Merchant, *Rewarding results: Motivating profit center managers* (Boston, Mass: Harvard Business School Press, 1989) at 47.

[188] *Ibid* at 91.

tion, the data subject must also establish, as a preliminary matter, that the defendant is (or was) acting as the controller of the processing。[189] The question inevitably arises as to the nature of the evidentiary burden of proof incumbent upon controllers. What evidence must controllers offer to successfully exempt themselves from liability, either for their own actions or for the actions performed by their processors or auxiliaries. In order to prove that the organization is "not responsible for the event giving rise to the damage," the controller must demonstrate three elements: (1) the occurrence of an event; (2) which caused the damage; and (3) which cannot be attributed to the controller, mere demonstration of an absence of a fault on the part of the controller is not sufficient.[190] The GDPR has introduced several changes to the allocation of responsibility and liability among controllers and processors. While the controller is still the party who carries primary responsibility for compliance, processors have become subject to a host of obligations and are directly liable towards data subjects in case of non-compliance (Article 82[2]). In situations involving more than one controller or processor, every controller or processor involved in the processing may in principle be held liable for the entire damage, provided the damage results from its failure to comply with an obligation to which it is subject (Article 82[4]).

> Where more than one controller or processor, or both a controller and a processor, are involved in the same processing and where they are, under paragraphs 2 and 3, responsible for any damage caused by processing, each controller or processor shall be held liable for the entire damage in order to ensure effective compensation of the data subject.[191]

The result is within a "cumulative liability regime", whereby each actor can be held liable in light of its role in the processing.[192] The liability model for controllers under the GDPR is essentially the same as under Directive 95/46. Article 82(2) of the GDPR provides that:

> Any controller involved in processing shall be liable for the damage caused by processing which infringes this Regulation.[193]

In other words, the controller remains generally liable for any damages arising from the unlawful processing personal data. The controller may be exempted from liability, in whole or in part, "if it proves that it is not in any way responsible for the event giving rise to the damage" (Article 82[3]).[194]

---

[189] Art. 6(102) of the Principles of European Tort Law (PETL). See also C. von Bar a.o. (eds.) "Principles, Definitions and Model Rules of European Private Law - Draft Common Frame of Reference (DCFR)", Study Group on a European Civil Code and the Research Group on EC Private Law, 2009 at 3318.

[190] Brendan Van Alsenoy, *Data Protection Law in the EU: Roles, Responsibilities and Liability* (Intersentia, 2019) at 23.

[191] Article 82 of GDPR

[192] Casey, Farhangi & Vogl, *supra* note 68 in Chap. 1.

[193] *Ibid.*

[194] Renata M de Carvalho et al., "Protecting Citizens' Personal Data and Privacy: Joint Effort from GDPR EU Cluster Research Projects" (2020) 1:4 SN Comput Sci 217 at 14.

A similar case occurred in the region of China following the adoption and implementation of the Personal Information Protection Law of People's republic of China (hereafter PIPL). The goal is to accurately interpret the rules governing civil liability for the infringement of personal information rights and interests. The understanding of civil liability for the infringement of personal information rights and interests by personal information handlers encompasses four main parts. Firstly, it identifies and delineates the status and object of civil liability in protecting the rights and interests of personal information. Secondly, it specifies the principles attributing civil liability for the infringement of personal information rights and interests by personal information processors. Thirdly, it outlines the constituent elements of the civil liability incurred by personal information processors when infringing upon the rights and interests of personal information. Lastly, it analyzes the rules governing the assumption of civil liability by personal information processors who infringe upon the rights and interests of personal information..[195] Due to the private nature of personal information rights and interests falling under private law, civil liability becomes the primary method for safeguarding these rights and interests. While the PIPL only explicitly addresses civil liability in Article 69, most of its provisions necessitate interpretation in the context of the Civil Code of the People's Republic of China. Consequently, claims corresponding to civil liability for protecting personal information rights and interests encompass tort claims and personality rights claims held by the right holder. The advantage of a tort claim lies in compensating for damages, while personality right claims aim to restore civil rights and interests to their original state of completeness. Considering the PIPL as a civil law regulating the infringement of personal information rights and interests mainly through civil liability implies that its regulatory focus should be the illegal acts of personal information handlers violating obligations stipulated in the law. The concept of infringement of personal information rights and interests requires a nuanced understanding, specifying that the subject of infringement is solely the personal information processor, excluding other entities. The rights and interests being infringed upon belong to natural persons, excluding legal persons and unincorporated organizations. The method of regulating these infringements involves bearing civil liability. Moving forward, a crucial aspect to explore is the principle of imputation of civil liability for the infringement of personal information rights and interests to ensure accurate application of specific rules. For example, Professor Yang Lixin argues that the PIPL incorporates the presumption of fault principle to address the unique requirements of protecting personal information rights and interests. This is grounded in three reasons: the special nature of the infringement subject, the natural person status of the right holder of personal information, and the unequal status of the two parties. Furthermore, when applying the presumption of fault principle, attention must be paid to three aspects: scope of application, responsibility, and burden of proof. It should be noted that the presumption of fault does not apply when a person with personal information rights seeks to exercise the right to claim

[195] Article 111 of Civil Code of the People's Republic of China.

personal rights for self-remedy. Regarding liability, compensation for the infringement of personal information rights and interests covers damages to personal information rights and interests, property rights and interests, and moral interests. As for the burden of proof, there is a shift in responsibility, with the burden borne by the personal information processor. The four constituent elements of the civil liability of the personal information processor for the infringement of personal information rights and interests are: first, the illegal acts of personal information handlers infringing on these rights and interests; second, the objective fact of the damage to the rights and interests of the right holder; third, the causal relationship between the infringement and the damage; and fourth, the fault in the infringement of personal information rights and interests. As the foundational law for personal information protection, the provisions of the PIPL regarding civil liability of personal information processors for infringement of personal information rights and interests possess a substantial jurisprudential basis. They align with the fundamental rules outlined in the Civil Code, contributing significantly to the protection of personal information rights and interests.[196]

2.2.2 Deconstructing Audit for Transparency

The two words "Transparency" and "accountability" are often used side by side in varies of legislation and regulation such as Federal Funding Accountability and Transparency Act and Honest Leadership and Open Government Act of the United States.[197] The content it reflected could be summarized as "requirement of disclosure" and "necessitate of control." Audit problem for deliver transparency in a ways that it cannot serve as a testimony to the emergence of a distinct managerial rationality centered in the notion that institutional behavior could be shaped if the right kind of reinforcement is combined with the appropriate information. Audit, on the contrary, may not generate transparency, or even worse, it mitigated transparency (Figs. 2.7 and 2.8).

2.2.2.1 Deconstructing the Concept of Transparency

[Two faces of transparency] If we back to a broader scope and more general sense for information disclosure, the concept of "right of information" is being escalated as a fundamental democratic right as declared in Article 19 of United Nationals

[196] Chinese Law & Government, "Tort Liability Law of the People's Republic of China [Article 36]" (2010) 43:5 Chin Law Gov at 82.

[197] Carolyn Ball, "What Is Transparency?" (2009) 11:4 Public Integrity 293–308. See online: <https://www.tandfonline.com/doi/abs/10.2753/PIN1099-9922110400> at 306 (Visited at 12 August, 2023).

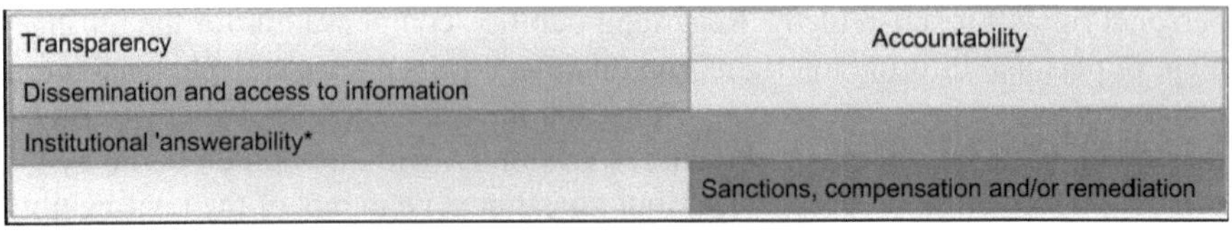

Fig. 2.7 Relationship between transparency and accountability (*Ibid* at 308)

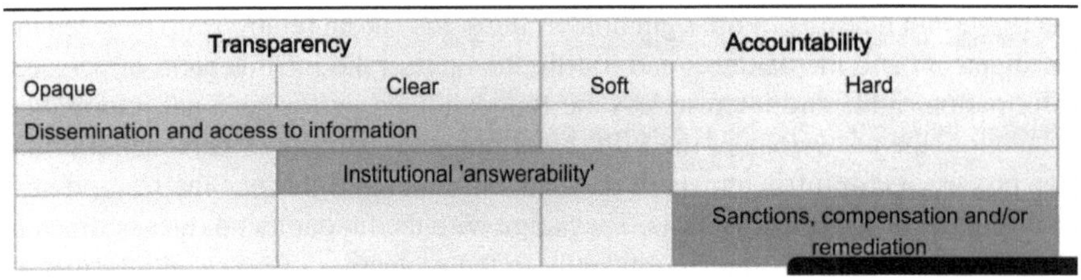

Fig. 2.8 The relationship between transparency and accountability (*Ibid* at 307)

Universal Declaration of Human Rights long time ago.[198] To have a deep dive of the meaning of transparency, as Greg Michener noted, transparency could be exemplified two essential sufficient conditions which adhere to the original literal meaning of the word:

> Visibility as in 'light rendering an object entirely visible'; and invariability, that which can be inferred with some degree of accuracy.[199]

Visibility could be explained as the degree to which information is complete and findable and invariability referred to the degree to which information is disaggregated, verified and simplified.[200] In other words, one leading assumption about transparency is that transparency has to be based on recorded information. In the 1980s the term first found as an accounting principle as "financial transparency."[201] The visibility of information – its presence as opposed to its absence – represented the recording requirement which many scholars mentioned. And "inferability" could be interpreted as the recorded information lending itself to verifiable inference or conclusions.[202] Indeed, "transparency" did not become popularized until seismic political and economic changes began to take shape at the dawn of the Twentieth Century's last decade. The democratic transitions of the late1980s and early 1990s

---

[198] United Nations, Article 19 of "Universal Declaration of Human Rights". See online: https://www.un.org/en/about-us/universal-declaration-of-human-rights/ (Visited at 19 Jan, 2023)

[199] Gregory Michener & Katherine Bersch, "Identifying Transparency" (2013) 18 Inf Polity at 234.

[200] Jon Gant and Nicol Turner-Lee, "Government Transparency: Six Strategies for More Open and Participatory Government" (2011). See online: <https://policycommons.net/artifacts/1302207/government-transparency/1905498/> at 14.

[201] Michener & Bersch, *supra* note 208 at 233.

[202] *Ibid* at 234.

spurred renewed interest in processes and concepts associated with democracy and institutions.[203] After financial crisis of the 1990s, international policy makers sought that visibility as a way of improving monitoring and visibility of information has become a well-established norm.[204] And then they soon realized that visibility is not enough, as announced by International Budget Partnership in 1997, where transparency advocates now seek standards to ensure the invariability of the information.[205] Succeeded by this trend, the reform of "right to know" started with Sweden now launched in varies perspectives such as financial regulation, environmental protection, anti-corruption as well as personal data protection, etc.[206] The promising nature of transparency initiatives is to some extent dart into doubt by dubious interpretations of 'transparency' and related concepts. The root problem is the term's consistent ambiguity. Much like sweeping words such as 'accountability,' 'transparency' offers a "nicely ambivalent" concept.[207] Many theories like "market for lemons"[208] are inherently foreground on the problem of "information asymmetry "where the problem of trust is the most crucial topic need to be judged for risk management purpose.[209] No matter on what purpose for any interest of stakeholders including individuals and institutional, transparency seemed to be an indispensable part for management and for governance. The ambivalent relationship between trust and openness is at the heart of about transparency.[210] Especially when the topic related to "modern transparency" where opponents have the first thought that traditional ways of producing trust are more accountable than of using ICTs since the 1980s.[211]

2.2.2.2 Deconstruct the Function of Audit for Transparency

[Audit for transparency] Like audit, transparency is less as a theoretical concept and more a descriptive heuristic. Just as Fox noted the "two faces" of transparency as "clear" and "opaque".[212] Coming to the topic of data protection, the transparency

---

[203] *Ibid* at 235.

[204] Alex Cukierman, *The Limits of Transparency* (Rochester, NY, 2008) at 21.

[205] Michener & Bersch, *supra* note 208 at 236.

[206] Jonathan Fox, "The unspecific relationship between transparency and accountability" (2007) 17:4–5DevelopmentinPractice663–671.See<https://doi.org/10.1080/09614520701469955>at666.

[207] Schedler, *supra* note 182 at 668.

[208] The market for lemons refers to a situation where sellers are better informed than buyers about the quality of the good for sale, like used cars. The informational asymmetry—sellers know more than buyers—causes the market to collapse. Inspections, warranties, and certification mitigate the lemons problem.

[209] Akerlof, *supra* note 73 at 248.

[210] Albert Meijer, "Understanding modern transparency" (2009) 75:2 International Review of AdministrativeSciences255–269.Seeonline:<https://doi.org/10.1177/0020852309104175>at261.

[211] Simon Nora, Alain Minc & Daniel Bell, *The Computerization of Society*, y first english language edition ed (Cambridge, Mass.: The MIT Press, 1981) at 43.

[212] Fox, *supra* note 215 at 667.

principle stated in the GDPR as "the right to be informed" in Article 13 and Article 14 of GDPR:

> Where personal data relating to a data subject are collected from the data subject, the controller shall, at the time when personal data are obtained, provide the data subject with all of the following information…which to obtain a copy of them or where they have been made available.[213]

The process of processing personal data shall be lawful, fair, and transparent to individuals regarding how their data is processed and under what conditions their data will be processed. The principle of transparency necessitates that information related to personal data processing is easily accessible and understandable, using clear and plain language. This applies to communications directed at the public or data subjects, requiring conciseness and accessibility, and to communication with children, using language suitable for their understanding. Individuals must be informed about risks, rules, safeguards, and rights concerning personal data processing, with explicit and legitimate purposes determined during data collection.[214]

Compared with GDPR, as stated in Article 18 of the PIPL of China, personal information processor, before processing personal information, shall prominently inform the individual, clear and understandable language of the following matters:

> (1) The identity and contact information of the personal information processor; (2) the purpose of processing personal information, the manner of processing, the type of personal information processed, the retention period; (3) the manner and procedures for the exercise of the rights of individuals under this Law; (4) laws, administrative regulations shall be informed of matters. Besides the general disclose requirements.[215]

PIPL required that, first, special notification of sensitive information: Before handling sensitive information, the subject of personal information shall be informed of the full necessity of handling sensitive information, and the impact on the individual. Second, exemption from informing the circumstances of the additional information: The law identifies two exemptions from informing the circumstances, respectively (a) the laws and administrative regulations shall be confidential or do not need to inform the circumstances; (b) emergency situations to protect the life and health of natural persons and property security cannot be informed in a timely manner to the individual. It should be noted that after eliminating of the emergency, the personal information processor shall promptly supplement the information.

Also, Article 54 of the PIPL proposed mechanism of audit for personal data protection:

> The personal information processor shall conduct regular compliance audits of its handling of personal information in compliance with laws and administrative regulations.[216]

Then, Article 64 of the law stated that:

---

[213] *Supra* note 106 at 213.

[214] *Ibid* at 233.

[215] Article 18 of Personal Information Protection Law of People's Republic of China

[216] Article 54 of personal information protection law of People's Republic of China

> The department responsible for the protection of personal information in the performance of duties, personal information processing activities found to be at greater risk or the occurrence of personal information security incidents, in accordance with the prescribed authority and procedures to the legal representative of the personal information processor or the main person in charge of the interview, or require the personal information processor to commission a professional organization to conduct a compliance audit of its personal information processing activities. The personal information processor shall take measures to rectify and eliminate hidden dangers in accordance with the requirements.[217]

The purpose of such an audit is for compliance checks instead of delivering transparency. As a result, transparency became the foundation of data compliance instead of the ultimate purpose under the topic of data governance. The strong demand for transparency has tended to augment the visibility of information rather than the invariability of information. Then, if audit, in some ways, could deliver transparency, what types of transparency did it deliver? Clear or opaque? Or we shall ask the question: "Can audit deliver transparency"? As this book noted before, the audit could not be defined as a verification tool for verifying that clear transparency could be achieved in some way, where it could deliver some kind of opaque transparency or visibility for the purpose of information disclosure. Especially when it related to data topics where computerized systems mitigated transparency.[218] Computerized system served as the medium could only serve "one-way" transparency whereas face-to-face transparency goes both ways. Another result of computer-mediated character of transparency is the decontextualized nature of information. Digitalized material created opportunities for presenting information in various ways. As for the result, the personal data could be processed through different mediums, which made the audit very difficult to conduct. The effectiveness of information as well as authenticity of the information is hard to guarantee for the purpose of verification. When it comes to the discussion of data protection, in response to the "right to be informed," it requires technical methods for algorithmic and data transparency. However, it must admit that the technical method could not be guaranteed to deliver clear transparency because of its digital medium lineage. Another consequence of the computer-mediated transparency character is the decontextualized nature of the information. The transparency is taken away from the context that it refers to the context which could be presented in different ways.[219] It would make the audit work more complex than the regular one. From this point of view, on the other hand, we are stuck in a situation where we are striving to turn all knowledge into making the information visible and undermining the real intention of an audit: Making the situation more understandable and building trust between different stakeholders. Bring things to the surface could make more information visible, In comparison, it is also nice problem of exegesis.[220] As Haridimos is concerned the problem of axiomatic

[217] Article 64 of Personal Information Protection Law of People's Republic of China.

[218] Meijer, *supra* note 219 at 259.

[219] *Ibid* at 260.

[220] Marilyn Strathern, "The Tyranny of Transparency" (2000) 26:3 British Educational Research Journal 309–321, See online: <https://doi.org/10.1080/713651562> at 315.

value given to increasing information where more information, less understanding, and more information, less trust.[221] He pointed out the audit problem for deliver transparency in a way that it cannot serve as a testimony to the emergence of distinct managerial rationality centered in the notion that institutional behavior can be shaped if the right kind of reinforcement is combined with the appropriate information.[222] A strict interpretation of algorithmic transparency demands the public release of a system's source code. While this represents a substantial stride towards transparency, it is seldom adequate on its own—provided that the shared code is not only accessible but also readable, well-documented, and comprehensive. One of the reasons for this, particularly relevant to the data management community, is that meaningful transparency of algorithmic processes cannot be achieved without data transparency.[223] Data transparency is indispensable in the context of more general problems such as data protection. For example, it allows data subjects to have a comprehensive view of how their personal data are being processed. It allows users of the data to obtain detailed information about the origin of the data as well as any changes made to the data as a way to assess trustworthiness and enhance quality. It also allows organizations with complex internal structures and processes to improve auditing activities for compliance with regulation.[224]

2.3 Deconstructing the Efficiency of Audit

For this part, the paper explores the efficiency of audits from various perspectives. It discusses how the audit process can be influenced by organizational structures and the roles of internal auditors and data protection officers. It also addresses the liability of external auditors and the challenges in managing statements and regulatory attention within audit processes. From a technical standpoint, the paper emphasizes the importance of effective technical methods to support auditing procedures, especially concerning algorithm audits and data management systems. From legal perspective, it explores the efficiency of regulatory connections and the incorporation of norms and principles within audits. It addresses the challenges in aligning technical standards with legal requirements, emphasizing the importance of

[221] Haridimos Tsoukas, "The tyranny of light: The temptations and the paradoxes of the information society" (1997) 29:9 Futures 827–843. See online: <https://www.sciencedirect.com/science/article/pii/S0016328797000359> at 839.

[222] *Ibid* at 831.

[223] Accenture publish, "Follow the Data – AI Matters", See online: <https://sigai.acm.org/aimatters/blog/2018/12/02/follow-the-data/> at 12 (Visited at 2 Feb, 2023). Also see: Julia Stoyanovich, Follow the data! Algorithmic transparency starts with data transparency, See online: Follow the Data! Algorithmic Transparency Starts with Data Transparency — The Ethical Machine (shorensteincenter.org) (Visited at Feb, 22023)

[224] Elisa Bertino et al., "Redefining Data Transparency: A Multidimensional Approach" (2019) 52:1 Computer 16–26 at 19.

evidence and compliance documentation in audits related to personal data protection. Overall, this part presents a comprehensive analysis of the complexities and challenges within the audit process, particularly in the realms of personal data protection, and exploring nuances in definitions, theories and the practical implementation of audits. All these are crucial under the explanation for the need to demonstrate compliance in the necessity of the "reversal of the burden of proof" in data protection regulations.

2.3.1 Deconstructing the Structure of Audit

From organizational perspective, the efficiency of audit could affect by structure of the audit process. From internal perspective, this part focused on the relating internal auditors such as specialist of audit and data protection officer regarding personal data protection. While practically, auditor's independence is irrespectively influenced by the hierarchical internal control of the company. From external perspective, this part focus on liability of external auditors.

2.3.1.1 Internal Perspective of Audit Process

[Corporate Governance] According to the definition given by the Institute of Chartered Accountants in England and Wales, efficiency can be regarded as a composite of competence, procedural arrangements, quality control, and quality assurance. The procedural arrangements can be regarded as the tools used by firms and individuals to ensure that audits comply with technical standards, i.e., legal requirements, regulators' requirements, and auditing standards set by the Auditing Practices Board (hereafter APB). Taking into account the supplementary material in APB Practice Notes and Bulletins.[225] A clear understanding of audit efficiency is a prerequisite of audit evaluation. Efficiency has many aspects, relating the audit and the audit firm in general. Furthermore, efficiency is to some extent in the eye of the beholder. It means different things to auditors and to audit committee chairs and may also differ between companies and over time.[226] There is no clear definition of "corporate governance," with the term always being defined as an "indefinable term," which we seem to know the nature of but does not provide an accurate picture.[227] In general, this term can be defined as the process of controlling management and of balancing the interest of all internal stakeholders and other parties who

---

[225] Evaluating your auditors: Institute of Chartered Accountants in England and Wales, 2003. See online: https://files.core.ac.uk/pdf/23/140331.pdf (Visited at 05 June, 2022).

[226] The comment reflects the discussions of a meeting of the Audit Committee Chair Forum (ACCF) held on second November 2006 to address the issue of audit effectiveness and evaluation.

[227] Jean du Plessis, James McConvill & Mirko Bagaric, "Principles of Contemporary Corporate Governance", See online: *Cambridge Core* <https://www.cambridge.org/core/books/principles-

can be affected by the corporation's conduct in order to ensure responsible behaviors by corporations and to achieve the maximum level of efficiency and profitability for a corporation.[228] Additionally, we can identify several essential components of this definition: corporate governance:

> A process of controlling management; takes into consideration the interest of internal stakeholders and other parties who can be affected by the corporation's conduct; aims at ensuring responsible behavior by corporations; and has the ultimate goal of achieving the maximum level of efficiency and profitability for a corporation.[229]

Some essential components of this definition are as follows:

> Control management, internal stakeholders, ensuring responsible behaviors as well as efficiency and profitability of a corporation.[230]

The connotation of this term has become increasingly multitudinous since the 1930s due to the "managerial revolution," as illustrated by Berle and Means.[231] The separation of ownership and control leads to the debate about corporate governance, which has changed companies' perception. Initially, shareholders who owned the company are the most important stakeholders, and the only goal of the company is the maximization of profits for shareholders.[232] Gradually, people began to realize that there are other stakeholders and that the balance needs to be rebuilt between shareholders and society, and thus, it is recognized that an "enterprise, private as well as public, because it both contribute to and benefits from society, can be said to have rights and duties that society, in somewhat the same way, as an individual.[233] In addition, the interests represented by the company are not only limited to shareholders but also to investors, outside creditors, employees, consumers and the public.[234] As a result, the concept of "managing the corporation" started to change the flavor of corporate governance where the interrelationships among the board of directors, shareholders, employees, managing directors, executive directors, nonexecutive directors, managers, audit committees and other committees of the board of directors need to be managed. As George Goyder noted:

---

of-contemporary-corporate-governance/73681FC8D4569775FF90843982CD5200> at 1 (Visited at 19 Mar, 2019).

[228] *Corporate Governance and the Judges*, SSRN Scholarly Paper, by John Hynes Farrar, papers.ssrn.com, SSRN Scholarly Paper ID 2146394 (Rochester, NY: Social Science Research Network, 2003) at 9.

[229] *Ibid* at 11.

[230] *Ibid.*

[231] Adolf A Berle et al., *The Modern Corporation and Private Property* (New Brunswick, N.J., U.S.A: Transaction Publishers, 1991) at 2.

[232] Margaret M Blair, *Ownership and Control: Rethinking Corporate Governance for the Twenty-First Century* (Washington, D.C.: Brookings Institution Press, 1995) at 175.

[233] C de Hoghton, *The Company: Law, Structure and Reform in Eleven Countries* (London: George Allen & Unwin, 1970) at 7.

[234] John H Farrar, *Farrar's Company law*, 3rd edition ed (London: Butterworths, 1991) at 13.

> The balancing of the company's responsibilities, to workers as members of the company, to consumers of the goods and services it provides, and to the community of which it is a citizen. Its primary goal of operating at maximum efficiency and the lowest cost, so as to make a profit and discharge its obligations to its shareholders, represents the full scope of management.[235]

For audit, the recognition of stakeholder concern is not only good business but also politically expedient and morally and ethically just, even if in the strict legal sense.[236] Following this trend, even the definition of corporation has transferred from "ownership-oriented" to "stakeholder-oriented."[237] Audits are now viewed as essential parts of corporate governance, more so than the basic role of "verifying," and the audit function is assimilated into the activities and affairs of institutions.[238] As Jean du Plessis noted, an audit is considered by some commentators to be a definitional and cardinal aspect of corporate governance.[239] As a matter of fact, auditors play a significant role in the internal management of the company and have significant impacts on corporate governance. A Cadbury report noted the following:

> The annual audit is one of the cornerstones of corporate governance…the audit provides an external and objective check on…have been prepared and presented, and it is an essential part of the checks and balances required. The question is not whether there should be an audit but how to ensure its objectivity and effectiveness.[240]

From a practical perspective, taking the financial sector as an example, the final financial report is not prepared by internal auditors but is board of directors' responsibility. Similar to the situation of an audit for personal data protection, the documentation process is not the duty of internal auditors or data protection officers, and audits provide independent assurance of the integrity of the way in which the company reports.

[Audit process] The audit process typically begins with an initial scoping exercise, where the audit team defines the scope and objectives of the audit, identifies the relevant legal and regulatory requirements, and determines the areas of focus. The audit team then performs a risk assessment to identify potential risks to personal data, such as unauthorized access, theft, loss, or misuse. Once the risks are identified, the audit team evaluates the organization's policies, procedures, and systems to assess their effectiveness in mitigating those risks. This may include a

---

[235] George Goyder, *The responsible company* (Oxford: Blackwell, 1961) at 45.

[236] Roberta Romano, *The Genius of American Corporate Law* (American Enterprise Institute, 1993) at 23.

[237] James E Post, Lee E Preston & Sybille Sauter-Sachs, *Redefining the Corporation: Stakeholder Management and Organizational Wealth* (Stanford University Press, 2002) at 17.

[238] Plessis, McConvill & Bagaric, *supra* note 236 at 240.

[239] *Ibid* at 241.

[240] Report of the HIH Royal Commission (2003) (Owen Report): On 16 April 2003, the final report of the HIH Royal Commission inquiring into the reasons for the collapse of one of Australia's largest insurance companies was publicly released. See online: https://parlinfo.aph.gov.au/parlInfo/search/display/display.w3p;query=Id:%22library/prspub/XZ896%22 (Visited on September 22, 2020).

review of data protection policies and procedures, data privacy notices, data retention policies, access controls, encryption and other technical measures, employee training programs, and incident response plans. During the audit, the team may also conduct interviews with key personnel to gain a better understanding of the organization's data protection practices and identify any issues or concerns. They may also perform testing and analysis of data protection controls to determine their effectiveness and identify any weaknesses. After completing the audit fieldwork, the team prepares a report that outlines the findings, conclusions, and recommendations. The report typically includes an executive summary, a description of the audit scope and objectives, a summary of the audit findings, a detailed analysis of the weaknesses identified, and recommendations for improvement. The report may also include a list of any regulatory or legal requirements that were not met and the associated risks. The organization then can review the report and respond to the findings and recommendations. This may involve implementing corrective actions, providing additional information or explanations, or disputing any findings they disagree with. The audit team may also perform a follow-up review to ensure that any recommended actions have been implemented and are effective. Audits for personal data protection are becoming increasingly important due to the growing concern around data privacy and security.

[Specialist of Audit Body] The competence of the auditor, as Power noted, is usually:

> Indicated by technical qualifications, membership of a recognized professional body or even experience and general reputation in the market.[241]

The competence of samples is usually examined and verified by auditors, which require different skills in information technology, management, production processes, data analysis, laws and regulations and a variety of abilities in other industries. As a result, audits are usually conducted by professional teams for a specific project. From this point of view, the samples' competence largely depends on the judgment of the auditors. Therefore, the qualifications of auditors are essential in the audit process. Accordingly, the auditor needs to provide evidence of professional qualifications to be considered legitimate for carrying out audits. For instance, in financial auditing, the formation of a viewpoint on financial statements is very specialized. Such accounting practices shall be audited by a competence auditor, who is usually required to be a certified practicing accountant in Britain, referred to as "chartered certified accountant." Their qualifications are recognized by the Companies Act of 1989, the Insolvency Act, and the Financial Services and Market Act.[242] Also, professional guidance has been developed to address the competence

[241] Power, *supra* note 10 in Chap. 1 at 80.

[242] In the UK and Ireland, according to the Companies Act of 1989, the Insolvency Act and the Financial Services and Markets Act, those certified as chartered certified accountants (ACCA), England and Wales chartered accountants (ACA), Scottish chartered accountants (CA), and Irish chartered accountants (CA) have the right to act as local statutory audit, bankruptcy management, and business investment consultants.

of auditors. For instance, there are standards and guidelines for financial auditors that have been published by the Financial Reporting Council of the U.K., such as ethical standards and guidance of practice notes.[243]

Compared with the financial sector, there also exists a certification body, like the International Association of Privacy Professionals (hereafterIAPP), which has provided certification programs for individuals to become certified professionals.[244] As the IAPP stated, its goal is to:

> Offer the most encompassing, up to date and sought-after global training and certification program for privacy and data protection...bolster compliance and risk mitigation practices.[245]

While from the audit perspective, to be certified by the IAPP does not mean that one is qualified as an auditor for personal data protection. Again, the GDPR needs to recognize such a professional body. Although such a qualification is well recognized by technology companies such as Microsoft, Amazon, and AT&T as a self-regulation approach,[246] GDPR or other relevant regulations do not recognize such qualifications. In other words, judiciary control needs to have the appropriate oversight in terms of the qualification of the auditor for personal data protection. In addition to these realities, the judgment made by auditors needs to be objective, and this book discusses this issue from both internal and external perspectives. The obscurity of auditing processes exists not only because of the information asymmetry needed to maintain auditor confidentiality but also due to the risk of undue responsibility that auditors have to overcome.[247] As a result, auditors rely heavily on internal statements from actors, and thus, the difference between internal and external audits has become increasingly vague, which has indeed impaired the effectiveness of the audit process.[248]

[Role of DPO] Under European regimes, the responsibility for the internal control for personal data protection is largely distributed to the data protection officer (DPO).[249] Chap. 4 of the GDPR introduces the requirement that organizations in which private or public bodies are being processed large scales of personal data need to appoint DPOs,[250] while most importantly, a DPO shall:

---

243 Financial Reporting Council, Audit, "Assurance and Ethics" See online: https://www.frc.org.uk/auditors/audit-assurance/standards-and-guidance (Visited on 28 August, 2020).

244 There are four CIPP concentrations, each focusing on a specific region: Asia (CIPP/A), Canada (CIPP/C), Europe (CIPP/E), and the US private sector (CIPP/US).

245 IAPP, IAPP membership page, See online: https://iapp.org/join/corporate/ (Visited on 2 February, 2024).

246 Ibid.

247 Power, *supra* note 10 in Chap. 1 at 65.

248 *Ibid* at 67.

249 Paul Lambert, *The Data Protection Officer : Profession, Rules, and Role* (Auerbach Publications, 2016) at 43.

250 Article 37 of the GDPR.

> In the performance of the tasks, have due regard of the risks associated with processing operations, taking into account the nature, scope, context, and purposes of processing.[251]

Regarding the responsibility of internal audits and personal data impact assessment, the GDPR also requires the DPO to carry out a compliance task. As the GDPR stated, the audit process and personal data impact assessment need to be carried out under the supervision of the DPO, which means that it links the position of the rule of audit and the rule of corporate governance.[252] The independence of the internal auditors and the DPO create ambiguous situations that need to be explained. Based on the explanation by the GDPR, the DPO must be allowed to act independently and not be under direction or instruction regarding his or her individual tasks.[253] In addition, the controller or processor shall ensure that the DPO does not receive any instructions regarding the exercising of his or her function. He or she shall not (ordinarily or at all) be dismissed by the controller or the processor for performing his or her tasks.[254] While practically, the DPO is designated by the processors and controllers and needs to report directly to the highest management level within the company, his or her independence, in truth, is irrespectively influenced by the hierarchical internal control of the company. In other words, from an internal perspective, auditors always have a close relationship with companies where the "conflict of interest" situation needs to be disclosed and managed. As a result, this book first tried to dig deeper into the concept of corporate governance to deconstruct internal auditors' liability regarding personal data protection.

[Liability of internal auditors] As essential stakeholders who aim to mitigate the risk of harm associated with the corporation, internal auditors play an indispensable role in terms of the benefits of the corporation, and the audit function has become integral to the daily activities of a company. As the Report of the H.I.H. Royal Commission noted:

> Auditors play a significant role in corporate governance. This is not surprising given the emphasis placed on integrity and on the need for financial reporting that is honest and that presents a balanced picture of the state of the company's affairs.[255]

From an internal perspective, auditors rely on their expertise to assist the governing body through communications and advice during the audit process. The communication process may be so intimately connected with the openness, integrity and accountability with which the financial state of the company is asspecific ed. and presented that it can be properly said to be part of corporate governance.[256] Like other stakeholders, internal auditors can be liable for their duties and responsible for

[251] Lambert, *supra* note 258 at 44.

[252] Plessis, McConvill & Bagaric, *supra* note 236 at 238.

[253] *Ibid* at 44.

[254] Article 38 (3) of the GDPR.

[255] Parliament of Australia: Report of Royal Commission into HIH Insurance. See online: https://parlinfo.aph.gov.au/parlInfo/search/display/display.w3p;query=Id:%22 library/prspub/XZ896%22 (Visited on October 7, 2020).

[256] Ibid.

their negligence or not properly discharging their legal duties. The liability originating internally can arise in three ways. First, it can be defined as "contract liability," where auditors engage in a contract with a company. Under this circumstance, internal auditors are subjected to employment relationships in relation to audit services, and the contract always requires the auditor to use "reasonable skills and care in the conducting of the audit."[257] A breach of the contract happens if auditors fail to perform audit functions adequately. Internal auditors can only be sued by the company, and other parties, such as shareholders, have no right to sue an internal auditor under the contract. Second, internal auditors may be liable for negligence to other stakeholders. For instance, in the financial sector, if internal auditors "do not complete the audit to the standard required of a professional auditor and the other party suffers a loss as a result of the negligent audit," then auditors may be sued.[258] Regarding the third perspective, auditors can be liable for breach of statutory duties, where an auditor breaches the duties imposed on them by a statute.[259] Under this circumstance, only companies can sue auditors for damages for breaching their duties.[260] In the context of auditing for personal data protection, the liability of internal auditors (also of personal data protection officers) needs to be analyzed under the regulations of the GDPR. First, internal auditors and data protection officers are always designated by companies as required by the GDPR. The requirements for internal auditing and for privacy impact assessment (hereafterPIA) are usually normed by the employment contract between companies and internal auditors. In addition, Article 28.3 of the GDPR states the following:

> Processing shall be governed by a contract or other legal regulation that stipulates that the processor makes available to the controller all information necessary to demonstrate compliance with the obligations laid down in this Article and allow for and contribute to audits.[261]

For the interest of companies, internal auditors shall use the best of their professional knowledge to audit the internal mechanism for the purpose of mitigating the risk associated with the processing of personal data. If internal auditors fail to fulfill the duty of auditing, then they may be liable for breaching contracts. While the GDPR requires that the DPO shall not be dismissed for performing his or her tasks and shall not receive any instructions regarding the tasks,[262] it seems that the GDPR guarantees the independence of internal auditors in performing their duties. This book found that the exemption of liability from the GDPR is difficult to achieve in reality. Although the DPO reports to the highest level of the management team of the data controller and is an executive at the company, this does not mean that the

---

[257] Power, *supra* note 10 in Chap. 1 at 42.

[258] Plessis, McConvill & Bagaric, *supra* note 236 at 250. Additionally, see Alexander v Cambridge Credit Corp. Ltd. (1987) 9 NSWL 310 at 97.

[259] *Ibid* at 251.

[260] *Ibid.*

[261] Article 28 of GDPR.

[262] GDPR, Article 38 (3).

DPO will be liable for his or her activities personally. In other words, DPOs and internal auditors are still liable for general employment contracts due to them poorly performing their duties. For instance, the DPO may breach a contract by breaching the duty of care required by a consultancy or an employment contract. Additionally, DPOs may be liable for negligence toward other stakeholders. Although the DPO is not personally liable for noncompliance with the GDPR, he or she is still liable for negligence for not performing tasks for other stakeholders.[263] Taking the Swedish Tort Liability Act (TLA) as an example, Chapter 4 (1) of the TLA provides a scenario for liabilities for employees, the conditions of which need to be met as follows:

> Damage has occurred to the employer; the damage has been caused because of the employees' fault or negligence. It is necessary that there is a link of causation between the actions of the DPO and the damage suffered; there are serious reasons.[264]

Based on the above-mentioned conditions, the DPO can be held liable for either intentional fault or negligence. As a matter of fact, there are two cases pending regarding decisions about personal liability for DPOs in both the UK and Switzerland. Although time is still needed for the final judgment, the tension between the "duty of care" in contract law and the exemption of the GDPR for DPOs are subsistent in reality.[265]

DPOs and internal auditors may also be held liable for criminal charges. For instance, in Ireland, the Data Protection Act of 2003 created the concept of criminal liability for both the company and its officers. As a matter of fact, criminal liability can be imposed at the individual level when an offense has been committed and the violation is found to have been committed with the director's or officer's consent or connivance and/or is attributable to any negligence on their part" (Table 2.2).[266]

As this book has noted, the independence of internal auditors and DPOs are required by the GDPR, while because of the affine relation between data processors and internal auditors, it is difficult to carry out tasks without the influence of data processors. As a result, the documentation process is necessary to mitigate the risk of internal auditors. For internal auditors, carrying out PIA or internal audits for compliance purposes is a function of compulsion by law, and it also ensures that data processors put in place proper privacy and security policies and strategies.[267]

---

[263] Article 29 Working Party addresses this issue in its Guidelines on Data Protection Officers of December 13, 2016. These guidelines state that the controller or the processor remains responsible for compliance with data protection laws, and accordingly, it will be up to the controller or processor to demonstrate compliance, regardless of how much autonomy the DPO is granted.

See online: https://www.lexology.com/library/detail.aspx?g=ef6f8142-9283-4a98-be5f-54d1054fd646 (Visited on October 18, 2020).

[264] Jan Hellner, "The New Swedish Tort Liability Act" (1974) 22:1 Am J Comp Law 1–16, See online: <https://academic.oup.com/ajcl/article/22/1/1/2585198> at 3 (Visited at 19 January, 2019).

[265] Data Protection Officers personally liable for fines, Aigine See online: https://aigine.se/en/data-protection-officers-personally-liable-for-fines/gdpr/ (Visited on 19 October, 2020).

[266] Criminal offenses are subject to a maximum fine of 3000 Euros for summary offenses and a maximum fine of 100,000 Euros for indictable offenses.

[267] David Wright & Paul de Hert, eds, *Privacy Impact Assessment*, Law, Governance and Technology Series (Springer Netherlands, 2012) at 480.

Table 2.2 Personal Liability for Privacy and DPOs in Different Legal Regimes (*Legal Risk to be a DPO*, by Hanratty Carissa (IAPP, 2017) at 1)

Country	Statute	Civil Liability	Criminal Liability	Penalty	Imprisonment
Canada	CASL (Section 31, currently suspended)	"[I]f directed, authorized, assented to, acquiesced in or participated in" violation of CASL	N/A	Statutory damages and compensation for actual loss or damage	N/A
Hong Kong	PDPO	"Subject to subsection (4), an individual who suffers damage by reason of a contravention of a requirement under this Ordinance: (a) by a data user; and (b) which relates, whether in whole or in part, to personal data of which that individual is the data subject, shall be entitled to compensation from that data user for that damage."	Data user: "a person who, either alone or jointly or in common with other persons, controls the collection, holding, processing or use of the data." "If the data is provided for gain, to a fine of $1,000,000 and to imprisonment for 5 years"	Statutory damages and compensation for damage	Up to 5 years
Ireland	Data Protection (Amendment) Act 2003 (Section 29)	N/A	"[C]ommitted with the consent or connivance of or to be attributable to any neglect on the part of a person"	Statutory Damages	N/A
Malaysia	PDPA (Part X, Section 133)	N/A	"[W]as in any manner or to any extent responsible for the management of any of the affairs of the body corporate or was assisting in such management … (a) may be charged severally or jointly"	Statutory Damages	Up to 2 years
Philippines	DPA (Rule XIII, Section 61)	"The penalty shall be imposed upon the responsible officers, as the case may be, who participated in, or by their gross negligence, allowed the commission of the crime."	"The penalty shall be imposed upon the responsible officers, as the case may be, who participated in, or by their gross negligence, allowed the commission of the crime."	Statutory damages	6 months – 7 years

(continued)

Table 2.2 (continued)

Country	Statute	Civil Liability	Criminal Liability	Penalty	Imprisonment
Singapore	PDPA (Part X, Section 52 (1))	"Where an offence under this Act committed by a body corporate is proved to have been committed (a) with the consent or connivance of an officer; or (b) to be attributable to any neglect on his part…"	"The officer as well as the body corporate shall be guilty of the offence and shall be liable to be proceeded against and punished accordingly."	Statutory damages and private right of action	1–3 years
United Kingdom	DPA (Part VII, Section 55A)	N/A	"(a) [K]new or ought to have known (i) that there was a risk that the contravention would occur; (ii) that such a contravention would be of a kind likely to cause substantial damage or substantial distress, but (b) failed to take reasonable steps to prevent the contravention."	Statutory Damages	N/A

However, the reality is that according to the Swedish Data Protection Authority's Integrity Report, no organization in Sweden meets the requirements regarding PIA or records of processing activities.[268] There are still numerous challenges that DPOs will face. In addition to the internal responsibility that DPOs need to deliver, they also need to take external responsibility "To act as the contact point or the supervisory authority on issues relating to processing, including the prior consultation referred to in Article 36 of the GDPR, and to consult, where appropriate, with regard to any other matter."[269] This brings about another essential perspective of an efficiency audit, which is referred to as an "external audit."

2.3.1.2 External Perspective of Audit Process

[Liability of External Auditors] Compared with the internal role of auditors, external auditors' liability can also arise in three main ways, as previously mentioned, referring to contractual liability, law on negligence and breach of GDPR duties. Within the GDPR context, external auditors are always related to audit/certification bodies and supervisory bodies. As stated in Article 42 of the GDPR:

> The Board and the Commission shall encourage, in particular, at Union level, the establishment of data protection certification mechanisms and of data protection seals and marks.[270]

As stated in Article 24 of the GDPR:

> Adherence to approved codes of conduct, as referred to in Article 40, or approved certification mechanisms, as referred to in Article 42, may be used as an element by which to demonstrate compliance with the obligations of the controller.[271]

Article 25 of the GDPR regards a certification mechanism as an element in demonstrating the requirement of "Data Protection by Design."[272] Regarding a supervisory body as an external auditor, Article 58 of the GDPR states that:

> Each supervisory authority shall have investigative powers to carry out investigations in the form of data protection audits.[273]

Additionally, Article 47 of the GDPR also gives power to competent supervisory authorities to review or approve the binding corporate rules for the purpose of data transaction across datasets.[274] Moreover, data protection audits are regarded as mechanisms for ensuring the verification of compliance with binding corporate

---

[268] Ibid.

[269] Lambert, *supra* note 258 at 44. Additionally, see Article 39 (1) of the GDPR.

[270] GDPR: Article 42 (2).

[271] GDPR: Article 24 (3).

[272] GDPR: Article 25 (3).

[273] GDPR: Article 58 1(b).

[274] GDPR: Article 47 (1).

rules.[275] As this book has demonstrated, an external audit body is indispensable for the demonstrable part of accountability, which is required by the GDPR. The liabilities of different external parties may need to be distinguished from each other, as stated in the GDPR. Third parties, such as certification bodies, may be involved in contractual liability and laws of negligence because they need to provide compliance as a service for data controllers or data processors. The GDPR also states that a certification pursuant to the GDPR does not diminish the liability of the controller for compliance with the GDPR.[276] In other words, the Board and the Commission encourage the data controller to employ a certification process, but the deployment of such a process does not equal compliance with the supervisory body. As a matter of fact, this actually creates a very tricky zone for the distribution of the liability of the external body as a third party for the certification process. If a competence certification body verifies the compliance of the data controller, then the company receives a seal of compliance. During the three-year certification period, it was found that the company breached the requirement. Thus, shall the certification body be liable for this kind of breach? For example, regarding this circumstance, we have already seen that TRUSTe was held liable for deceiving consumers about its recertification program and for misrepresentation.[277] Under the GDPR, the data controller is still liable for the breach of the data protection rule, and then, the controller can sue the certification body for negligence or for contractual liability. This leads to a trend that is very similar to that within the financial sector, where external audits pay more attention to the arrangement of data protection procedures in auditee organizations. Internal audits are regarded as internal controls, and external audit agencies have become the "controllers of control" for Internet companies.[278] The complexity of the process of personal data protection internally may drive the external audit body to reduce its work in terms of checking the details of how the company processes its clients' data to check that the company is compliant with personal data protection guidelines. In other words, the data management system has become an auditable object for the external audit body. External audit bodies need feedback from internal audit bodies on different kinds of statements to achieve the objectives of internal audits, the standards for processing personal data to which they adhere, the audit trial result from the monitoring of the data process, etc. In general, there are two omnipotent components of the ISO audit process: the information management standard and the requirements for this standard. To carry out audits, all the external checking and management procedures rely on the internal statements of "system documents," which need to be prepared under the guidance of an external audit body. In other words, from an external perspective, the audit process can be interpreted as a process of the "management of statements." While in theory, this

[275] GDPR: Article 47 (1).

[276] Article 42 of the GDPR.

[277] TRUSTe Settles FTC Charges it Deceived Consumers Through Its Privacy Seal Program. FTC: See online: https://www.ftc.gov/news-events/press-releases/2014/11/truste-settles-ftc-charges-it-deceived-consumers-through-its (Visited on November 14, 2020).

[278] Power, *supra* note 10 in Chap. 1 at 82.

can be a perfect regulatory scheme, where internal auditors cooperate with external standard bodies to achieve regulatory goals, but in reality, this scheme may also redirect the regulatory attention from the compliance of personal data processing toward a series of abstract statement arrangements.[279] From this point of view, Power noted the following:

> The abstract system tends to become the primary external auditable object, rather than the output of the organization itself, and this adds to the obscurity of the audit as a process which provides assurance about systems elements and little else.[280]

An expectation gap between auditing practices is formed between the internal and external regulatory layers. The public expects the external body to contribute directly to a substantive part of the data processing arrangement, while As a matter of fact, the audit of the external body becomes an "audit show" to check different kinds of documents, and the outcome of external auditing is converted into a mere "verification of the surface." The result of the certification mechanism makes a direct declaration of compliance, raising the question of whether the "effectiveness" of internal control can be objectively verified.[281] As a result, the liability of the external certification body becomes very nebulous for the internal body, third party and supervisory body. The regulatory safety of such a certification mechanism can also lead to public suspicion of such a system. Regarding other external audit parties mentioned in the GDPR, which referred to them as the competent supervisory authority and the European Data Protection Board (EDPB), the guidelines propose that these external bodies carry out audits to verify their compliance with the regulations. The problem they face is their ability to regulate the processing of personal data. In other words, the "regulability," as proposed by Lessig, is a concern of many scholars when the supervisory body faces the development of tools to deal with personal data.[282] It is similar to a matrix we faced twenty years ago, and as Lessig stated:

> It is that the government's power to regulate this space turns not just on whether it can regulate behavior directly; rather, its power turns as well on the ability to regulate code. By regulating code, it can regulate behavior, by changing the incentives that the code would otherwise produce.[283]

The efficiency of regulation depends on its architecture, where for the protection of personal data, some bodies are not convinced of the competency of the supervisory body. For instance, France's highest administrative court upheld a 50-million-euro fine against Google for violating the GDPR due to its alleged failure to comply with

---

[279] *Ibid* at 85. This idea has also been noted by Power.

[280] *Ibid.*

[281] Piper A and Jones: *"Auditors review of Cadbury compliance statements"* Tonkin and Skerratt (1995) at 29.

[282] Victoria Smith Ekstrand, "Lessig, Lawrence. The Law of the Horse: What Cyberlaw Might Teach, 113 Harv. L. Rev. 501 (1999)" (2020) 25:3 Communication Law and Policy 406–411, See online: <https://doi.org/10.1080/10811680.2020.1767414> at 409 (Visited 1 July, 2022).

[283] *Ibid* at 24.

the transparency and notice requirements,[284] while Google appealed that the CNIL did not have appropriate evidence and an investigative procedure to identify a violation of the GDPR transparency principles. It should be noted that the purpose of such an economic sanction is not to prorogue the processing of personal data for these companies because it is impossible for them to provide their services without using the data of the users within the European regime. The purpose of such punishment is to urge data controllers and processors to comply with the requirements of the GDPR. Regulatory bodies must be able to show how data processors violate the rules of the GDPR and to teach regulatory subjects how to demonstrate their compliance. To conduct an audit for personal data protection to deliver accountability, both counters and accounted need to be fully prepared for the audit process from both management and compliance perspectives. Another case occurred in Canada, which showed the lack of ability of the supervisory body to verify its compliance with the regulatory object. Moreover, the "COVI app," which uses artificial intelligence to predict a user's risk level for COVID-19, will not be recommended by the federal government. One reason for the refusal to adopt this app is that the federal government has concerns about the protection of privacy issues in the app.[285] Sometimes, the outcome is not because the law cannot be adapted to the new circumstance brought about by the technology but because of the lack of regulation ability of the supervisory body.[286]

2.3.2 *Deconstructing the Audit Process*

For this part, this book perceived that the process of audit for personal data protection faced more "digital challenges" compared with financial sector. From technical side, audit faced challenges both from data, algorithm and system level. From legal side, greater challenge are encountered when audit served as process to build connection between law, regulation and standards. Practically, difficulties to acquired evidence and to recognized of electronic documentations as well as the problem of burden of proof will affect the efficiency of audit process.

---

[284] French Highest Administrative Court Upholds 50 Million Euro Fine against Google for Alleged GDPR Violations. HUNTON, See online: https://www.huntonprivacyblog.com/2020/06/23/french-highest-administrative-court-upholds-50-million-euro-fine-against-google-for-alleged-gdpr-violations/ (Visited on 24 November, 2020).

[285] Vincent Gautrais, COVI, dommage! Blog of Prof. Vincent, Gautrais, See online: https://www.gautrais.com/blogue/2020/06/05/covi-pourquoi-pas/ (Visited on 4 February, 2024).

[286] The federal government has ruled out an endorsement of one of the highest-profile Canadian efforts to develop a COVID-19 contact-tracing smartphone app. The Covi Canada app, developed by Montreal's Mila Institute, uses artificial intelligence to predict a user's risk level. The decision against adopting Mila's app, which is based on the protocols developed by Britain's National Health Service, strongly suggests that the federal government will instead endorse an app based on the exposed notification application programming interface of Apple or Google.

2.3.2.1 Deconstruct the Technical Challenge of Audit Process

[Dataset problem for auditing] For personal data protection, obtaining samples involves to evaluating different kinds of datasets, pointing to multifold documentation that makes the process and transfer of personal data both visible and auditable.[287] As a matter of fact, large volumes of personal data have been processed by organizations. As a result, various datasets of personal data have been produced, such as those of medical records and social interactions. These datasets are multifarious in nature, with their sizes ranging from small to large, and are also evolving due to increased demand over time.[288] For different purposes, these datasets are subject to collaborative analysis through tools, programs and parameters.[289] To make the process of personal data visible, it requires the ability to keep track of the datasets being used. The GDPR introduced the principle of explanation, specific calling for algorithmic accountability, which can be briefly described as involving tools that allow the person who is subject to automated decision-making to be informed about this fact and about the reasoning behind this decision.[290] As for a premise, to explain to an individual how the decision was made by algorithms, it is crucial to clearly indicate from where the data came since transparency is often deemed an element of accountability. The difficulty faced was that current data management systems are usually inadequate at supporting these types of collaborative environments.[291] For the purpose of audits, such a system is necessary in essence. In other words, the data sheet itself is not an auditable object, and the records of using these data and of using data sets that can manifest as the purpose of using personal data are subject to audits. In this way, this approach can avoid the problem of trade secrets, and it also prevents the acquisition of the data from datasheets or databases directly.

While comparing mature industries that have developed standardized methods of benchmarking under different circumstances, it should be noted that for personal data protection, the absence of such a system or standardized format is the reality.[292] Thus, providing benchmarked documentation is essential to achieve an auditable environment.[293] As a matter of fact, scholars from both the Eastern and Western

---

[287] Mitchell et al., *supra* note 8 in Chap. 1 at 5.

[288] Anant Bhardwaj et al., "DataHub: Collaborative Data Science & Dataset Version Management at Scale" (2014) at 3 See online: <http://arxiv.org/abs/1409.0798> (Visited at 4 February, 2024).

[289] Bhardwaj et al., "DataHub", *supra* note 16 in Chap. 1.

[290] *Right to Access Information As a Collective-Based Approach to the GDPR's Right to Explanation in European Law*, SSRN Scholarly Paper, by Joanna Mazur, papers.ssrn.com, SSRN Scholarly Paper ID 3356770 (Rochester, NY: Social Science Research Network, 2018) at 2.

[291] Bhardwaj et al., "DataHub", *supra* note 16 in Chap. 1.

[292] Mitchell et al., *supra* note 8 in Chap. 1.

[293] Timnit Gebru et al., "Datasheets for Datasets" (2020). See online: <http://arxiv.org/abs/1803.09010> at 13 (Visited at 21 July, 2020).

worlds have called for transparency in different ways.[294] Some of these scholars believe that all stages of the processing of personal data should be subject to public scrutiny, while the present paper favors another method because full transparency will encounter problems by enumerate risks at different levels. For instance, Joshua Kroll resisted the call for transparency for both policy reasons and technical reasons. First, transparency often conflicts with important interests, such as the protection of trade secrets. In addition, just looking at algorithms may not allow for the easy identification of where the problem is.[295] Instead, some scholars have proposed relying on technological tools to ensure algorithm accountability.

This book suggests that transparency should take the form of enabling the expert oversight of auditors.[296] This is very similar to what the GDPR has established, which is called "qualified transparency," referring to "a system of targeted revelations of different degrees of depth and scope aimed at different recipients."[297] In other words, transparency in practice includes the consideration of the interest of the public, of companies and of regulators, which will involve oversight by different parties.

[Problem of algorithm auditing] Regarding the algorithm, four articles address algorithmic decision-making in the GDPR: Articles 22, 13, 14 and 15.[298] Article 22 states the following:

> Individuals have the right not to be subject to a decision based solely on automated processing.[299]

This article limits companies to using algorithms for making decisions only if individuals let them to do so in practice. In addition to Article 22, Articles 13 and 14 of GDPR for establishing notification rights when personal data are being processed through individuals or third parties.[300] Article 15 establishes access rights for individuals regarding "the existence of automated decision-making, including profiling."[301] Furthermore, Article 15 also states that the data subject has the right to have information about the recipients or categories of recipients' personal data, and in addition, the source of the personal data when they are not collected from the data subject needs to be provided upon request. Thus, a clear connection between other

---

294 Mireille Hildebrandt, "The Dawn of a Critical Transparency Right for the Profiling Era" (2012), See online: <https://works.bepress.com/mireille_hildebrandt/40/> at 17 (Visited at 21 July, 2020).

295 Pauline Kim, "Auditing Algorithms for Discrimination" (2017) 166:1 University of Pennsylvania Law Review See online: <https://scholarship.law.upenn.edu/penn_law_review_online/vol166/iss1/10> at 192 (Visited at 22 July, 2020).

296 *Ibid* at 189.

297 Frank Pasquale, *The Black Box Society: The Secret Algorithms That Control Money and Information*, reprint edition ed (Cambridge, Massachusetts London, England: Harvard University Press, 2016) at 140.

298 Casey, Farhangi & Vogl, *supra* note 68 in Chap. 1.

299 *Ibid.*

300 *Ibid* at 199.

301 Mazur, *supra* note 300.

individual rights established by the GDPR and the individualized transparency required has been established, suggesting an interesting point in terms of transparency: "The substance of other underlying legal rights often determines transparency's substance."[302] As Kaminski argued:

> If one has a right of correction, then one needs to see errors. If one has a right against discrimination, then one needs to see what factors are used in decision-making. Otherwise, information asymmetries render underlying rights effectively void.[303]

For the GDPR to establish "individualized transparency," as stated in relevant articles, processors are responsible for making such information understandable for individuals, which involves far more than providing an explanation of counterfactuals.[304] The data protection working party published Article 29, providing guidelines on "automated individual decision-making and profiling for the purpose of regulation, which noted the following:

> Controllers may want to consider implementing a mechanism for data subjects to check their profile, including details of the information and sources used to develop it.[305]

In other words, this article suggests that processors should offer interactive tools for individuals to manage their personal data, as it is the processors' duty to notify individuals about how they process personal information and ensure their understanding. As this book has pointed out, the GDPR establishes systemic transparency through Article 22's safeguards, the interpretation of the Working Party, and the requirement for impact assessments.[306] Systemic transparency can be carried out in many ways. First, as Article 58 of the GDPR states:

> Each supervisory authority shall have all of the following investigative powers: (a) to order the controller and the processor…to provide any information it requires for the performance of its tasks and (e) to obtain from the controllers…access to all personal and to all information necessary for the performance of its tasks.[307]

This implies that regulators have the authority to directly access information about algorithms processing personal data. The GDPR also mandates data processors to conduct a 'data protection impact assessment' when processing personal data likely

[302] *Binary Governance: Lessons from the GDPR's Approach to Algorithmic Accountability*, SSRN Scholarly Paper, by Margot E Kaminski, papers.ssrn.com, SSRN Scholarly Paper ID 3351404 (Rochester, NY: Social Science Research Network, 2019) at 1120.

[303] Casey, Farhangi & Vogl, *supra* note 68 in Chap. 1 at 213.

[304] Sandra Wachter, Brent Mittelstadt & Chris Russell, "Counterfactual Explanations without Opening the Black Box: Automated Decisions and the GDPR" (2018) ArXiv171100399 Cs, online: <http://arxiv.org/abs/1711.00399> at 12 (Visited at 12 June, 2020).

[305] European Commission, Guidelines on Automated individual decision-making and profiling for the purposes of regulation 2016/679:: https://ec.europa.eu/newsroom/article29/item-detail.cfm?item_id=612053 (Visited on 17 June, 2020).

[306] See Article 35, Article 38 of GDPR. Additionally, see Article 28, Article 32 of Guidelines on automated individual decision-making.

[307] Mazur, *supra* note 300.

to result in high risk.[308] Moreover, the GDPR proposes general data protection audits conducted by government authorities.[309] Additionally, the guidelines suggest that companies that process personal data use independent third party auditing and provide auditors with all necessary information about how the algorithm or machine learning systems works.[310] All these measures imply that the GDPR actuates third party and regulatory oversight over the development of the processing of personal data. By relying on sophisticated algorithm systems trained on massive datasets, we are at risk of making decisions based on systems that we do not truly understand.[311] How can individuals trust companies without understanding how their personal data are being used? How do regulators believe that companies comply with rules if they do not have the prowess to demonstrate the function of their model? As a result, explanation becomes the core of the responsibility and accountability of personal data processing. While the reality is that the mechanisms of accountability cannot keep up with technology development, to make the process of personal data explainable, technical tools are needed to verify and demonstrate compliance with rules and standards. As Kroll put it:

> Computer scientists may tend to think of accountability in terms of compliance with a detailed specification set forth before the creation of algorithms.[312]

Generally, from the perspective of computer science techniques, there are two ways to evaluate software: static analysis and dynamic analysis.[313] Static analysis involves reviewing source code, enabling analysts to learn how the programs work, but this method cannot identify how the programs interact with the environment.[314] Dynamic analysis tests and runs the program, but it is limited by the finite number of inputs that can be tested or outputs that can be observed.[315] Dynamic analysis is always divided into the "black-box test" and "white-box test," and the difference between them is that the former only considers the input and output of a system, while the

---

[308] GDPR, Article 31 (1) stated the following: "Where a type of processing, in particular, using new technologies and taking into account the nature, scope, context and purposes of the processing, is likely to result in a high risk to the rights and freedoms of natural persons, the controller shall, prior to processing, carry out an assessment of the impact of the envisaged processing operations on the protection of personal data. A single assessment may address a set of similar processing operations that present similar high risks."

[309] GDPR, Article 58 (b), Supervisory authority shall have all of the following investigative powers to carry out investigations in the form of data protection audits.

[310] Margot E Kaminski, *The Right to Explanation, Explained*, SSRN Scholarly Paper, SSRN Scholarly Paper ID 3196985 (Rochester, NY: Social Science Research Network, 2018) at 216.

[311] Riccardo Guidotti et al., "A Survey Of Methods For Explaining Black Box Models" (2018). See online: <http://arxiv.org/abs/1802.01933> at 64 (Visited at 13 June 2021).

[312] Kroll et al., *supra* note 40 in Chap. 1 at 695.

[313] Joshua Kroll et al., "Accountable Algorithms" (2017) 165:3 Univ Pa Law Rev. 633 at 14.

[314] Gary R McGraw, *Software Security: Building Security In*, 1 edition ed (Upper Saddle River, NJ: Addison-Wesley Professional, 2006) at 201.

[315] Kroll et al., *supra* note 40 in Chap. 1 at 650.

latter also considers the structure of the system.[316] In computer science, audits always treat the program as a black box, the inputs and outputs of which are visible but the inner parts of which are invisible.[317] However, it has been shown that:

> The black-box evaluation is the least powerful of a set of available methods for understanding and verifying system behavior.[318]

As a result, the complete coverage of a program's behavior cannot be provided because this methodology has a deficiency, in that it "explains little about what happens to the inputs that have not been tested."[319] Again, we face the same problem that is common among datasets. What is the proper audit object for auditing algorithms? What can be constituted as samples or documentation that can sufficiently support the idea that the program is in compliance with detailed specifications? As this book has noted, both static analysis and dynamic analysis belong to the method of "after the fact," which takes the program as a whole and tests it when the program is being developed.[320] However, the computer system may not be fully analyzed or explained only by relying on testing. Thus, it is essential to understand the design of the system and test it on a smaller scale.[321] As a matter of fact, relying on computational methods, there are several advanced techniques that provide accountability for auditing. For instance, software verification can mathematically provide proven invariants of a program.[322] Compared with software testing, software verification does not intend to use a specific input to verify that the program meets specific functional requirements, and it aims to demonstrate that the systems have specific invariants through mathematically checkable proofs.[323] However, the verification of a program can prove that it is in compliance with its technical specification, but it does not guarantee that such a specification is in compliance with rules or policies. To resolve this problem, the concept of "zero-knowledge proof" allows a personal data processor to prove that the algorithm decision was made in compliance with specific policies, without disclosing datasheets or algorithms.[324] To explain how the concept of zero-knowledge proof applies in the context of personal data protection, this book

---

[316] McGraw, *supra* note 324 at 106.

[317] Christian Sandvig et al., "Auditing Algorithms: Research Methods for Detecting Discrimination on Internet Platforms" (2014) Data Discrim Convert Crit Concerns Product Inq at 211.

[318] Amit Datta, Michael Carl Tschantz & Anupam Datta, "Automated Experiments on Ad Privacy Settings: A Tale of Opacity, Choice, and Discrimination" (2015) arXiv:14086491 [cs]. See online: <http://arxiv.org/abs/1408.6491> at 106 (Visited 22 August, 2022).

[319] A M Turing, "On Computable Numbers, with an Application to the Entscheidungsproblem" (1937) s2–42:1 Proc London Math Soc. See online: <https://academic.oup.com/plms/article/s2-42/1/230/1491926> at 259 (Visited 15 April, 2022).

[320] Kroll et al., *supra* note 40 in Chap. 1 at 653.

[321] Steve McConnell, *Code Complete*, 2 edition ed (Redmond, Wash: Microsoft Press, 2004) at 528.

[322] Jean Souyris et al., *Formal Verification of Avionics Software Products* (Berlin, Heidelberg: Springer, 2009) at 532.

[323] C A R Hoare, "An axiomatic basis for computer programming" (1969) 12:10 Commun ACM 576–580. See online: <https://doi.org/10.1145/363235.363259> at 576 (Visited at 15 August, 2023).

[324] Oded Goldreich, *Foundations of Cryptography: A Primer* (Boston: Now Pub, 2005) at 19.

provides an example. If the processor makes commitments A, B, and C—where A involves a commitment to a specific data protection policy, B involves a commitment to the datasets from which the personal data originated, and C involves a commitment to the process of how to handle personal data—zero-knowledge proof can enable auditors to verify that A, B, and C correspond with each other. This verification allows processors to build audit logs without disclosing personal data, which may be included in the input or outcome.[325] Another straightforward way to deal with this issue is to audit the practice of logging or recording specific actions in a file.[326] Analysis of logging messages is a common method for reviewing software programs, but it also requires technicians to set up what needs to be written when performing specific functions. In addition, similar to other electronic documents, logging messages can be easily modified or hidden. As a result, the auditing of logs requires specific internal management or the sending of logging messages to remote systems designed for reviews or audits.[327] While the reality is that for instance, until 2013, the existing log systems in hospital information systems faced difficulty in guaranteeing traceability.[328] In sum, for the purpose of obtaining proper samples, choosing the right audit object for personal data protection, and designing a proper documentation process, it is essential to set up a data protection procedure before starting to design the software. The enormous difference between selective testing in financial auditing and in personal data protection auditing is that for the former, auditors need to statically select a small number of transactions to draw conclusions about all the transactions as a whole, while for personal data protection auditing, the relevant and reliable evidence that can prove the compliance of the specification shall be considered when building the program. To select proper audit objects for procedural regularity, personal data processors shall prepare proper audit trails and relevant documents for performing efficient audit processes. For the GDPR, more important than the information itself is the knowledge of who, when and with what purpose the information is accessed and where it is stored and used.[329] Therefore, the GDPR requires computational methods and the collaboration of professionals.

2.3.2.2 Deconstructing the Legal Challenge of Audit Process

[From Law to Lex Informatica] Concerning this topic, the question is not which norms provide the best protection for personal information, as regulation can stem from technological standards, management norms, and legal rules.[330] Effective nor-

---

[325] Kroll et al., *supra* note 40 in Chap. 1 at 668.

[326] Ronald E Rice & Christine L Borgman, "The use of computer-monitored data in information science and communication research" (1983) at 252.

[327] Eric Cole, *Network Security Bible*, 2 edition ed (Indianapolis, IN: Wiley, 2009) at 198.

[328] Ricardo Cruz-Correia et al., "Analysis of the quality of hospital information systems Audit Trails" (2013) 13 BMC Med Inform Decis Mak 84 at 13.

[329] Duarte Gonçalves-Ferreira et al., "HS.Register - An Audit-Trail Tool to Respond to the General Data Protection Regulation (GDPR)" (2018) at 85.

[330] Trudel, *supra* note 100 in Chap. 1 at 16.

mativity relies on the ability to incorporate different Internet norms and principles. The dilemma we face is referred to by Brownswords as the "challenge of regulatory connection." Lyria Bennett Moses noted the following:[331] Lyria Bennett Moses noted the following:

> The law should not race ahead by anticipating technological trajectories that may never come to pass. Rather, a useful goal should be to have mechanisms in place to ensure that law is designed around the sociotechnical landscape of the present or, more realistically, the recent past.[332]

The "authority" of law explains the coercive nature of the law, where it serves as an interpretative tool to explain the idea of law normativity. Many statutes have been codified in a formal way to achieve legal unity, and formal authority was equally viewed as legal authority by many authors in nineteenth-century and twentieth-century jurisprudence.[333] However, authority cannot be maintained at the point when the law is open to parties' choices and serves as an "expression of what normally constitutes a fair balance of citizens' rights and duties."[334] This is significant, especially in the field of informal authority such as contract, certification, and internal controls. From this point of view, legal authority does not require formality, as illustrated by the key insights of legal pluralism:

> A recognition that multiple normative orders exist and a focus on the dialectical interaction between and among these normative orders.[335]

Paul Berman noted the following:

> We inhabit a word of multiple normative communities; some of those communities impose their norms through officially sanctioned coercive force and formal legal processes...but of course, many other normative communities articulate norms without formal state power behind them. Law is constantly constructed through the contesting of these various norm-generating communities.[336]

Along with formal normative tools, the growing number of informal norms is enriched by regulatory layers, such as mechanisms of mutual regulation and governance.[337] This trend calls for regulations to be redesigned to ensure that the incentive nature of technology can be understood. Michael Power noted the following:

---

[331] Brownsword, *supra* note 101 in Chap. 1.

[332] Moses, "Agents of Change", *supra* note 102 in Chap. 1 at 788.

[333] Joseph Raz, *The authority of law: Essays on law and morality* (Oxford University Press, 1979) at 233.Another idea, which has often been associated with formal conceptions of legal authority, is the assumption that the validity of law derives from the state alone.

[334] Leone Niglia, ed., *Pluralism and European Private Law* (Oxford ; Portland, Or: Hart Publishing, 2013) at 116.

[335] Sally Engle Merry, "Legal Pluralism" (1988) 22:5 Law & Society Review. See online: <https://www.jstor.org/stable/3053638> at 873 (Visited at 14 Nov, 2022).

[336] Paul Schiff Berman, *Global Legal Pluralism*, (Rochester, NY: Social Science Research Network, 2007) at 13.

[337] Rose & Miller, "Political Power beyond the State", *supra* note 103 in Chap. 1.

> The growing formalization of regulatory layers has generated interest in the internalization of control mechanisms and the validation of this internalization by internal and external audits.[338]

An increase in audits has been triggered by this formalization of regulatory layers, wherein record keeping and disclosure requirements become important ways of connecting the different layers of encouraging a specific kind of organizational introspection.[339] Nevertheless, this approach is carried out in a relatively autonomous way and is bereft of legal oversight.[340]

Many statutes were codified in formally in order to achieve legal unity and formal authority has been equally viewed as a legal authority by many authors in nineteenth-century and twentieth-century jurisprudence.[341] However, authority cannot be maintained at the point when the law is open to parties' choices and serves as an expression of what constitutes typically a fair balance of citizens' rights and duties.[342] This is a significant fact, especially in the field of informal authority such as contract,certification and internal control. From this point of view, legal authority does not require formality, as illustrated by the key insights of legal pluralism:

> A recognition that multiple normative order exists and a focus on the dialectical interaction between and among these normative orders.[343]

Back to the Middle Ages of the twenties, common ground rules were needed for international commercial trade across Europe, where:

> Dissimilarity among "local, feudal, royal, and ecclesiastical law provided a significant degree of unspecific ty and difficulty for merchants. Customs and practices evolved into a distinct body of law known as the 'Lex Mercatoria.'[344]

It was distinguished from substantive law, which assured universal applicability in different legal regimes. Regarding the era of information technology, the difficulty confronted by Internet companies is that different governing laws and conflicting regulations coexist, which causes unstable and unspecific compliance environments. Therefore, the default technical standards are just as essential for internet companies as Lex Mercatoria was for merchants.[345] Regarding audit trails for personal data protection, similar dilemmas involving law and government regulation

---

338 Power, *supra* note 10 in Chap. 1 at 53.

339 Grabosky, *supra* note 106 in Chap. 1 at 531.

340 Vincent Gautrais, "Normativité et droit du technique", See online: <https://www.gautrais.com/publications/normativite-et-droit-du-technique/> at 330 (Visited on 4 Feburary, 2019).

341 Raz, *supra* note 343. Another idea, which was often associated with formal conceptions of legal authority, is the assumption that the validity of law derives from the State alone.

342 Niglia, *supra* note 344 at 116.

343 Merry, *supra* note 345 at 873.

344 Joel R Reidenberg, "Lex Informatica: The Formulation of Information Policy Rules through Technology" (1997) Texas Law Review at 553.

345 Joel Reidenberg, "The Fundamental Role of Privacy and Confidence in the Network" (1995) 30 Wake Forest L Rev 105. See online: <https://ir.lawnet.fordham.edu/faculty_scholarship/799> at 105 (Visited at 10 February, 2019).

not recognizing technological standards and information policies embedded in the designs or system configurations have emerged. Although substantive standards, jurisdictional authority and enforcement powers all clash in terms of protecting personal data, technologies also offer new solutions to legal compliance. Law-makers must understand that technical standards will be the source of rule-making. As Reidenberg noted:

> In essence, that the set of rules for information flows imposed by technology and communications networks form a 'Lex Informatica' that policymakers must understand, consciously recognize and encourage.[346]

It provides the flexibility of the information required, whereas substantive norms are usually scarce.[347] For instance, technical content is more executable than are laws and regulations, which may lead to a problem of unspecific.[348] Technical content allows for customized rules for each personal data processor, as Reidenberg pointed out the following:

> Lex Informatica can provide for this flexibility a customization through the adoption of technological standards and configurations that may tailor roles to the precise circumstances or that may empower individual participants to make their own decisions.[349]

In addition, Lex Informatica can be delivered on a transnational basis, but it will exhibit the problem of the choice of law, with which legal regimes must deal. Additionally, Lex Informatica also has enforcement advantages compared with legal regimes, which are usually criticized as ex-post actions against violations. As Frydman Benoît interpreted:

> The performativity of a science is its capacity to act on the world from its statements.[350]

By creating standardization auditing trials, automatic monitoring and compliance executions can be completed through ex-ante measures.[351]

[From Lex Informatica to Standardization] Although a wealth of privileges may be gained through encouraging Lex Informatica, time is needed for an industrial standard to evolve into Lex informatics (Table 2.3). As a matter of fact, the centers of technical standards institutions such as ISO, ETSI, or Internet societies are not usually comforted by having a regulatory relationship with their clients. Standard bodies usually have few requirements for their relationships. Compared with law and regulations, openness, which is innate to these standard bodies, has few prerequisites other than membership to have enough money to attend the

[346] Joel R. Reidenberg, *supra* note 354 at 555.

[347] *Ibid* at 577.

[348] *Ibid.*

[349] *Ibid* at 579.

[350] Frydman Benoit et Van Waeyenbergen Arnaud, "Gouverner par les standards et les indicateurs". See online: *Droit Société* <https://ds.hypotheses.org/959> at 12 (Visited on 20 August, 2020).

[351] Pandit Harshavardhan, "Test-driven Approach Towards GDPR Compliance, Semantic systems: the power of AI and knowledge graphs". 15th International conference at 32.

Table 2.3 Lex Informatica (Reidenberg, *Supra* note 354 at 593)

	Legal Regulation	Lex Informatica
Framework	Law	Architecture standards
Jurisdiction	Physical Territory	Network
Content	Statutory/Court Expression	Technical Capabilities Customary Practice
Source	State	Technologists
Customized Rules	Contract	Configuration
Customization Process	Low Cost Moderate cost standard	Off-the-shelf configuration Installable configuration User choice
Primary Enforcement	Court	Automated, Self-execution

various meetings.[352] To benefit from technical standards, law needs to play an essential role in promoting Lex Informatica. In other words, laws and regulations need to confirm the existence of Lex Informatica. For instance, in the case of the audit trails of personal data, laws can impose liability on personal data producers to adhere to specific technical standards to comply with the auditing of regulatory bodies. For instance, in the UK, the financial reporting standards issued by the Accounting Standards Board (ASB) recognized by the Company Act, required that except for small companies, the financial statements of any company shall state whether it complies with accounting standards.[353] In other words, accounting standards are not only authoritative statements of accounting practice but also legally putative according to the Company Act. The Company Law recognizes the existence of accounting standards and affirms their beneficial effects on financial reporting. The financial sector has had clear accounting rules that led to the prosperity of the financial auditing market in the twentieth century. Ground rules for audit trail will also shape solid digital auditing markets. It takes a long time for accounting standards to be recognized by the Company Act. As mentioned above, before 1990, the British Accounting Standards were formulated by the Accounting Standards Committee (ASC).[354] However, these standards were never mentioned by any Company Act before 1990.[355] Therefore, these standards did not actually have legal effects at that time. After that, the Company Act of 1985 was amended by the Company Act of 1989 in

[352] Joel R. Reidenberg, *supra* note 354 at 592.

[353] Beginning on August 1, 1990, all UK accounting standards were issued by the Accounting Standards Board (ASB). In 2012, however, the FRC Board assumed responsibility for setting accounting standards. All accounting standards developed and issued by the ASB are known as Financial Reporting Standards (FRSs).

[354] Accounting Standards Committee (ASC). "What it is, How it Works". See online: https://www.investopedia.com/terms/a/accounting-standards-committee/asc.asp (Visited on August 24, 2020).

[355] Robert Day, "UK Accounting Regulation: An Historical Perspective", (2000). See online: </paper/UK-Accounting-Regulation%3A-An-Historical-Perspective-Day/cb21aae40a89fb8b6ed-d8a973498837d77b6a822> (Visited on August 24, 2020).

the UK, introducing the definition of accounting standards for the first time and requiring company directors to state whether their financial statements were prepared in accordance with applicable accounting standards.[356] In other words, since that time, accounting standards in the UK have not only been authoritative but also legally recognized.[357] In the European jurisdiction, the International Accounting Standards (hereafter IAS), published by the International Accounting Standards Board (hereafter IASB), were adopted by the European Union, requiring the consolidated financial statements of companies with debt or equity securities listed on a regulated EU market.[358] The IASB stated the aim of the regulation as follows:

> This regulation has as its objective the adoption and use of international accounting standards in the community to harmonize the financial information presented by the companies…in order to ensure a high degree of transparency and comparability of financial statements and hence an efficient functioning of the community capital market and of the internal market.[359]

Compared with the reality of the standards of audit trails for personal data protection, it shall be noted that it will take time for the technical society to select which standards are the best for practice in the form of Lex Informatica. Thus, the legal system must begin to take a look at these technical standards, as stated in the table below. The shortcomings of these technical standards are that they lack enforcement forces. If one wants the standards to be an effective norm, then the violators have to pay a price for it. The legal consequences of admitting these standards are essential for carrying out a successful audit. Although the GDPR requires a documentation process, it does not recognize the standard for such records. Compared with

[356] For instance, the Company Act of 1989 mentioned accounting standards in many places such as paragraph 36A of Schedule 4, Part 1 of Schedule 9, 49 other paragraphs, and paragraph 18B of Part 1 of Schedule 9A.

[357] Usually, within the UN regime, Company Act accounts are prepared in accordance with the accounting and disclosure requirements of the Company Act and with the Financial Reporting Standards (FRSs) published by the Financial Reporting Council (FRC) or in according with IAS Accounting Standards.

[358] Regulation (EC) No 1606/2002 of the European Parliament and of the Council of 19 July 2002 on the application of international accounting standards European Union Law. See online: https://eur-lex.europa.eu/legal-content/en/ALL/?uri=CELEX%3A32002R1606 (Visited on August 24, 2020).

Additionally, see the accounting requirements of the Company Act. See Online: https://www.charteredaccountants.ie/Member/Technical/Irish-and-UK-Financial-Reporting/Company-Law-accounting-requirements/Accounting-requirements-of-company-law-in-the-UK (Visited on August 24, 2020).

[359] Regulation (EC) No 1606/2002 of the European Parliament and of the Council of 19 July 2002 on the application of international accounting standards. European Union Law. See online https://eur-lex.europa.eu/legal-content/en/ALL/?uri=CELEX%3A32002R1606 (Visited on August 24, 2020).

Additionally, see the accounting requirements of the Company Act. See online: https://www.charteredaccountants.ie/Member/Technical/Irish-and-UK-Financial-Reporting/Company-Law-accounting-requirements/Accounting-requirements-of-company-law-in-the-UK (Visited on August 24, 2020).

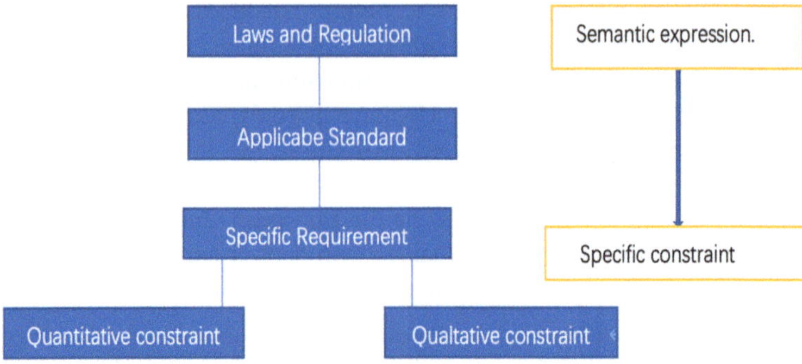

Fig. 2.9 From Applicable Laws to Executable Constraints (Picture draw by author)

financial audits, technical standards refer to the documentation of detailed transactions that support auditors' opinions on financial statements. It is widely acknowledged that the opinion given by auditors can not only rely on subjective judgment but also explain why the formalization of the auditing process and the auditing craft increase over time. As Power noted:

> Standard operating procedures also enable large auditing firms to control individual practitioners.[360]

Again, this shows the nature of an audit: An audit is As a matter of fact an arrangement for the purpose of standardization, not only for the audit but also for the audit process itself (Fig. 2.9). As Trudel observed the following:

> Regulations can flow from technological standards, management norms and legal rules. There is no reason to consider that legal or other norms are always dominant.[361]

From personal data protection perspective, either for legal compliance or for user satisfaction, the demonstration of accountability and control is vital for protecting personal data. There are several stakeholders involved in the documentation process, such as supervisory authorities (hereafterSA), data subjects (hereafterDAs), data controllers (hereafterDC), data processors (hereafterDPs), and third parties for accountability (Fig. 2.10). Stakeholders interact with others that have been affected by several GDPR clauses. Typically, there are four types of statements that can be identified within the GDPR. The first type is a requirement statement, in which stakeholders need to provide evidence that they have fulfilled the requirements for compliance; the second type can be an action that needs to be recorded for the sake of relating to the use, sharing or exchange of personal data; the third type involves the information that is categorically mentioned in the GDPR; and the last type is the format requirement, in which an explicit data format is mentioned within the GDPR.[362] Based on these four types of statements, several pieces of information need to be recorded, such as the provenance

[360] Power, *supra* note 10 in Chap. 1 at 74.

[361] Trudel, *supra* note 41 in Chap. 1 at 330.

[362] Harshavardhan, *supra* note 361 at 6.

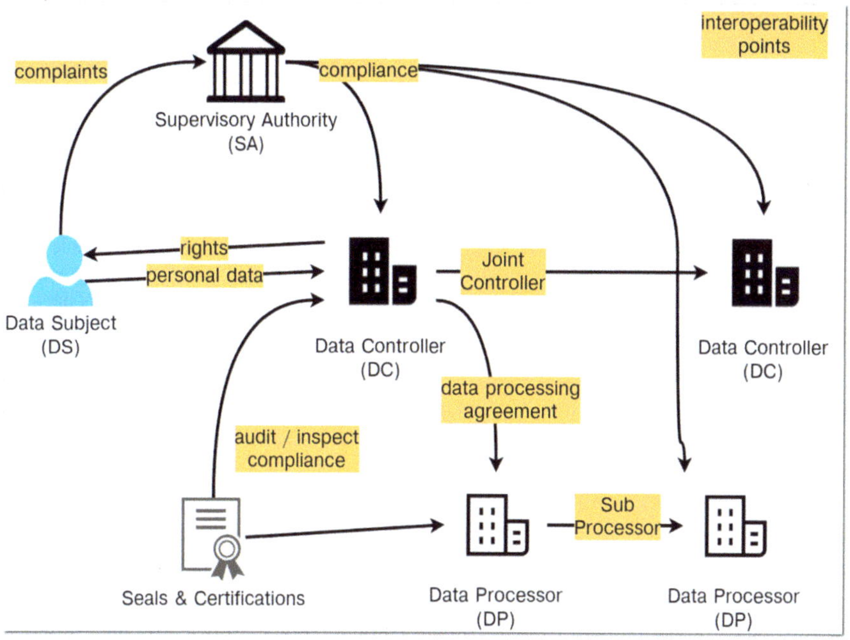

Fig. 2.10 Entities and Information Flows Based on the GDPR (Picture provided by Harshavardhan, *supra* note 361. See online: https://harshp.com/research/publications/035-representing-activities-processing-personal-data-consent-semweb-gdpr-compliance (Visited on July 9, 2020))

information of personal data,[363] the agreements relating to data transfer, the consent process for data subjects, and the compliance that need to be demonstrated. Although the GDPR does not give explicit specific standards for representing these documents, all these types of statements associated with processing can be used to formulate documents into more structured information, which can be helpful for the standardization process. Structural information is also helpful for building audit trails for the purpose of compliance checks in a systematic manner. For instance, it is possible for an auditor to check logs to see whether consent was obtained. The logical behind such documentation is that it is essential to have a systematic view of the information flow between different entities regarding GDPR compliance. As a matter of fact, compliance is an ongoing process that needs to be ensured by a data protection officer (DPO). Compliance assessments usually need to be implemented as part of audit practices. As a result, the record of such activities is an indispensable outcome.[364]

[363] The provenance information category, as defined by provenance, refers to information about the entities and activities involved in producing some data or artifacts, which can be used to form assessments about their quality, reliability or trustworthiness.

[364] An example can be seen in the case of the acquisition of consent, where consent is represented as an agreement that references the processes that will employ the data using provenance information, while the given consent itself is also recorded as an event using the same or similar provenance mechanisms. This explicit linking of inherently related information allows for a better representation of information and leads to semantic systems that are capable of intelligent operations.

Generally, Article 24 of the GDPR clearly demonstrates its intention to implement accountability legislation as a liability,[365] where "demonstrable accountability" is commonly noted in the article listed above.[366] With the consequence of failing to display demonstrable accountability, the supervisory authority is entitled to punish the processor via an administrative fine[367] and can order the processor to bring his/her processing operations into compliance.[368] In sum, from an audit perspective, demonstrable accountability has become a unique obligation for data controllers. As Christopher stated:

> The proactive obligation to adopt appropriate measures and the obligation to be able to demonstrate compliance are new obligations which, quite apart from any failure to respect applicable accountability-related obligations, would in themselves render controllers liable for noncompliance.[369]

[Problem of making things auditable] An audit system shall be built for fulfilling the purpose of mitigating the risk associated with the processing of personal data. Practically speaking, it is consequential to "make things auditable," which always refers to samples and specialists.[370] The Competition Bureau of Canada recently announced a settlement with Facebook Inc. in the amount of $9 million, with an additional $500,000 in investigation costs; this penalty was applied because of the false or misleading claims made by Facebook about the privacy of Canadians' personal information on Facebook and Facebook Messenger.[371] The bureau claimed that Facebook misled users by giving them false information about having control over their personal data on the platform.[372] Additionally, Facebook claimed to the public that it had stopped sharing personal data with specific third-party developers, whereas As a matter of fact, Facebook continued to share user information until 2018.[373] These misleading practices were also the subject of a joint investigation by the Privacy Commissioner of Canada and the Information and Privacy Commissioner for British Columbia.[374] The results showed that *Facebook* had contravened PIPEDA and Canada's federal privacy sector privacy law. As a matter of fact, the data controller had the liability to provide true and sufficient information to the public about the state of the processing of their personal data. Misleading information and deceptive practices are not only regulated by data

---

[365] Graham Greenleaf, "Accountability Without Liability: 'To Whom' and 'With What Consequences'" (Questions for the 2019 OECD Privacy Guidelines Review), (Rochester, NY: Social Science Research Network, 2019) at 2.

[366] Christopher Kuner, "The EU Gen*eral Data Protection Regulation (GDPR): A Commentary*" (Oxford, New York: Oxford University Press, 2020) at 323.

[367] Article 58 (2) (d) and (i) of the GDPR.

[368] Greenleaf, *supra* note 378 at 2.

[369] *Supra* note 379: At Article 24: "Responsibility of the controller" at 15.

[370] Power, *supra* note 10 in Chap. 1 at 88.

[371] Misleading Privacy Claims Results in $nine Million Dollar Penalty for Facebook. Mondaq Insights See online: https://www.bereskinparr.com/doc/misleading-privacy-claims-results-in-9-million-dollar-penalty-for-facebook?utm_source=Mondaq&utm_medium=syndication&utm_campaign=LinkedIn-integration (Visited on December 2, 2020).

[372] Ibid.

[373] Ibid.

[374] Ibid.

protection laws but also equally prohibited by the Competition Act. Regarding laws for personal data protection, misleading information will lead to a breach of data protection principles and rules of law. The GDPR has introduced can be interpreted as a series of documentation requirements concerning the processing of personal data and a mechanism for informing personal data users.[375] The GDPR explicitly requires documentation of the processing method in Articles 82 and 30 and for the recording of consent in Articles 42 and 7. In particular, the documentation requirements and processing requirements are mainly discussed in Articles 6 and 30 of the GDPR.[376] Article 6 specifies the compliance bases for the processing of personal data. In contrast, Article 30 outlines what institutions shall record for data processing, and the records should, at a minimum, contain the information of stakeholders, the purpose for the data processing, the logs of data transfers, etc.[377] All these recording requirements constitute the state of the art for the accountability of the GDPR. As a matter of fact, the accountability principle already existed in the previous personal data directive, such as lawfulness, transparency, data minimization, and accuracy.[378] Within the GDPR, the requirements for documentation are new. Additionally, the GDPR requires that the documentation process be auditable by supervisory authorities. Some countries, such as Spain and Slovakia, give supervisory authorities the right to impose fines if the records are not decorous for auditing.[379] In addition, data controllers are required to review the appropriate measures for the processing of personal data following the requirements stated in Articles 5 and 24 of the GDPR. Therefore, the process of assessing, maintaining, and demonstrating compliance with GDPR is tightly coupled with operational workflows involving personal data.[380] During a GDPR audit, it is essential to provide a lawful basis for processing data, the type of data they have and an explanation for how they process personal data. To meet the requirements of the GDPR, the documentation procedure goes through the whole process of data flow, and the

[375] For defining "GDPR documentation", this book considers the following meaning: "Documentation, directly or indirectly listed in articles or recitals or documentation that is deemed necessary or advisable to use for compliance." See Pidhainyi Illia, *GDPR Documentation* Ukrainian Catholic University, 2019) [unpublished].

[376] Maribel Acosta et al., eds, *Semantic Systems. The Power of AI and Knowledge Graphs.* (Springer International Publishing, 2019) at 19.

[377] UK Information Commissioner's Office, Guide to the General Data Protection Regulation: Legitimate Interests. See online: https://ico.org.uk/for-organisations/guide-to-the-general-data-protection-regulation-gdpr/lawful-basis-for-processing/legitimate-interests/ (Visited on June 30, 2020). Additionally, see Article 29 Working Party Opinion 06/2014 on the notion of legitimate interests of the data controller under Article 7 of Directive 95/46/EC. EC Data Protection Working Party 2014. See online: https://ec.europa.eu/justice/article-29/press-material/public-consultation/notion-legitimate-interests/files/20141126_overview_relating_to_consultation_on_opinion_legitimate_interest_.pdf at 84 (Visited on June 30, 2020).

[378] Directive 95/46/EC of the European Parliament and of the Council of 24 October 1995 on the protection of individuals with regard to the processing of personal data and on the free movement of such data 1995. See online: http://data.europa.eu/eli/dir/1995/46/oj (Visited on June 25, 2020).

[379] Parliament of Spain Cortes Generales. The Organic Law 3/2018 of 5 December on the Protection of Personal Data and the Guarantee of Digital Rights Act 74(12)[in Spanish]. 2018. See online: https://www.boe.es/boe/dias/2018/12/06/pdfs/BOE-A-2018-16673.pdf (Visited on June 30, 2020).

[380] Acosta et al., *supra* note 84 in Chap. 1 at 19.

Table 2.4 List of GDPR Documentation Requirements

Article 13	Privacy notice	The privacy notice shall be delivered to data subject "at the time when personal data obtained."
Article 6	Consent Requirement	Consent is the lawful basis for processing personal data
Article 24	Data Protection Policy	Contract between data subject and data Controller
Article 30	Record of Processing	Documentation of information about processing personal data
Article 5	Accountability	Responsible for demonstrating compliance
Article 7	Records of consent	Demonstration of consent
Article 33	Reporting data breaches	Report data breaches to supervisory authority
Article 15, 16, 17, 21	Data subject request policy	Recording the response to data subject request
Article 40, 42	Data transfers policy	Required security measures to transferring personal data

institution needs to extract all necessary information from both human and machine sources (Table 2.4).[381]

From standardization perspective, to conduct tests for conformance and compliance, it is essential to establish links between constraints, forming "dependency relationships" that enable the creation of a model for automated auditing.[382] Audit systems, at least in regard to security matters in computer science, are not new. Through the collection of security events, user access records, system operation logs, system operation status and other information in the computer system, audit software can analyze the security of the computer through filtering and merging the log data.[383] For personal data protection, such an audit system has not been as commonly used. The GDPR specifies that the sharing, provision, or communication of personal data between entities is an integral aspect of its operation and compliance.[384] According to the result, documentation became necessary with the emergence of the processing of personal data. Documentation is usually involved in formatting data-sharing agreements, recording compliance audits and producing reports.[385] To support the conclusions of these reports, evidence needs to be provided based on various procedures outlined for the process of data flows, and the standardization of such records will impact how to interpret or formulate such records and activities. In addition, this evidence and these records will be required

381 Regina Becker et al., "DAISY: A Data Information System for accountability under the General Data Protection Regulation" (2019) 8:12 GigaScience. See online: <https://academic.oup.com/gigascience/article/8/12/giz140/5652251> at 2.

382 Acosta et al., *supra* note 84 in Chap. 1 at 21.

383 Audit log system: Seeo online: https://translate.google.cn/#view=home&op=translate&sl=auto&tl=en&text=综合日志审计平台. [Translated by author] (Visited on August 24, 2020).

384 Harshavardhan, *supra* note 361.

385 *Ibid* at 5.

to be shared with other entities or regulatory authorities for auditing purposes or compliance requirements, which also presents the need to utilize the formation of such evidence. For instance, taking consent as an example, users give their consent for their personal information to be processed, where the activity of consent will be recorded as an event based on specific standards, so it will be possible to identify the specific consent given by a specific user by checking the logs. First, this book explores the standards published by the World Wide Web Consortium (W3C), which is the primary standard body responsible for information exchange.[386] For different types of data that may be included in audit trails, the W3C has different standards suitable for recommendation. For instance, since 2013, the W3C has provided a Provence data model, which provides a framework for the interchange of Provence data related to the GDPR.[387] To represent the statement of the processing of personal data, the W3C proposed recommendation policies such as open digital rights language (ODRL) to provide an interoperable information model.[388] In addition, ODRL can be used to represent data-sharing and consent agreements. To incarnate the information itself, the W3C has standards such as RDF, OWL, and XML to provide structuring information for querying and auditing, and for auditing entities, it provides mechanisms such as SPARQL and XQuery, corresponding to the structural information standards for querying the information and shape constraint language (SHACL) for validation.[389] Another critical standardization body impacting GDPR compliance is the European Committee for Standardization (hereafterCEN), which consists of thirty-four national members who work together, although the standards have substantial overlap between the CEN and the International Standard Organization (ISO).[390] In addition, there are several institutions that have made these standards national or international organizations, such as "American National Standards and Institute," "Standards Australia" and "International Standard Organization." These institutions have made specific standards for subdivided sectors. Taking the health sector as an example, there are standards for health information logs such as ASTM: E2147 (Standard Specification for Audit and Disclosure Logs for Use In Health Information Systems), ISO/TS 18308:2011 (Health Informatics-Requirements for an Electronic Health Record Architecture), and ISO/IEC 27001:2006 (Information Technology-Security Techniques-Information Security Management Systems-Requirements) in the healthcare industry.[391] All these standards are aimed at building principles for developing and implementing audit logs or data for the storing and processing of health information. In addition,

[386] *Ibid* at 6

[387] Harshvardhan J Pandit & Dave Lewis, *Modelling Provenance for GDPR Compliance using Linked Open Data Vocabularies* (2017) at 13.

[388] *Ibid.*

[389] Acosta et al., *supra* note 84 in Chap. 1.

[390] *Ibid.*

[391] Gonçalves-Ferreira et al., *supra* note 57 in Chap. 1.

standards set up procedures to specify how to design audit logs for auditing. For instance, standard "ASTM:E2147" aims to:

> Develop policies, procedures and functions of health information logs to document all actions regarding identifiable health information for use in both manually entered and computer systems as well as designing the audit log to record all activities.[392]

Although the goal of these standards seems compatible with the requirements of the GDPR, it has not been updated since it was published and has not been broadly known since 2013.[393] As mentioned above, these standards are essential for auditing purposes from both internal and external perspectives. These standards foster the interoperability of the audit trail and make it possible for external auditors to evaluate the samples properly, which helps them understand the action of the audit. However, it should be noted that the GDPR does not explicitly require entities to adopt these standards for the exchange of data or for the documentation process; in other words, it is not mandatory for processors to adopt any of these standards. For instance, Article 30 (1) requires that the controllers maintain their information associated with processing activities, which will be helpful for the external control of personal data processing,[394] but it does not identify any standardization of such records. In reality, this leads to the problem of commonality for auditing and for reusing such records because such records, whether internal of an organization or external of third parties, form part of the documentation process, proving their GDPR compliance. As a matter of fact, technical standards are urgently needed for executable explanations of the semantic expressions of the GDPR. Regulatory authorities such as the European Data Protection Board (EDPB) should recognize this trend.

[Problem of evidence gathering for audit process] External auditors lack authority to access samples and data internally and are regarded as having an inherent paucity of external audits.[395] For data protection auditing, external auditors do not have the authority to obtain a close look as to how the processor processes their personal data or obtain access to training algorithms or data, which are often regarded as trade secrets.[396] Moreover, complex interactions between users and data processors exist in each stage of data processing. However, first, it should be noted that a systematic question involving the efficiency of data protection audits is as

---

[392] ANTS, Standard Specification For Audit And Disclosure Logs For Use In Health Information Systems. See online: https://webstore.ansi.org/Standards/ASTM/ASTME214718?gclid=CjwKCAjwmrn5BRB2EiwAZgL9osWSjNToFm_HyVeABvxCQyp3HJDPSKj5efW-35KQZt2yXiDjWlemHRoCvqoQAvD_BwE (Visited on August 8, 2020).

[393] Gonçalves-Ferreira et al., *supra* note 57 in Chap. 1.

[394] Pidhainyi Illia, *GDPR Documentation* (Ukrainian Catholic University, 2019) at 293 [unpublished].

[395] Inioluwa Deborah Raji & Joy Buolamwini, *Actionable Auditing: Investigating the Impact of Publicly Naming Biased Performance Results of Commercial AI Products* (Honolulu, HI, USA: Association for Computing Machinery, 2019).

[396] Jenna Burrell, "How the machine 'thinks': Understanding opacity in machine learning algorithms" (2016) at 13.

follows: what kind of samples can be considered an effective system for proving data protection compliance? In other words, what kind of documentation is required at each step of the audit cycle? What kinds of documentation procedures need to be normalized for standardization?[397] The concept of evidence is crucial for auditing operations in practice.[398] In the financial sector, the forming of an opinion regarding a financial statement usually needs reliable and supportive evidence. In addition, auditors must provide:

> A trail of evidence and procedure to be verified.[399]

As a matter of fact, the process of sampling is always used for solving practical problems. As Hansen argued:

> A sample survey is an economic production process intended to make the most efficient use of limited resources in order to achieve specified goals.[400]

However, in the absence of a whole picture of audit objects, it was difficult to know what an "adequate sample" truly was. As Power argued:

> Sampling seemed to be paradoxical because one had to know the population in some sense before the sample could be credible, but if one knew the population, then the sampling was redundant.[401]

Moreover, the idea of "statistical sampling" emerged as an attempt to address the dilemma of defining selective samples by the items being tested being so chosen that they cover the whole field to be examined, or, in other words, they ought to be, in the statistical sense, fair samples of the whole group.[402] In other words, artifact collections, which ought to adhere to specific statistical standards. The idea of statistical sampling entails the scientific rationalized perspective of financial audits. Auditors' judgments usually refer to structured samples, and incomplete audit trails are conducive to unaudited financial statements, which is why auditors' compliance with an organization is usually unaudited because of the quality of record keeping.[403] From this point of view, the decisions made by auditors are influenced not only by their subjective expertise but also by the objective scientific samples gathered by the audit subject and audit institutions. However, by the mid-1980s, statistical sampling had fallen out of favor in the financial sector due to practical reasons, such as atypical errors often appearing and effective samples not often being easy to

---

[397] Margaret Mitchell et al., "Model Cards for Model Reporting" (2019) Proc Conf Fairness Account Transpar - FAT 19220–229 at 226.

[398] Flint, *supra* note 1 in Chap. 1.

[399] American Accounting Association & Committee on Basic Auditing Concepts, *A statement of basic auditing concepts,* (Sarasota, Fla.: American Accounting Association, 1973) at 14.

[400] Morris H Hansen, "Some History and Reminiscences on Survey Sampling" (1987) 2:2 Statistical Science 180–190. See online: <https://www.jstor.org/stable/2245667> at 187.

[401] Power, *supra* note 10 in Chap. 1 at 72.

[402] Dicksee & Rowland, *supra* note 20 in Chap. 1 at 49.

[403] Power, *supra* note 10 in Chap. 1 at 87.

Table 2.5 Example of Subset of Constraints and Assumptions regarding Given Consent (Pandit, Supra note 361 at 32)

GDPR	Constraint
A1-11	Consent must be associated with only one Data Subject
R32, A4-11	Consent must have one or more categories or types of personal data associated with it
R32, R42	Consent must have one or more purposes associated with it
R32, A4-11	Consent must have one or more processing associated with it
A7-3	Consent must have one and only one state/status
A7-2	Consent is given by exactly one Person
	Given consent must have information on how it was obtained
	Consent must have artefacts associated with how it was obtained
	Consent must have information on what choices provided
	Consent must have affirmative statement or affirmative action
	Consent must have information about right to withdraw
R32, A7-2	Consent must not have more than one medium when it was provided
	Consent must have a timestamp indicating when it was given
	Purpose or processing associated with Third Party must specify role played by the Third Party
	If data is being stored, it must have information on how long it will be stored for
	Storage of data must have information on its storage location
R71, A9-2c, A22-2	Automated processing of personal data must be clearly indicated
R111, A49-1a	Data transfer to third country or international organisation must specify identity of recipient
R51, A8-2a	Personal data belonging to a special category must be clearly indicated

obtain information. Traditional documents are easier to access when they are handwritten. Electronic evidence always relies on hardware or software to obtain access. As a matter of fact, electronic documents are better understood as a "process" where unintelligible pieces of data that are distributed over the storage medium are assembled, processed and rendered legible for a human user.[414] In other words, electronic documents must be rendered readable through other technologies, while the mediation of such technologies may display different results in different situations.[415] Second, for the same reason as that for establishing new legislation for electronic evidence, the features of electronic documents will affect the authenticity (provenance) of such evidence. For instance, a document examiner can test the chemical element of the ink on a paper document to determine if it is consistent with the time

[414] Mason, *supra* note 93 in Chap. 1 at Chapter 2, 2.2.

[415] Bonnie Malkin, "Water pistol emoji replaces revolver as Apple enters gun violence debate", *The Guardian* (2 August 2016). See online: <https://www.theguardian.com/technology/2016/aug/02/apple-replaces-gun-emoji-water-pistol-revolver-violence-debate> at 12 (Visited at October 22, 2021).

it was allegedly written, while authenticity can become problematic in electronic documents where copies are difficult to distinguish from the original documents and, the time when the documents are created is difficult to trace. As a matter of fact, electronic documents are easier to modify in a way that the changes and alterations are difficult to trace. They can be easily copied, altered, updated or deleted. Additionally, it is easier for electronic documents, compared to traditional documents, to cross physical and geographical boundaries. Third, electronic documents are unstable, and the storage of electronic evidence is at risk of accidental or deliberate damage. For the purpose of mitigating this risk, procedures to prevent the destruction of evidence, such as back-up plans and third parties in off-site remote storage facilities, must be established; of course, these measures usually mean increased expenses. Moreover, the fragility and the ubiquity of electronic storage have made the modern-day discovery exercise a formidable process.[416] These characteristics, to some extent, may affect the legal value of electronic documents, as confirmed by the legal system. Electronic evidence is relatively new as a means of proof in legal proceedings. Different legal systems have various ways to address this new challenge. Some jurisdictions have introduced new legislation specifically focused on electronic evidence, while others have tried to "establish the closest match to existing evidentiary concepts and have applied wherever possible existing rules analogously."[417] These two methods have been adopted in a combinatorial way in most jurisdictions. Mason argued the following:

> Where new legislation is introduced, the emphasis is on the differences between electronic and traditional forms of evidence; this can prevent lawyers from utilizing their collective institutional experience in evaluating and interpreting such evidence, often creating a sense of confusion and unspecific ty...Where analogous approaches are used, the emphasis is on the similarities between traditional and digital evidence.[418]

Within the legal regimes of the European Union, according to the Guidelines for Electronic Evidence in Civil and Administrative Proceedings, announced by the Council of Europe, "electronic evidence" refers to:

> Any evidence derived from data contained in or produced by any device, the functioning of which depends on a software program or data stored on or transmitted over a computer system or network.[419]

The guidelines also established "functional equivalence" principles, where electronic evidence should be evaluated in the same way as other types of evidence, in particular, regarding its admissibility, authenticity, accuracy and integrity. Considering the higher risk of the destruction or alteration of electronic evidence, the guidelines also announced several requirements for the collection, seizure and transmission of electronic evidence. For instance, member states should "establish

[416] Mason, *supra* note 396 at Chapter two, at 44.

[417] *Ibid* at Chapter 2, 2.2.

[418] *Ibid.*

[419] *Guidelines of the Committee of Ministers of the Council of Europe on electronic evidence in civil and administrative proceedings*, 2019.

procedures for the secure seizure and collection of electronic evidence."[420] As a matter of fact, the probative value of electronic evidence depends on the judgment of national laws and traditions, which vary across member states of the European Union, and there is no international or European legal framework relating to electronic evidence.[421] However, legal instruments and policy documents, like the "European Convention for the Protection of Human Rights and Fundamental Freedoms" promote the harmonization of electronic evidence at the national law level.[422] Compared with civil and administration procedures, in which traditional procedurals may not specifically cover electronic evidence, electronic evidence relating to criminal law is subject to national law, which has a longer history and more engrained legal traditions. Some criminal laws were written long before the Internet existed. Within civil proceedings, three types of evidence can be obtained: (1) evidence from publicly available websites, such as blog postings and images uploaded to social networking websites; (2) substantive evidence, that is, the e-emails or documents in digital format that are not made publicly available and which are held on a server; and (3) purported user identity and traffic data that are used to help identify a person by identifying the source of the communication but not the content.[423] As for the documentation made for personal data compliance, most are subject to the second evidence category.

By comparing the legal regimes of Canada, it can be seen that, for instance, in Quebec, the Federal Evidence Act provides for several legal regimes decided on by the rules of the division of jurisdiction, such as criminal law, whereas in a residual manner, disputes are governed by the Civil Code of Quebec and the law concerning the legal framework of information technologies.[424] Unlike the European Union, in Quebec, the act respecting the legal framework for technological information used the word "technological documents" instead of "electronic evidence," although the act did not give a clear definition.[425] However, a technological document was interpreted as a "subset forms part of the concept of a document within the meaning of

[420] *Ibid.*

[421] Jeanne Pia Mifsud Bonnici, Melania Tudorica & Joseph A Cannataci, "The European Legal Framework on Electronic Evidence: Complex and in Need of Reform" (2018) Handling and Exchanging Electronic Evidence Across Europe 189–235. See online: <https://www.rug.nl/research/portal/en/publications/the-european-legal-framework-on-electronic-evidence(135ebdcb-2d62-4c1e-8820-2f8889eda63b).html> at 192.

[422] Bonnici, Tudorica & Cannataci, "The European Legal Framework on Electronic Evidence", *supra* note 435.

[423] Mason Stephen, The use of electronic evidence in civil and administrative law proceedings and its effect on the rules of evidence and modes of proof. (European committee on legal co-operation (CDCJ, 2016) at 23.

[424] LCCJTI.ca, La loi federale sur la preuve a-t-elle une incidence au Quebec? See online: https://www.lccjti.ca/faq/ (Visited on July 17, 2020).

[425] Vincent Gautrais, "La preuve technologique". See online: <https://www.gautrais.com/publications/la-preuve-technologique/> at 307. Additionally, see: https://www.lccjti.ca/doctrine/gautrais-gingras/ (Visited on July 17, 2020).

the Act."[426] As a result, the concept of technological documents relies on the definition of "technological," according to Fabien, which refers to the following:

> The expression indicates, in a general way, all the supports of information, other than paper, created by modern science and likely to be used as evidence before the courts.[427]

In addition, as stated by Article 7 of the act stated:

> There is no need to prove that the medium of the document or that the processes, systems or technologies used to communicate by means of a document ensure its integrity…unless the document establishes, on a preponderance of evidence, that the integrity of the document has been infringed.[428]

In which an exemption for proving the integrity of the electronic document as a premise is introduced. As Gautrais noted, this is:

> An exemption from proof aimed at facilitating the use of information technologies when presenting a technological document as a proof.[429]

[Problem of "burden of Proof"] Another explanation for the need to demonstrate compliance according to the GDPR is the necessity of the "reversal of the burden of proof" for the benefit of personal data owners. Generally, the GDPR consists of a directive proposal involving accountability principles while also adding several principles of importance. The first of such principles can be stated as the lawfulness process, in which personal data s"hall be processed in a manner that is compatible with GDPR requirements. The second principle can be summarized as a data confidentiality principle, according to which personal data shall be processed in a manner through which appropriate security can be ensured. The third principle can be described as the personal data controller being responsible for demonstrating compliance with the general principles of data processing, although it can be interpreted by an accountability principle, according to which the GDPR explicitly announced the demonstration parts of accountability. Usually, it is the liability of the victim to submit a claim to provide supporting evidence; however, sometimes the law will introduce variations to facilitate the burden of proof of the victim. Such variations may place the liability with the defendant to prove himself or herself innocent, which is usually called the reversal of the burden of proof.[430] This reversal usually responds to circumstances where disadvantages exist between the two parties. Under the GDPR, a data protection officer may face is the situation in which once

---

[426] Ibid.

[427] Fabein Claude, The proof of technical document, (2004) 38 RJT 533 at 127.

[428] Lccgti.Ca, Loi concernant le cadre juridique des technologies de l'information. See online: https://www.lccjti.ca/articles/article-7/ (Visited on October 28, 2020).

[429] Vincent Gautrais & Patrick Gingras, "La preuve des documents technologiques" (2017) 22:22--2 Les Cahiers de propriété intellectuelle. See online: <https://www.lescpi.ca/articles/v22/volume-22-numero-2/la-preuve-des-documents-technologiques/> at 12. Additionally, see https://www.lccjti.ca/articles/article-7/ at 13.

[430] Andrej Orel & Igor Bernik, "GDPR and Health Personal Data; Tricks and Traps of Compliance" (2018) at 257.

there is a breach event of GDPR principles, if the data protection officer failed to provide evidence to prove his or her compliance, then he or she is deemed liable for the data breach because the data subjects have little information about how the institutions process their personal data. All these new requirements show the same trend, where regardless of internal or external oversight, documentation is indispensable for compliance with GDPR requirements. As mentioned above, to constitute an efficient auditing process, documentation not only shows compliance with the applicable law but also provides an opportunity for data protection officers to demonstrate their competence. Despite many scholars criticizing the limitation of the capability of individuals in managing their personal information, this book notes that the GDPR tries to create ideally, at least, where a tension between regulatory oversight and individual oversight coexists to predict systemic accountability. Individual accountability usually occurs after software development; as a result, it is impossible for individuals to rebut or correct the deficiency of the system at the development level. Regulatory oversight grants the possibility of impacting systems before the deployment of the algorithm. Systemic accountability measures are envisioned as:

> Ongoing, continuous, and being implemented early on in an algorithm's development.[431]

From another perspective, although there are limitations in terms of individual accountability and transparency, systemic accountability is an indispensable part of managing personal data. Individual transparency, from one perspective, is an essential measure that guarantees the protection of personal data as a fundamental right within European regimes. From another perspective, individual transparency is a safeguard for the efficiency of the auditing system, and it prompts the transparency of the audit system. However, it should be noted that the discussion of these measures in this book is quite different from their operation in practice. The proposals of the GDPR heavily rely on collaborative governance, which requires different regulatory stakeholders to be toiled together.

[431] Kaminski, *supra* note 320 at 217.

Part III
Redefining Audit

Chapter 3
Reconstructing the Definition of Audit

3.1 Implementing Function Approach to the Notion of Audit

In this section, the paper explores the concept of functionalism and analyzes the function of personal data protection laws in mitigating the risk of harm when processing personal data. The paper then proposes leveraging a functional approach for analyzing the function of audits as a form of control. Through an analysis of both internal and external audit processes, the paper further proposes two main perspectives of control: management control and legal control for the function of audits.

3.1.1 Proposing Interpretation Model for Audit Considering Functional Approach

The definition of functionalism given by Cambridge Dictionary explained as:

> The principle that the most important thing about an object such as a building is its use rather than what it looks like.

The history of functionalism can be traced back to nineteenth century, when economic and political conditions played an essential role on emergence of sociology as well as the functionalism. The "science of society" were born with the French revolution of 1789 and was associated with the Industrial Revolution.[1] From creation of Comte as positive philosophy, which contained the seed of functional theorizing to the work of Emile Durkheim as a codification of the functional orientation. As it has been noted, functionalism has been distinguished between cause and

[1] Jonathan Turner & Alexandra Maryanski, *Functionalism-the Book* (1979) at 9.

H. Wu, C. Zhang, *Audit the Audit*, https://doi.org/10.1007/978-981-95-2473-0_3

function.[2] With development of the functionalism, it has been viewed as an explanatory theory.[3]

3.1.1.1 Proposing Functional Approach

[Functionalism] Konrad Zweigert theorized functionalism as "The basic methodological principle of all comparative law is that of functionality."[4] Although such claims seem too absolute or superficial for the discipline, it remark the significance of the functional approach. Indeed, the more precise concepts of functionalism in different fields have been assembled. As Ralf Michaels distinguished, at least seven prospects existed in different disciplines of functionalism as an explanatory theory:

> Finalism. Classical functionalism, adoptionism, instrumentalism, refined functionalism, epistemological functionalism, equivalence functionalism.[5]

Finalism, adoptionism, and classical functionalism all enclose the same logic as determinism, which means if the problems could be solved in a similar way, then the solutions must have similar functions that the same type of institution could accomplish. In contrast, equivalence functionalism rejected this idea by proclaiming that different institutions performed similar functions in different societies.[6] As proposed from the comparative law perspective of functional equivalence, Ralf deepen into the "function of functionalism from seven perspectives:

> The epistemological function of understanding legal rules and institutions; The comparative function of achieving comparability; The presumptive function of emphasizing similarity; The formalizing function of system building; The evaluative function of determining the better law; The universalizing function of preparing legal unification an The critical function of providing tools for the critique of law[7]

Functionalism has been exceedingly distinguished by legal actors, beginning with Montesquieu and Adam Smith and continuing with Karl Llewellyn and Franz Neumann.[8] As Gordon noted:

> The general functionalist method is to construct (or, as is rather more common, to assume without much discussion) a typology of stages of social development and then to show how

---

[2] *Ibid* at 26.

[3] *Ibid* at 93.

[4] Ralf Michaels, "The Functional Method of Comparative Law". *The Oxford Handbook of Comparative Law* (Oxford University Press, 2006) at 346.

[5] *Ibid* at 344.

[6] Walter Rochs Goldschmidt, *Comparative Functionalism: An Essay in Anthropological Theory*, first edition ed. (University of California Press, 1966) at 30.

[7] Michaels, *supra* note 5 at 363.

[8] Peter Stein, *Legal Evolution: The Story of an Idea*, first edition ed. (Cambridge: Cambridge University Press, 2009) at 122.

> legal forms and institutions have satisfied, or failed to satisfy, the functional requirements of each stage.[9]

As perceived in a functional approach to law, the strength of the functional method is periodized on emphasized differences within similarity. And the use of functional approach in law, as proposed by Cohen, is classified as:

> The definition of law, The nature of legal rules and concepts, The theory of legal decisions, and The role of legal criticism.[10]

The meaning of the definition, as proposed by functionalists, can be found in its consequences.

[Function of data protection law] The consequence of law from judicial decisions may arise to define "contract", "responsibility", and "right". From legislative perspective, it usually referred to the actions in which the legislators tried to avoid. Taking the "risk-of-harm" as an example, Gratton proposed the use of this approach to analyze the definition of personal information under the data protection law, which is based on functionalism:

> Attempt to explain…legal forms or practices by reference to social purposes or interest.[11]

She then stated that:

> The ultimate purpose of data protection law is to address or avoid the risk of harm to individuals triggered by organizations handing their personal information.[12]

As Gratton proposed, the discourse of personal data protection issues frequently involves the deployment the term of harm. The ICO published "Overview of data protection harms and the ICO's Taxonomy," which set the framework for harms.[13] As noted, the general framework for considering risk and consequences can be found in organizational risk management guidance, which makes the distinction between cause, events and consequences.[14] Causes itself are not harmed, it only arose the risk which may result negative consequences and impacts of the events. Also, events also may not lead to a harm. In other words, the harm could be interpreted as the negative consequence of the event.

On the other hand, the objective of the GDPR is stated as follows:

---

[9] Robert W Gordon, "Critical Legal Histories Critical Legal Studies Symposium" (1984) 36: Issues 1 & 2 Stanford Law Rev. 57–126 at 64.

[10] Felix S Cohen, "Transcendental Nonsense and the Functional Approach" (1935) 35:6 Colum L Rev. See online: <https://heinonline.org/HOL/P?h=hein.journals/clr35&i=897> at 834 (Visited at November 13, 2022).

[11] Gordon, *supra* note 10 at 11.

[12] Eloïse Gratton: *If Personal Information is Privacy's Gatekeeper, then Risk of Harm is the Key: A Proposed Method for Determining What Counts as Personal Information.* (Rochester, NY: Social Science Research Network, 2013) at 88.

[13] Information Commissioner's Office: Overview of Data Protection Harms and ICO's Taxonomy. See online: https://ico.org.uk/media/about-the-ico/documents/4020144/overview-of-data-protection-harms-and-the-ico-taxonomy-v1-202204.pdf (Visited at November 23, 2022).

[14] Ibid.

> This regulation lays down rules relating to the protection of natural persons with regards to the processing of personal data and rules relating to the free movement of personal data. This regulation protects the fundamental rights and freedoms of natural persons and their right to the protection of personal data.[15]

The GDPR establishes positive rights for personal data protection, which require the data processor to demonstrate his or her compliance with the regulation. The purpose of such legislation is not just to avoid harm to individuals but also to maximize social benefits, which refer to the free movement of personal data within European regimes. Obviously, the tension between individual interest and social benefit is subject to observation by the legislator.

3.1.1.2 Analyzing the Function of Audit System

[Functional analysis of audit system] The function of internal audit is being explained as redundant part which served as the similar function as external audit, and the whole audit system has been criticized as "a ritual of verification" originated from the "comfort zone" of internal control. As power argued:

> Internal audits will soon substituted by external audits and the distinction between them will become extremely vague. Internal auditors will play a role in matters of regulation and internal oversight will be outsourced to external agencies.[16]

While is it a true story under the analysis of the function approach for audit system? As Reiner Wiehl noted, the shift from essentialist to functionalist could be perceived through the observation of focusing on the object itself to of focusing on their relations amongst each other and to the whole since the nineteenth and twentieth centuries.[17] For its development, "functional analysis on system level" developed in the fields of engineering, business information systems, and computer programming specifically to manage complexity. Instead of screening complexity out, the systems analyst attempts to accommodate as much complexity as possible. A comprehensive description of the system's function is a precondition to the analysis.[18] Given by the explanation from Lynn M. Lopucki, system view will benefit from identifying systems, discovering their goals or attributing goals to them, mapping their subsystems and the functions each performs, determining their internal structures, depicting them with attention paid to efficiency of presentation, and searching for internal inconsistencies.[19] As Lopucki noted:

---

[15] Article 1 of GDPR.

[16] Power, *supra* note 10 in Chap. 1 at 67.

[17] Reiner Wiehl, *Subjektivität und System*, 1. edition ed. (Frankfurt am Main: Suhrkamp, 2000) at 375.

[18] Lynn M LoPucki, "Systems Approach to Law" (1996) 82:3 Cornell L Rev. 479–522. See online: <https://heinonline.org/HOL/P?h=hein.journals/clqv82&i=509> at 481 (Visited at March 1, 2023).

[19] *Ibid* at 481.

> Systems shake into place" as their components and environments interact...the system evolves a state in which no one who has the power to impose changes on the system would choose to do so.[20]

Analyzed function of audit system proceeded by identifying the goal of the audit, the performance of each subsystem of audit, depicting the internal structures of the system to improve the efficiency, consistency as well as effectiveness of the system internally and externally. This book analyzes the function of personal data protection compliance audit as a "law-related system" for the purpose of understanding the rationale behind what rendered it inefficient, disrupting its functioning, or destroying it. A "law-related system" could be interpreted as the law playing a role within the system, where

> The goal of the system are not goals primarily associated with the law, and the important elements are not legal in nature.[21]

Law within law-related systems performed its role as an element by which governments and legislators could intervene the systems. From this point of view, the system could be interpreted as a context for law to act on or contribute. To do this at least has two advantages. First, the law-related system could be observed objectivity. Second, it could be empirically verified whether particular reformed for the system are effective.[22] The emphasis on system is on relationship of the components rather than the components themselves, the advantages of functional approach also manifested through perspective of "empirically verifiable," which means the goal of the system could be verified practically.[23] It emphasized on how different parts within the law-related system interacted with other parts of the system which gave a comprehensive understanding how law-related system worked. When service of internal audit outsourced by external body, it usually referred to one audit firm to perform both internal management as well as the external verification, which leads the risk of non-neutral conclusion for the statement. As a matter of fact, the internal audit function has become a major support function for management, the board of directors, the external auditors. As Keeneth noted:

> Control often described as a function of management, rather than as a synonym of "power." Managers implement controls, or sets of controls, to help attain these results and to protect against the threats to the achievement of good performance.[24]

As defined by the institute of internal auditors, a key element of the new definition for internal audit is the focus on designing to add value and improve an

---

[20] *Ibid* at 487.

[21] *Ibid* at 488.

[22] *Ibid* at 491.

[23] Gordon, *supra* note 12 at 64.

[24] Keenneth A. Merchant, "A review of the literature on control and accountability" (2007), Handbook of Management Accounting Research, 785–802 at 796.

organization's operations.[25] Internal auditors recognized and familiar with the value of the organizations based on their depth knowledge throughout their careers. As Flemming Ruud noted:

> Just as crucial as it is to understand an organization goals, is it crucial for an internal audit function to understand the risks that either treat the achievement of objectives and goals or that fail to identify and explore new opportunities for the organization. Internal auditing is therefore expected to apply an integrated, process-oriented approach to the evaluation of risks in order to evaluate both upside and downside risks.[26]

In other words, the unique position which internal auditor could be summarized as advantage position within organization which has a complete and sound understanding of the governance structure of the organization. For governance of an organization, as given by Cadbury Report, could be defined as:

> System by which companies are directed and controlled.[27]

To be more specific, how the objectives of governance are achieved and monitored are emphasized through this definition. To ensure the strategic could be turned into operating value-creating measures, a comprehensive understanding of the risk threatening the whole organization thereof is need. As noted both from Rittenberg and Jordan Lowe, the outcome of outsourcing of the internal audit function to an external audit body, auditor performance had a significantly negative impact on users' perceptions of auditor independence as well as the reliability of audit statement, and resulted in the lowest percentage of loan approvals.[28] From systemic perspective, the characterization of internal audit can thus contribute both by evaluating different parts of the internal control for the purpose of delivering accountability. Based on the objective and goal of an organization, management strategy develops and implements through the operating measures of management teams, whether based on centralized or decentralized structure. As for the result, the goal of the internal audit shall be consistent with the goal of the organization, rather accompanied by universal external entity. From this point of view, the management function

---

[25] Definition of Internal Auditors: Internal auditing is an independent, objective assurance and consulting activity designed to add value and improve an organization's operations. It helps an organization accomplish its objectives by bringing a systemic, disciplined approach to evaluate and improve the effectiveness of risk management, control, and governance processes. The Institute of Internal Auditors. See online: https://na.theiia.org/standards-guidance/mandatory-guidance/Pages/Definition-of-Internal-Auditing.aspx (Visited at 24 January, 2021).

[26] Flemming Ruud, "The Internal Audit Function : An Integral Part of Organizational Governance" in Andrew Bailey, Audrey Gramling & Sridhar Ramamoorti, eds, *Res Oppor Intern Audit* (Altamonte Springs: IIA - The Institute of Internal Auditors, 2003) at 78.

[27] *The Financial Aspects of Corporate Governance* (London: The Committee on the Financial Aspects of Corporate Governance and Gee and Co. Ltd., 1992)at 12.

[28] D Lowe, Marshall Geiger & Kurt Pany, "The Effects of Internal Audit Outsourcing on Perceived External Auditor Independence" (1999) 18 Auditing: A Journal of Practice & Theory 41–44 at 41. Also see: Larry E Rittenberg, *The Outsourcing Dilemma: What's Best for Internal Auditing* (Institute of Internal Auditors Research Foundation, 1997).

of internal audit could be regarded as designed control system. As Cecily Raiborn argues:

> When external auditors serve as internal auditors, as was the case with Enron, the corporate governance process can fail.[29]

The function of audit is not just served as verification tool, but also, it is an essential part of organizational governance. In other words, it played critical onus as management and it is a prerequisite for good governance.[30] Distinguished from external audit, responsibilities of internal control extend far beyond statement to management, control and governance processes throughout the organizations.[31]

3.1.2 *Interpret Audit as Function of Control*

As perceived by this book, we are facing a systemic failure when protects personal data with different layers from law, management and technology. As control revolution triggered by the evolvement of digitalization, either from top-down approach or bottom-up for regulating cyberspace and data, they both called for different types of control. As paper perceived, function of audit defines as a system for control. This part explores the meaning of control both from management perspective and legal perspective.

3.1.2.1 Interpret the Meaning of Control for Personal Data Protection

[Systemic failure of personal data protection] Until May 2022, European Data Protection Authorities imposed over 900 fines because of failure of protecting personal data.[32] As it had been shown, the reason for the penalty varies case by case. For instance, Amazon punished for the reason of "cookie consent." What's App fined because of failing to properly explain its data processing practice in its privacy notice as well as "legitimate interests." Google Ireland was issued fined for the reason of failing to provide easy way to refuse cookie. Facebook also, failed to obtain proper cookie consent from its users. H&M's GDPR violations involved the monitoring of several hundred employees; TIM's infraction for unlawful actions including aggressive marketing strategy; British Airways was considerably $238 million fine that the ICO originally found 400,000 customers' data breach; Marriott also,

[29] Rossiter C, "How internal audit adds value to the governance process" (2011) Protiviti. See online: https://www.protiviti.com/US-en/insights (Visited at 24 January, 2021).

[30] Cecily Raiborn et al., "The Internal Audit Function: A Prerequisite for Good Governance" (2017) at 17.

[31] *Ibid* at 3.

[32] 30 Biggest GDPR Fines So Far.TESSIAN News, See online: www,tessian,.com/blog/biggest gdpr fines 2020. (Oct 10, 2022).

acquired fines for data breach; Clearview AI fined because of unlawful processing of personal biometric and geolocation data; Vodafone Italia was issued fined because of failing to properly secure customer data, sharing personal data with third-party call centers, and processing without a legal basis. Austrian Post sanctioned for allegedly failing to facilitate data subject rights requested properly. Notebooksbilliger.de's penalty related to use CCTV cameras to monitor its employees and customers; Meta Ireland fined because of failing to demonstrate the security measures that it implemented to protect EU users' data.[33] All these penalties could write the book of "interpretation of GDPR," the failure of personal data protection could also be interpreted as "systemic failure" with different layers of digital transformation. It could be within business architecture, data architecture as well as technical architecture (Fig. 3.1).

For instance, business partners are always defined as third parties which may generate the risk such as losing control of data. To find the scope of digital risk associated with business partners, it usually starts with the definition of basic assumptions for our organization external and internal environments and overall objectives of risk management process and activities, which may consequently become the basic parameter to define the scope of audit associated with business partners. The definition of external environments typically included external stakeholders, social and cultural conditions, law and regulation environments, political

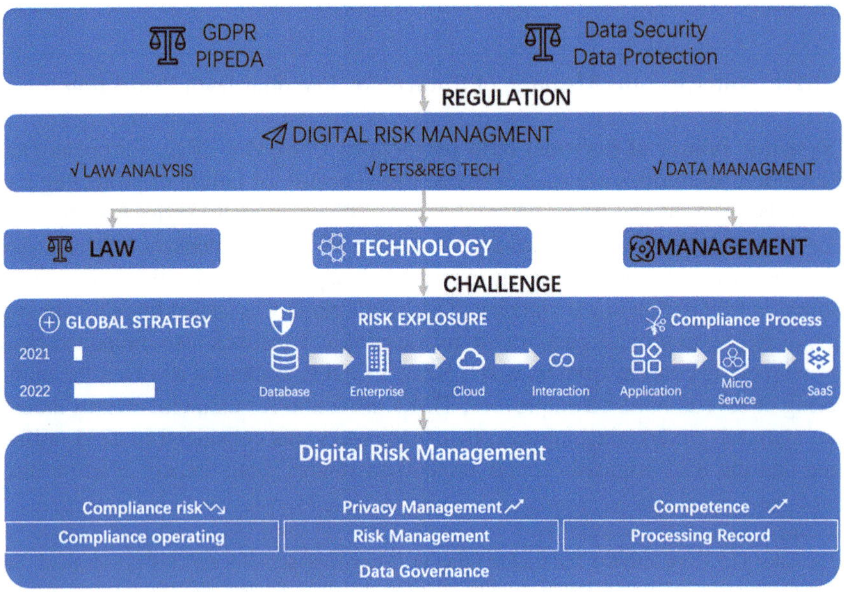

Fig. 3.1 Pictures provide by the author

[33] Ibid.

environments as well as market conditions. The internal environments shall provide a comprehensive view of key business drivers, organization structure, digital assets as well as opportunities and threats. From contractual perspective, it usually involved with DPA agreement, and NDA agreement, which clearly define the responsibilities and rules for data controller, data subjects as well as data processors. It also defines the scope of digital risk from legal perspective. For technical architecture, it usually involves with the risk of third parties such as cyberattacks, algorithms accountability, both for HW/SW solutions for internal management and external use for consumers and vehicles. To define the digital risk associate with technical architecture, risk due to changes in implementation, deployment and or management of new IT systems. For instance, it involves with identity management where the risk posed by third parties having access to the organization's sensitive information.[34] Also, it involves the vulnerable of third parties of cybersecurity issues. It also involved the workforce control which could be dynamic risk for intellectual property. For data architecture, to define the scope of digital risk, it usually starts with data mapping where you need to clearly acknowledge the data flow between venders and our entity. It usually involves the risk of unlawful data processing by third parties and as well as compliance issues. Although this book proposed audit as possible solution for the designing, implementing, and reforming personal data protection policies, it is the fact that: there is no mechanism either for public or for regulatory agencies, can obtain expert and independent assessment of audit system itself.

[Control revolution] As risk became so important in the language of data management, risk associated with personal data has shifted from one of the calculations to tone of accountability, a process that has been shaped by the growth of regulation and governance in response to organizational and systemic failure.The importance of management for mitigating risk has been found since the mid-1990s, and the difference between risk analysis and risk management has been much debated. The scientific purity for risk analysis, as well as the degree of precaution and multiplicity of principles for determining acceptability, have been understood as boundaries of formal risk analysis. These debates demand improved risk communication and greater transparency of the risk analysis process. With regard to this topic, this book discusses the design of a regulated entity for protecting personal data, the quality of data management and the effectiveness of internal control. As Power noted:

> Risk analysis in private sector management thinking has also become transformed within a broader governance setting, which focuses on matters of organizational design, the quality of senior management and accountability for the effectiveness of internal controls.[35]

As highlighted, there exist different risks associated with personal data, and the first step of "risk identification" requires that the data controller consider different concentrations of miasma to avoid harm associated with processing personal data. When the audit system serves as a regulatory system, it encountered rockiness in

---

[34] Ishaq Azhar Mohammed, "Systemic review of identity access management in information security." (2017) at 4.

[35] Power, *supra* note 10 in Chap. 1 at 32.

terms of how legal and policy processes respond to the digital environment, which have evolved rapidly. "The control revolution," proposed by James Beniger, was used to describe the process in which organizations undergo profound changes because of the revolution of technology.[36] This idea was often studied in fields such as technology, labor history and economic sociology. "The control revolution" has two distinct meanings. First, it changes how organizations produce outputs, and it also changes what organizations produce. Second, it changes why organizations produce. In retrospect, it seems naïve to have thought that these meanings would not apply to the organizational forms of legal institutions. When an audit served as control function for an organization, it encountered both problems from legal perspective and management perspective for the purpose of personal data protection. However, regulatory system may lose focus in the digital code, and regulatory institutions may find regulatory subjects escape oversight. "Lex Informatica" explored the ways in which governance entities may reassert themselves within pathways defined by the digital code proposed by Joel Reidenberg. Another paper written by Lawrence Lessig, "Code and other laws of cyberspace," asserted that digital codes serve as a normative tool that may frustrate other processes traditionally located in the domain of law.[37] If one accepts that technological activities require new types of response from law, two papers mentioned respond with two different approaches. "Lex Informatica" was the product of great minds in both "North America" and "Europe," automatically turned mechanics of grabbing regulatory authority into a process of developing standards. The code foregrounded the influence of the marketplace offering a new approach for theorizing the regulatory properties of technology. One way was from the top-down and the other was from the bottom-up, and they both manifested different regulatory layers for control.

3.1.2.2 Audit for Management and Legal Control

[Meaning of Control] According to etymology studies, the word "control" originated from the Anglo-French term "controller," which means to control; from medieval Latin word "contrarotulus," which means 'register'; and from the late Latin word "rotulus," which means 'wheel.'[38] Moreover, the term "control" means:

> To order, limit, or rule something or someone's actions or behavior, demonstrating the ability or power to decide or strongly influence the particular way in which something will happen or someone will behave or the condition of having such power or the act of controlling something or someone, as well as the power to do this.[39]

---

[36] James R Beniger, *The Control Revolution: Technological and Economic Origins of the Information Society* (Cambridge, Mass.: Harvard University Press, 1986) at 21.

[37] Lawrence Lessig, *Code: And Other Laws Of Cyberspace*, first edition ed. (New York: Basic Books, 1999) at 13.

[38] Webster, *supra* note 135 in Chap. 2.

[39] IDM, *supra* note 25 in Chap. 2.

Therefore, the meaning of control always consists of the power to exercise authority or the ability to influence or limit something. For instance:

> Control of an organization, place, or system is the power to make all the important decisions about the way that it is run. If you have control of something or someone, then you are able to make them do what you want them to do. To control a piece of equipment, a process or system means to make it work in the way that you want it to work.[40]

Control always refers to an organization, in which the concept of control always implies the control of a corporation. The term "corporate control" refers to the right to exercise the power to operate a corporation or the ownership of a company.[41] As a matter of fact, the term is used in three different senses: as "an agreement for the naked transfer of the corporate office"; as "the group of individuals who, for practical purposes, can be regarded as 'the control';[42] and most famously, as an "official relation as a fiduciary relationship to the corporation" (this last sense was characterized by Judge Clark). David defined corporate control as follows:

> Corporate control is a relation of total custody, subsisting between the office of the controller and the corporation, giving rise to a complex of duties and a corresponding complex of rights.[43]

From the perspective of corporate governance, corporate control can be divided into internal aspects and external aspects.[44] Regarding internal aspects, the research has been more focused on management and organization-based mechanisms, such as authorization, documentation, reconciliation, security and the separation of duties. Regarding the subject of audits in this book, audit professionals are not responsible for constructing and administering corporate control,[45] and corporate managers are responsible for the arrangement of this control,[46] so a well-organized interpretation of control in the audit context regards control as a process. According to the U.S. Committee of Sponsoring Organizations (hereafterCOSO), internal corporate control is defined as follows:

> Internal control is a process, affected by an entity's board of directors, management, and other personnel, designed to provide reasonable assurance regarding the achievement of

---

[40] Collins Dictionaries, *Collins English Dictionary and Thesaurus Boxed Set: All the words you need, every day*, third edition edition ed. (Collins, 2019).

[41] C L Pass, Bryan Lowes & Leslie Davies, *Collins Dictionary of Economics*, 2 edition ed. (Glasgow: Harpercollins Pub Ltd., 1991). Corporate control means the ability to exercise control over a public joint-stock company. In countries where shares in a large company are freely traded, if the incumbent directors and senior managers fail to achieve good profit and dividend performances will fall.

[42] David C Bayne, "The Definition of Corporate Control" (1964) 9:4 St Louis U LJ 445–463. See online: <https://heinonline.org/HOL/P?h=hein.journals/stlulj9&i=455> at 446 (Visited at 4 Feb, 2024).

[43] *Ibid.*

[44] OECD, *The OECD Principles of Corporate Governance* (2004).

[45] Noel O'Sullivan & Pauline Wong, "Internal versus External Control: An Analysis of Board Composition and Ownership in UK Takeovers" (1998) 2:1 J Manag Gov at 28.

[46] Moeller, *supra* note 118 in Chap. 2 at 3.

Fig. 3.2 COSO Internal Control Framework

> objectives in the following categories: the effectiveness and efficiency of operations, the reliability of financial reporting, and compliance with applicable laws and regulations.[47]

The COSO provides a three-dimensional framework to illustrate this definition (Fig. 3.2).

[Audit for management control] Management, as interpreted by Cambridge English Dictionary, could be defined as:

> The group of people who control a company or organization.[48]

To explain and recognized as midst function of management can be retrospect back to the early 1990s.[49] The literature of Scott for organization theory always being identified as a benchmark for the development of "management control system" (hereafterMCS) research.[50] Scott pointed that the control process moved from imposed process into a natural evolving process.[51] Anthony first dismembered

[47] *Ibid.*

[48] IDM, *supra* note 25 in Chap. 2.

[49] Giovanni B Giglioni & Arthur G Bedeian, "A Conspectus of Management Control Theory: 1900–1972" (1974) 17:2 AMJ. See online: <https://journals.aom.org/doi/abs/10.5465/254981> at 297 (Visited at February 4, 2024).

[50] W Richard Scott, "Developments in Organization Theory, 1960–1980" (1981) 24:3 American Behavioral Scientist 407–422. See online: <https://doi.org/10.1177/000276428102400306> at 413 (Visited a February 4, 2024).

[51] *Ibid* at 414.

management control into three stages: *"strategic planning, management control and operational control.*"[52] Strategic planning is future oriented, and sets the overall strategies and plans that then require to be implemented. Management control processes, which are focused on ensuring that resources are obtained and used effectively and efficiently to achieve the organization's objectives, relied heavily on accounting measures of performance and financial accountability. Operational control processes are highly dependent on the situation and tend to rely heavily on nonfinancial measures of performance.[53] Ouchi focused on specific control tools for management purpose, he initiated a control framework which identified three forms of control:

> behavior control, outcome control and clan control.[54]

Similar with Ouchi's argument, Simons' framework posits that organizations must make explicit decisions regarding their preferences for each of the four distinct types of control:

> belief systems, boundary systems, interactive controls, and diagnostic controls.[55]

Belief systems serve as the foundation for an organization's core values, contributing to its overall culture and ethos. These systems are often expressed through tools such as mission statements and corporate policies. It is crucial for senior managers to embody these values, ensuring that organizational statements align with actual practices. In contrast, boundary systems define the limits of acceptable activity and behavior within the organization. This type of control is exemplified by compliance systems and quality control mechanisms.[56] While diagnostic control involves routine variance accounting and management-by-exception reporting, interactive control plays a unique role in distinguishing between strategic failure and insufficient strategic implementation. This differentiation helps organizations address issues at a more strategic level. In other words, interactive controls are intended to provide early warning that a given strategy is no longer appropriate and needs revision. However, the term 'interactive' also covers other types of behavior (the term comes from intensive and interactive discussions between senior and junior managers).[57] Then Otley proposed another framework that seeks to ensure that a comprehensive

---

[52] Robert N Anthony, *Planning and control systems; a framework for analysis* (Boston: Division of Research, Graduate School of Business Administration, Harvard University, 1965) at 41.

[53] *Ibid* at 19.

[54] William G Ouchi, "A Conceptual Framework for the Design of Organizational Control Mechanisms". (1979) 25:9 Management Science 833–848. See online: <https://pubsonline.informs.org/doi/abs/10.1287/mnsc.25.9.833> at 840 (Visited at March 21, 2024).

[55] Robert Simons, *Levers of control: how managers use innovative control systems to drive strategic renewal* (Boston, Mass.: Harvard Business School Press, 1995) at 34.

[56] *Ibid* at 44.

[57] *Ibid.*

view of the control system which could be preserved.[58] A final body of literature review which taken a contingency theory approach to design of controlling systems. Contingency research was motivated by the generally correct belief that no single control or MCS is optimal in all situations and that the control choices depend on any of a number of situational.[59] Which means that drawing upon earlier developments in organization theory, contingency theory has made some progress in determining the most important contingent variables. Certain control systems primarily aim to enforce accountability for individuals or groups, holding them responsible for their actions or the outcomes they, or their organizations, generate. Accountability involves rewarding individuals for positive outcomes and penalizing them for negative ones. This emphasis on accountability is prevalent in many organizations. In an accountability-oriented control system, individuals subject to control are typically, though not universally, informed in advance of the expectations for their performance during a specific period. Alternatively, these expectations can be implicit, becoming apparent only after the performance period concludes. This dynamic underscores the proactive nature of accountability systems, where individuals are made aware of the standards against which their actions or outcomes will be measured.[60] The main objective of good management is to ensure that shareholders and all stakeholders have confidence in the perpetuity of the organization.[61] Management has been described as a social process involving responsibility for economical and effective planning and regulation of operation of an enterprise in the fulfillment of given purposes. Control function is being defined as one of four functions of management as: "planning, organizing, leading, and controlling."[62] The goal and task of

[58] David Otley, "Performance management: a framework for management control systems research" (1999) 10:4 Management Accounting Research 363–382. See online: <https://linkinghub.elsevier.com/retrieve/pii/S1044500599901154> at 367.: "He proposes a descriptive framework structured around five fundamental questions: Key Objectives and Evaluation: What are the central objectives critical to the organization's long-term success? How does the organization assess its performance in achieving each of these objectives? Strategies, Plans, and Performance Measurement: What strategies and plans has the organization adopted to implement its objectives? What processes and activities are deemed necessary for successful implementation, and how is the performance of these activities measured? **Performance Targets:** What level of performance is deemed necessary for success in each identified area? How does the organization establish appropriate performance targets for these areas? **Rewards for Performance:** What rewards, both for managers and other employees, are associated with the achievement of these performance targets? **Information Flows and Learning**: What information flows, including feedback and feed-forward loops, are essential for the organization to learn from its experiences? How does the organization adapt its current behavior based on this experiential learning."

[59] Joseph Fisher, "Contingency-Based Research on Management Control Systems: Categorization by Level of Complexity" (1995) at 6.

[60] Ibid

[61] Narasimha Rao Vajjhala, *Cybersecurity and Decision Makers*, first ed. (John Wiley & Sons, Ltd., 2020) at 39.

[62] "Functions and management of affect: Applications to economic behavior" (1988) 9:2 Journal of Economic Psychology 251–282. See online: <https://www.sciencedirect.com/science/article/pii/0167487088900542> at 255 (Visited at 4 February 2024).

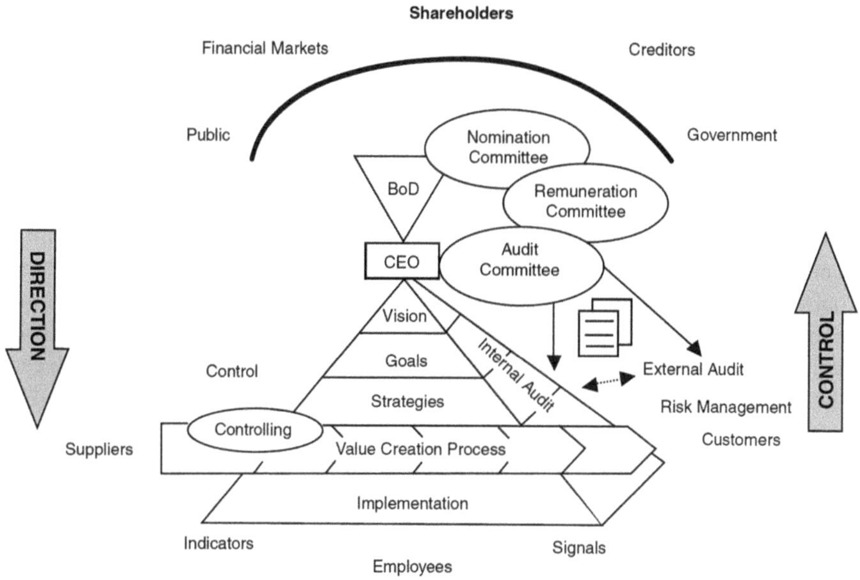

Fig. 3.3 Management Structure (Ruud Flemming, "Corporate Governance und Interne Revision" (2001) 75 Der Schweizer Treuhander 521–534 at 522)

an organization which need to be achieved, are carried out through the task of the basic control process usually involved three steps: (1) Establishing standards, (2) measuring performance against these standards, and (3) correcting deviations from standards and plans.[63] As noted from this definition, internal audit is naturally divulged the control function of management (Fig. 3.3).

[Audit for legal Control] Legal control, as discussed with many scholars, leveraged its influence over subjects for two concurrence facts: it stipulated certain behaviors and made the subjects in conformity with such stipulation.[64] The functionalist asserted that the legal rules performed their rule effectively to provide certainty. While another type of voice could be heard soundly: "Law is marginal."[65] The struggles from legal regulation and effective control have been proposed in many areas of law.[66] The term "formalism of law" has been defined as "lies the

[63] Harold Koontz & Heinz Weihrich, *Management*, ninth edition ed. (New York: McGraw-Hill Inc.,US, 1988) at 722.

[64] Daniel Ward, "A Taxonomy of Legal Control". (2018) 31:2 Canadian Journal of Law & Jurisprudence 431–457, See online: <https://www.cambridge.org/core/journals/canadian-journal-of-law-and-jurisprudence/article/abs/taxonomy-of-legal-control/8B9A2A597702B988F8F4BB14FD2ABA65> at 4 (Visited at 4 Feb 2024).

[65] Harold Canfield Havighurst, *The Nature of Private Contract* (F.B. Rothman, 1981) at 65.

[66] Doreen McBarent & Christopher J. Whelan, "The Elusive Spirit of the Law: Formalism and the Struggle for Legal Control 54 Modern Law Review 1991". See online: <https://heinonline.org/HOL/LandingPage?handle=hein.journals/modlr54&div=61&id=&page=> at 848 (Visited 4 Feb 2024).

concept of decision making according to rule."[67] Whereas "creative compliance" use formalism to avoid control such as avoiding tax.[68] By stated that is not to compromise the value of the law, instead, it is to declare the formal law is not what structure the society.[69] As it could be perceived, the behavior of individuals is often constrained by different norms. As Lawrence Lessig noted: *"Behavior, we might say, is regulated by four kinds of constraints."*[70] Law is just one of them. There are also social norms, market as well as architecture.[71] These four types of norms controlled the behavior of individual in different types. Law controlled by threatening a punishment; Social norms controlled by threatening punishment ex-post; Market controlled through price; Architecture controlled by design.[72] These four constraints appeared both in real space and in cyberspace. To understand how these norms interacted with each other (sometimes they may complement or compete with each other), it usually put these modalities on the same field to observe them.[73] Also for the topic of this book, whether the behavior of the cyberspace can be regulated depends on the architecture "the code" which referred to the "regulability" manifested through the function of its design.[74] To increase regulability, As Gordon noted:

> Regular, patterned, and moderately predictable (at lease in the short-to -medium-term) causal relations are always springing up between specific and legal practices. Though the lessons of realism are that one must get down to very concrete situations before one can describe what they are.[75]

Law did not deliver its function solely, but collaboratively worked with other norms such as audit. There are other essential components between law and the architecture which shall not be undermined or weaken. For example, when businessman said they need an enforcement mechanism, it's usually referred to arbitration process. Lawyers will also promote their products, the common law of contracts, treaties, restatement, and commercial codifications to promote certainty of commercial transactions Control played an important role in explaining the effectiveness of the audit system in the personal data protection regime. From the principal-agent type of explanation, external auditors played an essential role in responding to the suspectable internal audit process to external stakeholders, as well as the public, and

---

[67] Frederick Schauer, "Formalism" (1988) 97:4 The Yale Law Journal 509–548. See online: <https://www.jstor.org/stable/796369> at 520 (Visited at 4 Feb 2024).

[68] Note 68 at 849.

[69] Havighurst, *supra* note 67.

[70] Ekstrand, "Lessig, Lawrence. The Law of the Horse", *supra* note 292 in Chap. 2 at 7.

[71] *Ibid* at 8.

[72] *Ibid.*

[73] Lawrence Lessig, "The Law of the Horse: What Cyberlaw Might Teach" (1999) 113:2 Harvard Law Review 501–549. See online: <https://www.jstor.org/stable/1342331> at 512 (Visited 4 Feb 2024).

[74] *Ibid* at 518.

[75] Gordon, *supra* note 10 at 81.

became an important external control method for persona data protection.[76] Serving as an oversight method, the effectiveness of external audits is crucial for executable internal audit management. Compared with internal audits, external audits cover more issues related to the external market, laws and regulations.[77] Risk management internally relies on internal procedures, such as Privacy Impact Assessment (hereafter PIA) from an engineering perspective, whereas from an audit perspective, internal management procedures need to be verified from external audits to ensure that internal execution is aligned with legal requirement. Regarding the topic of this book, the definition of "control" can be interpreted from the perspectives of the owners and processors of personal data.[78] Regulators have endeavored to increase individual control over personal data as one of the most crucial solutions for tackling emergent technologies. Control over personal data is often conceived as "the claim of individuals to determine for themselves when, how, and to what extent data about them are communicated to others."[79] As a matter of fact, "data protection as a control" theory, which was proposed by A. Westin, has been endorsed by a broad range of scholars.[80] It emphasizes the discretion of individuals over their data. For instance, the protection of personal data, stated in the EU Charter of Fundamental Rights, is defined as follows: "Everyone has the right to the protection of personal data concerning him or her. Such data must be processed fairly for specified purposes and on the basis of the consent of the person concerned or some other legitimate basis laid down by law. Everyone has the right to access data that have been collected concerning him or her and the right to have it rectified."[81] In other words, the right to process personal data is established on the basis of individual consent or consent by law, while the right to process personal data, constrained by the right to the protection of personal data, is established on the basis of the user's right to access and rectify these data as well as set a rule with a legitimate and specific purpose. In this regard, "control" can be described as an information management pro-

---

[76] Gene A Brewer et al., "External Control and Red Tape: The Mediating Effects of Client and Organizational Feedback" (2012) 15:3 International Public Management Journal 288–314. See online: <https://doi.org/10.1080/10967494.2012.725291> at 357 (Visited at 22 February, 2024).

[77] Karthik Anand & Suremya S L, "External and Internal Rules of Corporate Governance" (2021) 4 Issue 4 Int'l JL Mgmt & Human 2887–2902. See online: <https://heinonline.org/HOL/P?h=hein.journals/ijlmhs12&i=2922> at 2887 (Visited at March 17, 2024).

[78] Christian Fuchs, "Towards an alternative concept of privacy" (2011) 9:4 Journal of Information, Communication and Ethics in Society 220–237. See online: <https://doi.org/10.1108/14779961111191039> at 233. In the field of privacy and data protection, the challenge of grasping the notion of control is reinforced by the fact that two totally different meanings are frequently ascribed to the concept of control.

[79] Alan Westin, "Privacy And Freedom" (1968) 25:1 Washington and Lee Law Review 166,See online: <https://scholarlycommons.law.wlu.edu/wlulr/vol25/iss1/20> (Visited at March 18, 2024). Also see: Christphe Lazaro & Daniel Le Métayer, "The control over personal data: True remedy or fairy tale ?" (2015). See online: <http://arxiv.org/abs/1504.03877> at 233 (Visited at March 17, 2024).

[80] Westin, *supra* note 81.

[81] *Ibid* at Article 8.

cess through self-management; in this sense, it is subject to the idea of "privacy as an agency," which refers to "self-determination over information about oneself and the self-management of privacy."[82] Personal data self-management is based on an individual's willingness to collect or use his/her personal information.[83] Although acknowledgement and consent from data subjects are one of the fundamental origins of grounds for processing personal information, we are still faced with cognitive problems, wherein people are reluctant to read privacy policies, or it is difficult for ordinary people to determine what is the "necessary and adequate" information for various purposes.[84] The purpose of consent is to ensure a certain degree of control concerning the personal information of the user, but practically, it has become a discretionary tool entitling Internet companies to circulate personal information; whether or not this processing action is justified hinges quite simply and exclusively on whether these companies have obtained user consent. As a matter of fact, negative situations exist in which personal information managers use contractual rules to protect themselves.[85] In sum, from legal perspective, regulation on personal data protection can be described as normative actions which resulted from risk management decisions made by regulators and stakeholders internally and externally of an organization. Taken the GDPR as an example, it identifies three main stakeholders in the process of data management as data subject, data controller as well as data processor.[86] For the explanation of the act, data controller played an important role in compliance with the requirement such as accountability of information shared by data subjects. "Accountability components" of the data controller shall be responsible to evaluate trust between data subjects and data processors considering GDPR principles and requirements.[87] The accountability components need to be managed from technical accountability to legal accountability for add value of organizational governance. For instance, the concept of trust, in computer science, is considered as:

---

[82] Lazaro & Métayer, "The control over personal data", *supra* note 81 at 5. "The second way to consider the notion of control is in an individual/subjective manner and relates to the multiple ways in which individuals interact with each other and communicate personal information: the ways in which they participate in the self-construction of their digital identities. In this sense, control as an agency refers to self-determination over information about oneself and the self-management of privacy."

[83] The idea is that it is possible or desirable for every individual to monitor and manage a shifting collection of privacy settings of which they may only be dimly aware.

[84] Sabine Trepte et al., "Do People Know About Privacy and Data Protection Strategies? Towards the 'Online Privacy Literacy Scale' (OPLIS)" in Serge Gutwirth, Ronald Leenes & Paul de Hert, eds, *Reforming Eur Data Prot Law* Law, Governance and Technology Series (Dordrecht: Springer Netherlands, 2015) at 333.

[85] Gautrais, *supra* note 39 in Chap. 1 at 178 (Visited on May 16, 2019).

[86] U Jayasinghe, G M Lee & A MacDermott, *Trust-Based Data Controller for Personal Information Management* (2018) at 124.

[87] LoPucki, *supra* note 19 at 489.

> A computational value depicted by a relationship between a trustor and a trustee, described in a specific context, measure by trust metric, and evaluated by a mechanism.[88]

From the management perspective, the technical value as well as management value are all need to be added through the process of internal audit. Besides, the sensitive personal data & model of process data for the company could not directly audit by an external party for security as well as trade secret reasons. Although the credible experts from third parties are least affected by internal considerations, they can only have very limited access to intermediate models or training data. Internal audit could have directly to the private protection process internally which could add management value by incorporating additional information typically unavailable for external evaluations to reveal unidentifiable risk for the board of directors.[89] As an essential part of the audit system, outsourcing the internal part of audit system would diminish the management function of the internal audit.

3.2 Interpret Audit from Function of Management Control

For this part, this book further explicated function of management control in the context of personal data protection audit. To conduct audit, audit trail need to be ready for different layers such as organization, data subject and algorithm perspective. Risk associate with the audit trail need to be identified and need to be managed.

3.2.1 Managing Audit Subject

The different colors of the personal data protection audit presented the discriminate function of the system: a compliance mechanism, a management tool and an accountability approach. As for the result, the audit served as a regulatory system for personal data protection and shall be interpreted as follows:

> For the purpose of reducing compliance risk, of ameliorating knowledge of personal data protection, of revealing deficiencies in management and control in the procession of personal data, audit body evaluated activities of data processors in accordance with laws, regulations, as well as standards.[90]

When an audit serves as management function to norms the procession of personal data, components served as a management tool to improve the maturity level of internal control for the purpose of protecting personal data. More precisely, data

[88] Upul Jayasinghe et al., "Machine Learning Based Trust Computational Model for IoT Services" (2019) 4:1 IEEE Trans Sustain Comput 39–52. See online: <https://ieeexplore.ieee.org/document/8364607/> at 47 (Visited at December 11, 2023).

[89] Raji et al., "Closing the AI Accountability Gap", *supra* note 86 in Chap. 1 at 4.

[90] Pandit & Lewis, *supra* note 400 in Chap. 2 at 5.

protection laws such as the GDPR often seek to regulate and control all flows of personal data from different perspectives, with various safeguards for individuals and entities who have the right to process personal data. From another perspective, personal data protection audits also serve as an interpretation tool to evince substantive compliance (Compliance Documentation). As for the result, the audit must be able to identify the following: (1) auditable organization supported the audit activities. (2) data containers, including the outcome of data processing, (3) processing relationship relating to the data, and (4) application contexts in which data have been processed.[91]

3.2.1.1 Towards an Auditable Body

[Towards an auditable organization] Many approaches of risk management try to understand the relationship between organizations and risk focused on the relationship between organizations and their environment. These theories entail a common reminder that risk management is "constitutive of organizations." As Power noted:

> Organizing and managing are fundamentally about individual and collective human efforts to process uncertainty… how specific uncertainties become objects, risk objects, for a management process demands an analysis of the manner in which they are represented and constructed within organizational and managerial fields.[92]

Formal entities always served as underpinnings to manage risk associated with data. When discussing personal data protection, first instincts refer to which organization, what context, and how to apply a data protection strategy. There exists a dilemma of where organizations are involved in the business scene. For instance, for an internet company, such as Xiaomi, it established the Privacy Protection Department under the Data Security Department. The Privacy Protection Department always needs to communicate with the Legal Department when facing compliance issues associated with protecting personal data. Due to management concerns, the company established the Xiaomi Privacy Committee at a higher level to make reasonable decisions when facing complicated issues. However, the efficiency of such a committee is questionable. It usually held the meeting for 2 or 3 weeks, where many of the cases did not have the chance to be discussed. The fact is that the business partners for privacy protection have faced a multitude of cases every day. This leads to the fundamental question of personal data protection from the perspective of practical issues: are problems of personal data protection on the legal side or security side within an organization? The scope of personal information protection compliance audit objects usually includes a description of organizational departments, activities, application systems, IT infrastructure, etc. As a matter of fact, legal departments could serve as agents to interpret the requirements of law and standards. However, it is insufficient for the Legal Department to implement these legal

[91] *Ibid.*

[92] Power, *supra* note 10 in Chap. 1 at 127.

requirements into IT infrastructure. Again, the same gap between law and technology was faced from the perspective of organizational design. An organization's personal data protection program may often go above or beyond what is required by law. To be effective, a protection program should usually operate on the implemented side to obtain substantive compliance results. Thus far, this book noted that it is essential for an organization to design organizational and management mechanisms, including roles and responsibilities for the protection of personal data (governance). Additionally, there is a structural system of procedures that control the risk detected, as well as constant monitoring of the correct implementation of this system in compliance with applicable regulatory requirements in the protection of personal data (Compliance). For instance, usually within a private organization, such as a corporation, under the evaluation of a data protection officer, the aspects concerning data protection are handled within the Legal Department, IT Department, Security Department and HR Department. The Legal Department and the HR Department handle the organizational aspects as follows:

(1) Constant updates and revision of the privacy document framework (e.g., information to the data subjects, appointments of external processors, processing authorizations, appointments of System Administrators, etc.).

(2) The establishment, maintenance, and updating of the Data Processing Register.

(3) The establishment of internal procedures for management of privacy compliance.

(4) The planning and provision of dedicated training on privacy to the employees authorized to process personal data.

(5) The planning of audits for periodic reviews of proper compliance with privacy laws and compliance with procedures and instructions by the employees authorized to process personal data.

The IT department is usually responsible for the monitoring and possible implementation of information system measures. As outlined in Section 24 of the GDPR, it is essential that reforms to data protection self-management mechanisms be complemented by appropriate organizational accountability obligations to ensure that the burden of proof and consenting to complicated practices does not fall solely on individuals, which is a crucial concern that data protection officers need to address. As Ann Cavoukian noted in her seven principles for privacy by design, accountability requires clear organizational rules with understandable descriptions of the policies for the rules, which should make clear that personal information shall only be collected and used in a manner that is respectful of individuals' expectations and within a safe information environment. From a practical perspective, the organization of constructed entities is usually based on business units, products or service lines, while from an audit perspective, an auditable entity may simply be constructed according to a key risk or control. Put simply, thinking of an organization as a cake, how best do you slice the cake into bite-sized pieces? In other words, how can an organization be easily and effectively audited to achieve an accountable environment for processing personal data? It is truly a subjective process. Once the nature and scope of these auditable entities are determined, internal audits assess the risk of each auditable entity to assist in producing a risk-based internal audit plan that lists the internal audits to be carried out. From a functional perspective, personal data protection auditors usually need to deal with databases, as well as algorithms. The database and algorithm are usually applied by different departments, as well as third parties. In addition, companies gradually adopted cloud-based architecture. As data owners no longer physically store their data simply downloading the data for its verification of processing is not a practical solution due to the high cost of input/output (I/O) and transmission across the network. It is often insufficient to detect data corruption only when accessing the data, as it does not give correctness assurance for un-accessed data and might be too late to recover the data lost or damaged. When these issues combine together, different from other industries, an internal audit is essentially needed for an organization to carry out a personal data audit process. And that is the trigger for why the digital companies like the "One Trust" thriller. The organization, not only included entities such as legal departments and IT departments, but also included virtual platforms, such as the "Data Compliance Center," which targeted the complicated context that data protection has encountered. Usually, when discussing organizational management, a "management system" is a tool for relation mapping for the organizational control structure. As Power put it, "Logic of audit ability which is hidden in more established contexts…is accomplished by auditable measures of performance, systems of control and reliance on experts." For personal data protection audits, digital platforms would like to give systemic approaches for shaping auditable organizations, as well as auditable systems. The virtual organization may serve as an indispensable part of organizational management, as well as compliance operations.

3.2.1.2 Building Audit Trial for Personal Data Protection

[Data Mapping] "compliance audit" became a mandatory requirement in some jurisdictions. For instance, Article 54 of the China Personal Information Protection Law noted that "personal data processors shall carry out compliance audits based on related regulations on a regular basis.[93] With the requirement of the law that PIPL involved, the compliance audit could be conducted by the processor; in other words, the compliance audit could be regarded as a type of internal audit. Although there is no specific article in the GDPR requiring that an organization conduct compliance audits, a similar obligation is placed on the side of the data processor, such as data protection impact assessment (hereafterDPIA), as part of the accountability

[93] Article 54 of Personal Information Protection Law of the People's Republic of China. See online: https://www.lawinfochina.com/display.aspx?id=36358&lib=law&SearchKeyword=&SearchCKeyword= (Visited at 09 Nov 2021):

PIPL specifies requirements on audit, including regular audit conducted by personal information processor, as well as ad hoc compliance audit of personal information processing activities conducted by the entrusted specialized institutions where relatively large risks exist in personal information processing activities or personal information security incidents occur. In addition, PIPL requires the personal information processor to implement categorized management of personal information.

principle.[94] As a matter of fact, the requirement of compliance audit differed from the requirement of PIA, which GDPR referenced. Compliance audits often ratify the procedural stage of personal information in operations, whereas PIA should be a prospective tool before it commences operations.[95] To identify an effective audit system for regulating personal data processing, the first step is to recognize the audit target. More specifically, it is essential to confirm what sort of data are being processed within an organization for the purpose of protecting personal data. Data mapping is the process of connecting a data field from one source to a data field in another source.[96] This helps standardization process and makes it easier to connect sensitive data to the identity of the person associated with it. Additionally, recordings of a person's voice could be personal data, even if they aren't talking about themselves.[97] Before considering what types of personal data your organization may hold, it is worth evaluating how personal data comes into your system. For instance, personal data could be presented through emails, websites, cookies, apps, third parties, social media, feedback and research surveys. In other words, it requires an understanding of the information flow both from inside and outside of an organization. Data mapping is also required to describe the information flow to ensure that the purpose of processing personal data can be identified. At this stage, there are usually two options for an organization to carry on data mapping. The first option is to conduct a manual information search, and personal data are analyzed based on an in-person survey. The other option is to engage in a technology-assisted approach that seeks to automate data mapping procedures to reduce human errors and remove subjectivity. As a matter of fact, this approach emerged as a solution to compliance challenges in the financial industry in the first place called "RegTech."[98] RegTech can be defined as:

> The use of technological solutions to facilitate compliance with and monitoring of regulatory requirements.[99]

---

94 Article 35 of GDPR: Where a type of processing in particular using new technologies, and taking into account the nature, scope, context and purposes of the processing, is likely to result in a high risk to the rights and freedoms of natural persons, the controller shall, prior to the processing, carry out an assessment of the impact of the envisaged processing operations on the protection of personal data. A single assessment may address a set of similar processing operations that present similar high risks.

95 David Wright & Paul De Hert, *Privacy impact assessment*, Law, governance and technology series v. 6 (Dordrecht ; Springer, 2012) at 56.

96 Definition of Data mapping, See online: https://www.informatica.com/resources/articles/data-mapping.html (2022) (Visited at 22 December 2022).

97 Conducting a GDPR Data Audit. See: https://www.termsfeed.com/blog/gdpr-data-audit/ (January 11, 2022).

98 Paul Ryan, Martin Crane & Rob Brennan, "Design Challenges for GDPR RegTech" (2020) Proc 22nd Int Conf Enterp Inf Syst 787–795 at 792.

99 Veerle Colaert, "Systematisation as a Response to Regulatory Expansion in the Financial Sector" SSRN Electron J. See online: <https://www.academia.edu/31897087/RegTech_as_a_response_to_regulatory_expansion_in_the_financial_sector> at 8 (Visited at 12 Feb 2022).

Table 3.1 Example of Data Mapping term sheet

Data Mapping Record	Created by	Input by	Date	Version
Source	Type of Personal data	The way you will store the data, how it will be processed, and who has access to it.	When will the data be disposed of	Consent obtained

RegTech could support the visualization component of data mapping. Data visualization could help data processors follow the personal data flows within organizations quickly and easily. The next step is to clarify where personal data might be stored within an organization. For instance, in electronic form on devices, on cloud servers or in physical form, such as paper records. This also means you should acknowledge the types of personal data you hold, such as names, contact details, biometrics and genetic information. In sum, the function of data mapping usually supports five perspectives: (1). Where is the personal data collected? (2) What types of personal data are collected? (3) Where is the data stored? (4) What is the purpose of processing personal data? (5) How long is the data retained? Although the GDPR was not expressly required by rule, it could be considered an essential part of GDPR compliance with Article 30, as well as Article 36[100] (Table 3.1).

Data mapping also serves as a management tool to carve out personal data. It provides a means to link seemingly disconnected bits of information to specific individuals. As part of the GDPR compliance requirement, individuals have the right to control their own data, which authorizes data owners to obtain an explanation of all the information that an organization has about them based on consent. They can also assert rights over their personal data, such as refusing to allow it to be sold to third parties, having it erased (the right to be forgotten), and taking their entire data record elsewhere (data portability). Data mapping could make it efficient and effective to manage the rights of individuals at scale. In addition, by enabling central management of personal data from a single location linked to all applications, data mapping makes it easier to apply subject rights processing in a consistent way.[101] Data mapping is also a preliminary step for personal data classification. For instance, entities handling the personal data of European data subjects are required to classify all collected data types. The GDPR categorizes specific data related to

[100] Article 30 requires documentation of certain organizations processing. Article36 requires organizations to conduct Data Protection Impact Assessments before engaging in certain processing.

[101] Informatica, What is data mapping See online: https://www.informatica.com/resources/articles/data-mapping.html (Visited at 12 January 2022).

Table 3.2 Best Practices for Data Mapping (Pribado news, Best Practices for Data Mapping. seeonline: https://www.privado.ai/post/gdpr-data-mapping#4 (12 January 2022))

Define Processing Activity	The biggest challenge in getting information for data mapping is an empty state, that leads to inertia for people in giving answers. This is why it is recommended breaking the questions down into two phases, with the first step to define key business processes.
Getting More Information	Once you have basic information, you can send a detailed assessment for each of these processes where you can ask questions about the purpose, legal basis, consent, and rights, among others.
Data Flow Mapping	The final step to complete is to map your internal assets, vendors, and third parties in each process. IT and engineering teams have this information. Leverage the asset register that IT might already have and start from there. Ensure that the location, as well as technical and organizational measures, is associated with the completed data map.
Finding Gaps	After the initial information collection, you will collate a large amount of data. It's important to find the gaps that currently exist in the data.

race, political opinions, health care, ethnic origin, and biometrics as "special." These data require additional protection[102] (Table 3.2).

As this book noted, data mapping manifests its essential aspect to identify a set of analysis and implementation functions related to personal data protection. However, several challenges influence the effectiveness and efficiency of audits at the data mapping stage. The first and foremost challenge originated from the definition of personal data. It is intricate for a data processor to provide an exhaustive list of personal data based on a broad definition. Isolated and related information may not be defined as personally identifiable information, whereas information combined as a dataset could become personally identifiable.[103] As a matter of fact, as Robert Gellman noted:

> Personal information that no longer contains overt identifiers (name, identification number, email address, telephone number)" can still be linked with known individuals.[104]

For instance, medical data are naturally distributed via different hospitals. In addition to direct identification information, if there is a unique combination of birthday, gender and ZIP code, the possibility of de-identification exists.[105] The technology for deidentification employed is one method for protecting personal data, as Paul Ohm noted:

---

[102] Article 9 of GDPR: Processing of personal data revealing racial or ethnic origin, political opinions, religious or philosophical beliefs, or trade union membership, and the processing of genetic data, biometric data for the purpose of uniquely identifying a natural person, data concerning health or data concerning a natural person's sex life or sexual orientation shall be prohibited.

[103] Robert Gellman, "The Deidentification Dilemma: A Legislative and Contractual Proposal" (2010).

[104] *Ibid* at 7.

[105] Mengchun Gong et al., "Evaluation of Privacy Risks of Patients' Data in China: Case Study" (2020) 8:2 JMIR Medical Informatics e13046. See online: <https://medinform.jmir.org/2020/2/e13046> at 6 (Visited at July 13, 2022).

> As a general proposition, for most personal data, deidentification maybe like absolute zero for temperature: a state that can be approached, but never achieved. Even if data could be fully deidentified, the prize may not be worth the effort in many cases.[106]

In other words, personal data shall be defined under a certain context with a certain dataset,[107] which requires identified activities within a certain scope.[108] From the management perspective, at the initial stage, identify activities and key stakeholders, both internally and externally, that need to be evinced (i.e., DPOs, IT managers, third-party providers).[109] Precisely recognizing all stakeholders, both internally and externally, is essential for the data mapping process. Luca Piras gave an example for data scope management, and he separated the management process into four phases: initial organization data collection, organization collection for profile creation, organization data collection of data processing activities, assessment translation and data synthesis.[110] From the compliance perspective, data mapping is setting the stage for the rest of the audit work; it needs to be legislative-based or contractual-based for conducting data mapping. While privacy by design is inherently human-oriented work, in the sense that personal data protection shall be proactively adopted and embedded into the design phase of new systems and services, subjective work has become an uncertain part of data mapping.[111] In sum, based on information obtained from the assessed system, it could decompose part of the audit process, referred to as the "description part" of data mapping, to enumerate its functions and components for the purpose of describing the information flows of personal data in the system.[112]

[Auditable Algorithm] All objects of control are executed through IT systems, which are usually referred to as transparency-enhancing technologies (TETs) and privacy-enhancing technologies (PETs).[113] Regarding the topic of this book, subject to the information technology (IT) environment, it is necessary to examine the meaning of control in the technical context. Control refers to "a procedure or policy

---

[106] Paul Ohm, *Broken Promises of Privacy: Responding to the Surprising Failure of Anonymization*, S (Rochester, NY: Social Science Research Network, 2009) at 40. Additionally, see: Gellman, "The Deidentification Dilemma", *supra* note 106.

[107] Aggeliki Tsohou et al., "Privacy, Security, Legal and Technology Acceptance Requirements for a GDPR Compliance Platform" (2020). (Lecture Notes in Computer Science 'including subseries Lecture Notes in Artificial Intelligence and Lecture Notes in Bioinformatics') at 212.

[108] National Institute of Standards and Technology, *NISTIR 8053 De-Identification of Personal Information: NiSTIR 8053* (CreateSpace Independent Publishing Platform, 2015) at 12.

[109] Luca Piras et al., "DEFeND DSM: a data scope management service for model-based privacy by design GDPR compliance." (2020). See online: <https://rgu-repository.worktribe.com/output/1003508/defend-dsm-a-data-scope-management-service-for-model-based-privacy-by-design-gdpr-compliance> at 233 (Visited at 16 May, 2023).

[110] *Ibid* at 155.

[111] Tsohou et al., *supra* note 110 at 2.

[112] Martin Horák, Václav Stupka & Martin Husák, *GDPR Compliance in Cybersecurity Software: A Case Study of DPIA in Information Sharing Platform* (New York, NY, USA: Association for Computing Machinery, 2019) at 4.

[113] Ian Goldberg, "Privacy Enhancing Technologies for the Internet III: Ten Years Later" at 14.

that provides a reasonable assurance that information technology used by an organization operates as intended, that data are reliable and that the organization is in compliance with applicable laws and regulations."[114] IT control is a subset of internal control and can be divided into two levels: application control, which covers a specific process and general control, which covers all aspects of IT operations, such as computer operations, access to programs and data, and network controls.[115] For the objective of control, the control objectives for information and related technology (hereafterCOBIT) framework has been widely promulgated by a large number of IT institutes, as it provides "A complete set of high-level requirements to be considered by management for the effective control of each IT process."[116] Additionally, management must respond to dynamic changes in the personal data sheet or field names in the data sheet. To tackle these management obstacles, Personal Data Enhancing Technologies (hereafterPDET) has been researched and elaborated, or so-called Privacy-Enhancing Technologies. The systematization of such knowledge has been discussed by some reviews and surveys.[117] These technologies have tended to move towards a "model-driven" design comprising different perspectives, such as architectural, functional, data, etc. The model serves as a structural tool to organize the information about the categories of personal information, as well as relevant IT properties for data protection, such as purpose limitation, data visibility, and accountability. Additionally, the automated model-based audit platform can be specifically addressed for the correct application of mechanisms for the control of personal data. For instance, European countries conducted a series of tools streaming for this issue. The MUSA DST demonstrated applicability to the safety or security of risk management. Papyrus and Sophia conducted model-driven analysis, design and verification. OpenCart conducted software and system assurance.[118] Additionally, a set of EU projects on the H 2020 DS-0802017 topic, namely BPR4GDPR, DEFeND, SMOOTH, PDP4E,[119] PAPAYA and PoSeID-on, aim to

[114] Steven De Haes et al., *Enterprise Governance of Information Technology: Achieving Alignment and Value in Digital Organizations*, 3d ed., Management for Professionals (Springer International Publishing, 2020). Additionally. See online: https://searchcompliance.techtarget.com/definition/IT-controls (Visited on April 13, 2020).

[115] Moeller, *supra* note 118 in Chap. 2 at 153.

[116] The COBIT framework was created by the ISACA for information technology management and IT governance and defines a set of generic processes for IT management, with each process defined together with process inputs and outputs, key process activities, process objectives, performance measures and an elementary maturity model. See online: https://www.isaca.org/resources/cobit (Visited on April 13, 2020).

[117] Johannes Heurix et al., "A taxonomy for privacy enhancing technologies" (2015) 53 Computers & Security 1–17. See online: <https://www.sciencedirect.com/science/article/pii/S0167404815000668> at 2 (Visited at April 13, 2020).

[118] Yod-Samuel Martin & Antonio Kung, *Methods and Tools for GDPR Compliance Through Privacy and Data Protection Engineering* (2018) at 110.

[119] PDP4E is an innovation action that will provide software and system engineers with methods and software tools to systemic ally apply data protection principles in the projects they carry out, so that the products they create comply with the General Data Protection Regulation (GDPR), thus

provide specific, operational solutions for the identified challenge of implementing GDPR requirements, either technical or organizational.[120] Taking PDP4E as an example, it provides four solutions: risk management, requirement engineering, privacy-aware design and assurance management.[121] For risk management, the project provided a risk management tool that enabled engineers to analyze software development risks related to data protection and privacy. Through the dashboard provided by the platform, the connection between legal perspective and points of view of engineers becomes stronger. The next step is software design; in any system or software development project, the elicitation of requirements serves as the essential part. It provided PDP4E-Req to guarantee a framework amenable for engineers not savvy on GDPR matters. "Privacy and Data Protection should be addressed "by design," that is, from the onset of a system or software project, rather than as an afterthought. To realize this precept, engineers need to be aware of at least three categories of essential knowledge. The first concerns the typical means to conduct system and software engineering (e.g., MBSE, formal methods), the second inherits the know-how related to privacy and data protection (e.g., anonymization, minimization, PETs), and the third is related to principles and provisions within regulations, such as GDPR (e.g., lawfulness, transparency, fairness). Mastering referred knowledge categories is critical to honor the tenets and to incorporate the necessary aspects to realize the "by design" precepts."[122] Most importantly, the auditable system must provide assurance management to fulfill accountability and transparency claims. The "assurance management" tool is a set of auditable claims, arguments and evidence created to support the claim that a defined system/service will satisfy a particular, given requirement. It provides four core functions: assurance project lifecycle, insurance case management, evidence management and insurance reporting. The platform must translate regulatory issues into operational work items and activities for the projects they manage. For instance, they must ensure that the GDPR requirement translates into backlog items, what specific threats their users

---

bringing the principles of Privacy and Data Protection by Design to practice. PDP4E will integrate privacy and data protection engineering functionalities into existent, mainstream software tools that are already in use by engineers, focusing on open-source tools that will be integrated in the Eclipse ecosystem. The approach will integrate methods proposed by the privacy engineering community (e.g., LINDDUN, ISO/IEC 27550 Privacy engineering), and the industry of software and system engineering tools (e.g., MUSE, PAPYRUS or OpenCert) using a model driven engineering approach. PDP4E will introduce privacy and data protection into software and system engineering disciplines (Risk Management, Requirements Engineering, Model-Driven Design, and Assurance), which drive the everyday activities of engineers. See online: https://cordis.europa.eu/project/id/787034 (April 30, 2022).

[120] Renata M de Carvalho et al., "Protecting Citizens' Personal Data and Privacy: Joint Effort from GDPR EU Cluster Research Projects" (2020) 1:4 SN COMPUT SCI 217. See online: <https://doi.org/10.1007/s42979-020-00218-8> (Visited at May 8, 2022).

[121] PDP4E Project: See online: https://www.pdp4e-project.eu/risk-management/ (Visited at May 8, 2022).

[122] PDP4E Project: See online: https://www.pdp4e-project.eu/risk-management/ (Visited at May 8, 2022).

face, what technical measures choose to meet user's rights, whether the rights to access or portability implies slit opening databases and revealing their witty algorithms.[123] From a management perspective for effective personal data auditing, as this study contends, a digitalized system must be used to ensure a systemic approach. However, it must be acknowledged that there are possible barriers to effective risk management, such as individual biases and cultural norms.[124] Although there are still strict rules adopted on how and what types of personal data could be processed, those procedures alone will not necessarily change a firm's decision regarding how to process personal data. Individuals still make those decisions, and their possible biases and surrounding environment may be more influential than any risk assessment reports.

3.2.2 Audit for Risk Management

In response to the risks associated with personal data, auditing serves not only as a verification process but also as a management tool for effectively protecting personal data. To control the risk of harm, there are four types of methods: preventive, corrective, directive, and detective. Due to the complexity of audit for personal data protection. This section viewed the audit system as a management control system.

3.2.2.1 Identify the Risk Associate with Personal Data

[Risk Identification] Based on the information that the data mapping stage has already collected, the data processor can obtain enough information for the purpose of identifying the risk of data subjects. An essential dilemma that needs to be conciliated is how to describe risk for the purpose of protecting personal data. Risk is based on the contrast between reality and possibility. As Andreas Kline noted:

> The prediction of possible hazards depends on the causal relation between the responsible party and the consequences. Because the consequences are unwelcome, risk always comprises a normative concept[125]

Theoretically, there are eight criteria that could be described as comprehensive risk classification: damage potential; probability of occurrence; incertitude; which defines the scope dispersion of potential damages; ubiquity, which defines the

---

[123] Martin & Kung, *supra* note 121 at 109.

[124] Michelle M Harner, "Barriers to Effective Risk Management Securities Regulation and the Global Economic Crisis: What Does the Future Hold" (2010) 40:4 Seton Hall Law Rev. 1323–1366 at 1326.

[125] A Klinke & O Renn, "Prometheus unbound - challenges of risk evaluation, risk classification, and risk management" (1999). See online: <https://www.osti.gov/etdeweb/biblio/20039357> at 14 (Visited at June 12, 2023).

temporal extension of potential damages; and irreversibility; which describes the impossible recovery of the situation before the damage occurred.[126] Based on the definition given by the ISO, risk is *"The effect of uncertainty on objectives."*[127] For the cybersecurity sector, in a risk-based approach, risk associated with IT resources is usually followed by the adoption of appropriate risk mitigation strategies.[128] Risk assessment usually serves as the first process in the risk management methodology. As noted by the National Institute of Standards and Technology (Fig. 3.4):

> Risk is a function of the likelihood of a given threat resource's exercising a particular potential vulnerability, and the resulting impact of that adverse event on the organization.[129]

Risk could be profiled based on the severity of its impact and likelihood of occurrence.[130] If the risk is high, then the data controller should implement measures to mitigate risk to a certain level at which risk can be accepted. The typical classification for the severity of risk was identified as high, medium and low. Thinking about personal data protection from a risk perspective is not new. The Security Safeguards Principle in the 2013 OECD Privacy Guidelines, dating from 1980, already refer to the need to protect personal data from the "risk" resulting from "unauthorized access, destruction, use, modification or disclosure of personal data."[131] As a matter of fact, the scope and effectiveness of personal data protection result from risk management decisions.[132] The core problem is how we can properly assess the risk associated with a different application context (Figs. 3.5 and 3.6). It has to encourage all stakeholders to minimize the risks flow in from situations over which they have some control and to maximize the risk incurred by stakeholders who choose to behave in ways that are harmful or unduly increase risks to legitimate users. For instance, the risk could be classified as follows:

> The inability of data subject to exercise rights; loss of control over the use of personal data; loss of confidentially. Inability to access services or opportunities; and other economic or social disadvantages.[133]

---

[126] *Ibid* at 1.

[127] Definition of Risk: See online: https://www.iso.org/standard/43170.html (Visited at January 24, 2022).

[128] Risk assessment, classification and mitigation See online: https://itsc.hkust.edu.hk/it-policies-guidelines/risk-assessment-classification-and-mitigation (Visited at January 24, 2022).

[129] Gary Stoneburner, Alice Goguen & Alexis Feringa, "Risk Management Guide for Information Technology Systems" 55. NIST, Special Publication 800–30. See online: https://www.hhs.gov/sites/default/files/ocr/privacy/hipaa/administrative/securityrule/nist800-30.pdf (Visited at January 24, 2022).

[130] Horák, Stupka & Husák, *supra* note 115 at 5.

[131] *Trade and Cross-Border Data Flows*, by Francesca Casalini & Javier López González, OECD iLibrary (Paris: OECD, 2019).

[132] Gratton, *supra* note 13.

[133] Vaclav Bartos et al., "Network entity characterization and attack prediction" (2019). See online: <https://arxiv.org/abs/1909.07694v1> at 2 (Visited at 4 Feb 2023).

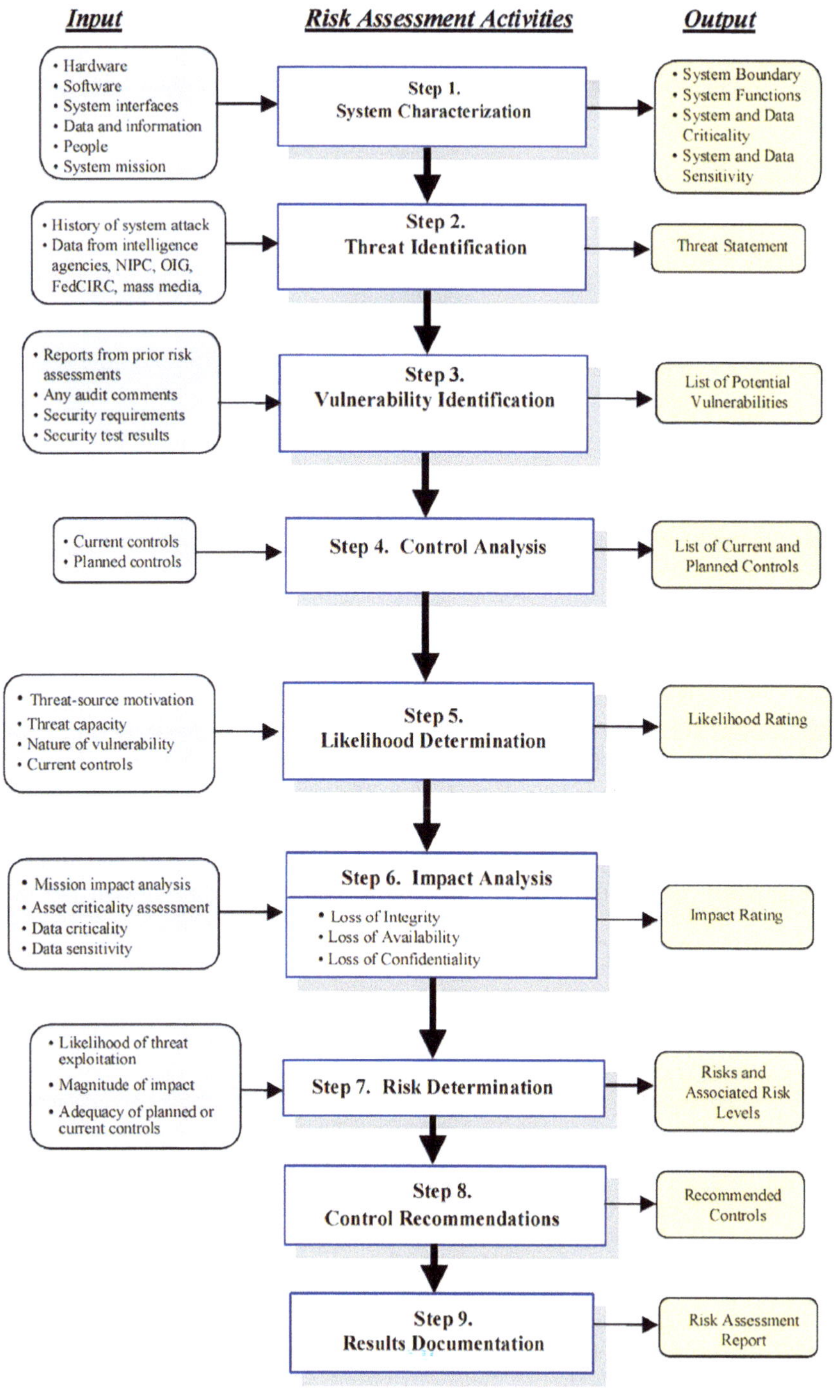

Fig. 3.4 Risk Assessment Methodology Flowchart Given by NIST (*Ibid* at 9)

Severity of impact	Serious harm	Low risk	High risk	High risk
	Some impact	Low risk	Medium risk	High risk
	Minimal impact	Low risk	Low risk	Low risk
		Improbable	Reasonably likely	More likely than not
		Likelihood of occurence		

Fig. 3.5 Example of the mechanism of risk evaluation

Fig. 3.6 Compliance Approach by PIA (Raphaël Gellert, "Understanding the notion of risk in the General Data Protection Regulation" (2018) 34:2 Computer Law & Security Review 279–288. See online: <https://www.sciencedirect.com/science/article/pii/S0267364917302698> at 283 (Visited at 25 March 2023))

The GDPR risk is always about "compliance risk" by using risk as a descriptive device.[134] In other words, the descriptive method entailed a twofold dimension of the risk analysis for risk compliance: risk assessment and risk management.[135] Risk assessment determines the level of risk, while risk management determines the circumstance under which to take the risk.[136] As Wright puts it: *"A PIA shall include a compliance check, but it should also go beyond."*[137] However, GDPR remained absolutely silent on how to perform the risk analysis exercise. As for the result, it left the gap between "risk to the data subjects rights" and "risk factor criteria." In other

[134] *Ibid* at 8. "It has used the constitutive elements of risk and risk analysis as a descriptive tool. Of particular importance is the mostly overlooked fact that risk is composed, not only of impacts (or consequences, also known as harms when they are negative), but also of events. This twofold composition of risk is used in order to analyze the notion of risk in the GDPR and to discuss the way in which a number of DPIA methodologies have appraised the said GDPR risk. More particularly, it has discussed two different approaches toward defining the GDPR risk. One keeps compliance issues out of the risk analysis process. Such an approach finds support in a number of DPIA methodologies and in some of the Art. 29 WP's documents and its 2017 DPIA Guidelines. The other approach, defended in the present contribution, argues instead that compliance should be directly integrated in the risk analysis process (as the "event") insofar as it is the only possible way to achieve a number of additional goals associated with the risk-based approach (protection on the ground and scalability of compliance obligations)."

[135] Michael Power: *Organized Uncertainty: Designing a World of Risk Management* (Oxford, New York: Oxford University Press, 2007) at 13.

[136] *Risk: Analysis, Perception and Management: Report of a Royal Society Study Group* (London: The Royal Society, 1992) at 13.

[137] David Wright, "The state of the art in privacy impact assessment" (2012) 28:1 Computer Law & Security Review 54–61.See online: <https://www.sciencedirect.com/science/article/pii/S026736491100183X> at 57 (Visited a 25 March, 2023).

words, it is muddled to build the connection between the event that targets the severity of the risk and the consequence (risk of harm). Additionally, it must be admitted that being effectively broad, taking into account a riot of harms to personal data and benefits, is a challenging task. Risk assessment can be subjective, which leads to an over simplification of the problem, often through quantification, disguising the full complexity of risks.[138] For instance, subjective harm associated with personal information could be classified into two stages: the harm resulting from collection and the harm resulting from disclosure.[139] "Collecting harm," could be interpreted as harm originating from surveillance or excessive collection.[140] "Disclosure harm," could be interpreted as psychological (harm directly linked to disclosure) and harm indirectly linked to information disclosure.[141] From an objective perspective, harm can be classified as financial harm, discrimination, or physical harm.[142] As ohm noted:

> Regulators need to shift away from thinking about regulation, privacy, and risk only from the point of view of the data, asking whether a particular field of data viewed in a vacuum is identifiable. Instead, regulators must ask a broader set of questions that helps reveal the risk of de-identification and threat of harm.[143]

Although privacy and personal data are two separate things, as this book previously discussed, there are also five indicators of the risk of privacy harm: Data-handing technologies; private versus public release; quantity; motive, as well as trust.[144] As a matter of fact, the harmful power of enormous platforms was recalled to reconsider regulatory tension, and most laws treated all regulated actors at the same time or assumed that "twice as large means twice as powerful and twice as harmful."[145] For personal data protection, the law failed to reflect how the power and harm of some increase more than a linear.[146] As ohm noted:

> A regulation that grows only at the rate of a company's user base or revenue cannot always serve its purposes given the way platform power grows. The time has come to ramp up regulation on platforms that grow to sizes once unimaginable in order to help stem the worst effect of the platform economy.[147]

---

[138] C Hood & D K C Jones, eds, *Accident And Design: Contemporary Debates On Risk Management* (London: Routledge, 1996) at 23.

[139] Eloïse Gratton, *Understanding Personal Information: Managing Privacy Risks* (Markham, Ont, 2013) at 248.

[140] *Ibid* at 252–286.

[141] *Ibid* at 284–286.

[142] *Ibid* at 362.

[143] Ohm, *supra* note 109 at 1742.

[144] Paul Ohm, "Broken promises of privacy: responsding to the surprising failure of anonymization." UCLA LAW REVIEW 77 at 1742.

[145] Ohm Paul, "Regulating At Scale" (2018) 546:2 Georget Law Technol Rev. at 546.

[146] *Ibid* at 546.

[147] *Ibid* at 556.

3.2.2.2 Control the Risk Associate with Personal Data

[Risk Management] The managerial logic concerned with values of audit ability and accountability for due process is that risk management may seek to align itself with enterprise values, but it is also central to a distinctive style of organizational discipline and accountability. As Power noted:

> a mass standard for organizational behavior, including codes of corporate governance, supports an increasingly 'self-reflective' and 'self-improving' organizational actor....Images organizations as capable of facing and managing uncertainties in a rational way, an image which will resurface in the various cases which follow.[148]

In other words, risk is, not only to be managed in the process for the sake of enhancing the capacity to avoid or mitigate harm, it is also to be done in the name of opportunity and enterprise as a notion of enterprise risk management that would increase the value of the organization.[149] From the management perspective, audits served as a regulatory tool to increase the capability of compliance, as well as manage capability. As a matter of fact, organizations encountered risk that could impact the outcome of protecting personal data. The desire overall strives for organizational objectives for risk management classified into three types: hazard risks, opportunity risks and control risks.[150] Hazard risk could be interpreted as organizations trying to avoid that which could cause the crash of the goals that the entities are trying to achieve. Opportunity risk could be risks that could enhance the aim of the organization. Control risk may create uncertainty about the outcomes.[151] Risk management necessitates providing a systemic approach for the purpose of evaluating, controlling and monitoring these three types of risk. Most risks associated with personal data could be classified as "hazard risk" and "control risk." Personal data risk events are always concerned with issues that could cause disruptions to the normal operations of organizations, as well as result in increased costs and poor publicity associated with disruptive events. It also has the features of business dependencies, including IT and other supporting services. In other words, these types of risk are highly sophisticated, where organizations may be unaware of the legal and contractual obligations that they face. In this case, it is necessary to inform organizations of their obligations in relation to the risk. As the level of sophistication develops, the organization will become aware of the need to comply with obligations and the general need for improved risk management. Once the organization is aware of obligations, there will be a need for the organization to reform in response to the hazard risk. As organizations respond to risk, they will seek to con-

---

[148] note 140 at 23.

[149] Pat O'Malley, "Uncertain subjects: risks, liberalism and contract" (2000) 29:4 Economy and Society. See online: <https://doi.org/10.1080/030851400501747 41> at 460 (Visited at July 23, 2023).

[150] Paul Hopkin, *Fundamentals of Risk Management: Understanding, Evaluating and Implementing Effective Risk Management*, fifth edition ed. (New York: Kogan Page, 2018) at 3.

[151] *Ibid.*

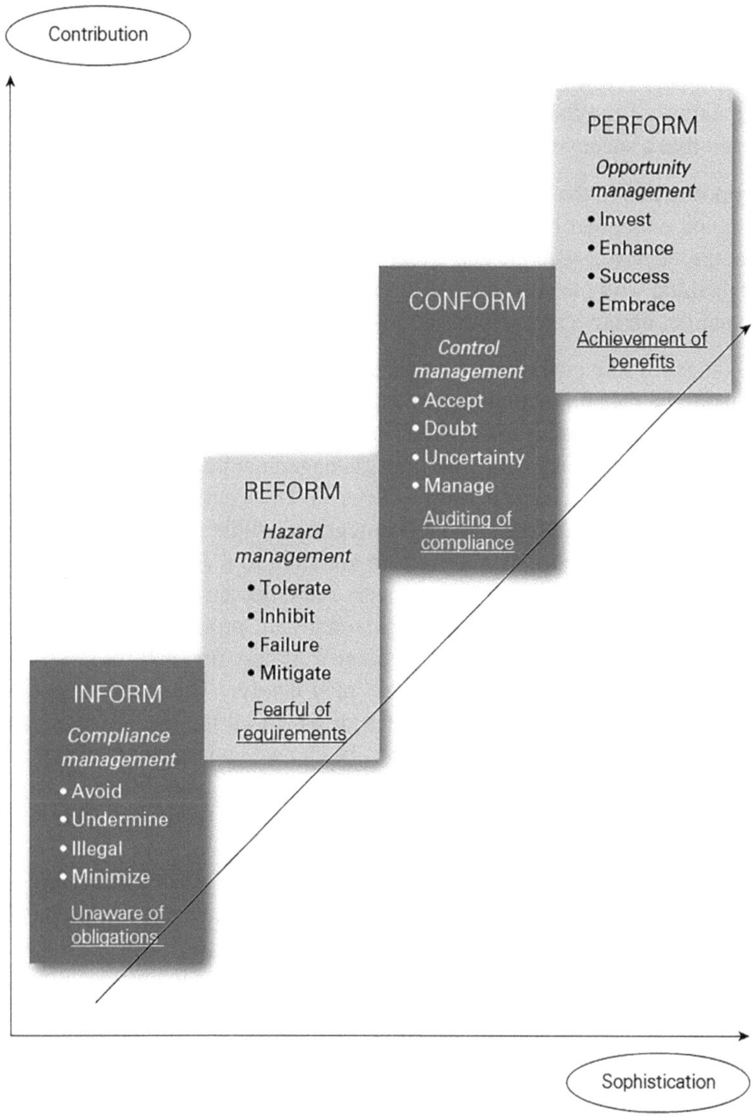

Fig. 3.7 Risk Management Sophistication

form to the appropriate risk control standards. After this stage, the realization may occur that there is benefit from the risk.[152] This is called "IRCPD," and refers to the process of inform, reform, conform, perform, and deform (Fig. 3.7).

[152] *Ibid* at 54.

The principle of risk management is to deliver value to an organization, and it involves a set of principles, such as ISO 31000.[153] Additionally, it is essential to distinguish between what the risk management initiative has been set up to achieve and the nature of the risk management framework that will be put into place. It is suggested that a successful risk management framework be "PACED" referred as:

(1) Proportionate to the level of risk within the organization.
(2) Aligned with other business activities.
(3) Comprehensive, systemic and structured.
(4) Embedded with business procedures and protocols.
(5) Dynamic, iterative and responsive to change.

In the context of risk management of personal data, the measures of privacy impact assessment, the data protection impact assessment and privacy by design or default, become part of risk management from both the personal data protection program management and personal data enterprise management perspectives.[154] These measures either addressed legal privacy offices or IT departments. Again, they just served as supporting roles that cannot be integrated within the engineering lifecycle. Consequently, privacy and data protection are alien to their work, but they seldom use these tools.[155] In other words, engineers must possess technological tools that allow for the systemic application of personal data protection principles for the purpose of compliance and risk management.[156] It may first call for risk classification based on the level of risk the context may involve. The management process needs to be based on a systemic approach in which all the data involved are covered.[157] The management structure needs to be cleared and executed, which involves many departments. Based on law and regulation, the organization shall propose related standardization, Standard Operation Protocols (hereafter HOP) and log record.[158]

[Control the risk] While risk management is the process of identifying, analyzing and treating the issue, risk control is part of risk treatment for the purpose of avoiding, accepting, mitigating, transferring or sharing each risk.[159] The wave of devolution of control downwards in organizations was due to changes in technologies and audit methodology, which rapidly enforced compliance with policies and

---

[153] ISO 31000 on risk management: See online: https://www.iso.org/iso-31000-risk-management.html (Visited at 22 March 2022).

[154] Martin & Kung, *supra* note 121.

[155] *Ibid* at 109.

[156] This idea has been widely recognized as the practical complement to PhD by the EDPS (European Data Protection Supervisor, which has created the internet Privacy Engineer Network-IPEN), ENISA (European Network and Information Security Agency). See: de Carvalho et al., "Protecting Citizens' Personal Data and Privacy", *supra* note 201 in Chap. 2.

[157] *Ibid.*

[158] Martin & Kung, *supra* note 121 at 110.

[159] Laura F Spira & Michael Page, "Risk management: The reinvention of internal control and the changing role of internal audit" (2003) 16:4 Account Audit Account J at 650.

procedures.[160] In 1992, it was the first time that "effectiveness" was added as an objective of internal control by COSO.[161] Additionally, the COSO framework identified risk management as one of five components of internal control, as Turnbull stated:

> A company's system of internal control plays a key role in the management of risks that are significant to the fulfillment of its business objectives.[162]

As COSO defined internal control as follows: effectiveness and efficacy of operations; reliability of reporting; and compliance with applicable laws and regulations,[163] where internal audits serve as part of the risk control function for companies to mitigate operational risk. Internal audits serve as an assurance and consulting role and emphasize adding value, as well as improving the effectiveness of risk management, control and governance processes.[164] The perception of risk will vary according to the characteristics of different risk regimes.[165] With the context of personal data protection, it required stakeholders of the organization to seek power by asserting how the risk should be managed. As Michel Page noted:

> Mapping the development of the conceptualization of risk against associated response and accountability mechanisms demonstrates that notions of risk are mutable and continue to evolve. The analysis offered by cultural theorists argues that the perception of appropriate regulation of risk will vary, according to the characteristics of specific risk regimes.[166]

For the hazard risk associated with personal data, the range of response available is often described as the 4 T: Tolerate, Treat, Transfer, and Terminate[167] (Fig. 3.8).

For risks that have low impact, the main response will be tolerated. Because risks have a high impact, the main response is to treat them. Personal data processed without consent or disclosed without appropriated protection may cause subjective or objective harm. For instance, data inappropriately disclosed associated with medical history may cause problems for data subjects with their social life. Financial information may cause data subjects to be involved in fraud. The effectiveness of operations relies on the efficient management of the corporation, reliability of the statement requiring the competence of officers and verification of external auditors. As this book has noted, the "theory of process" views control as an arrangement, while the "theory of relation" views control as a nexus. Therefore, the meaning of control implies the ability to manage the process to achieve the objective of the corporation. In other words, it is a more systemic sentiment to consider control as a

---

[160] *Ibid* at 647.

[161] *Internal Control, Integrated Framework: Executive Summary* (Committee of sponsoring Organizations of the Treadway Commission, 1992) at 9.

[162] Spira & Page, "Risk management", *supra* note 164 at 651.

[163] Note 166.

[164] Krogstad & Ridley, "Where we're going" (1999) Intern Audit at 31.

[165] Diane van Gils, Christian de Visscher & Gerrit Sarens, "Le dévelоppement de l'audit interne dans le secteur public belge" (2012) at 93.

[166] Spira & Page, "Risk management", *supra* note 164 at 656.

[167] Hopkin, *supra* note 155 at 176.

1	*Tolerate* Accept/retain	The exposure may be tolerable without any further action being taken. Even if it is not tolerable, the ability to do anything about some risks may be limited, or the cost of taking any action may be disproportionate to the potential benefit gained.
2	*Treat* Control/reduce	By far the greater number of risks will be addressed in this way. The purpose of treatment is that, whilst continuing within the organization with the activity giving rise to the risk, action (control) is taken to constrain the risk to an acceptable level.
3	*Transfer* Insurance/contract	For some risks the best response may be to transfer them. This might be done by conventional insurance, or it might be done by paying a third party to take the risk in another way. This option is particularly good for mitigating financial risks or risks to assets.
4	*Terminate* Avoid/eliminate	Some risks will only be treatable, or containable to acceptable levels, by terminating the activity. It should be noted that the option of termination of activities may be severely limited in government when compared to the private sector.

Fig. 3.8 Description of the 4 T of Hazard Response

process. Externally, control is more involved in market-based control mechanisms and external oversight mechanisms.[168] First, shareholders' interests can be an efficient source of power for manipulating corporate management. According to Fama's theory,[169] if a top manager engages in self-interested behavior that will diverge from the interest of the corporation, then the value of the corporation in the stock exchange market will decrease; under this circumstance, the corporation will likely change its management team. This phenomenon is called "the market for control."[170] In addition, due to the conflicts of interest between managers and shareholders,[171] external parties such as audit firms are always involved to deliver higher levels of accountability and reliability. In addition, the external control of a corporation is intertwined with the principles of corporate social responsibility.[172]

Taken cloud service as an example, it always needs cloud service providers provide enough choices for their customer to decide where the data shall be stored and how to control the process of data protection. Also, the cloud service providers need to have third-party certification to show their accountability. Also, it always encouraged to use encryption technology to give the control power for the data to their clients. Preventive controls are designed to limit the undesirable harm associated

[168] James P Walsh & James K Seward, "On the Efficiency of Internal and External Corporate Control Mechanisms" (1990) 15:3 Acad Manage Rev. at 442.

[169] Eugene F Fama, "Agency Problems and the Theory of the Firm" (1980) 88:2 J Polit Econ at 292.

[170] Walsh & Seward, *supra* note 173.

[171] *The Modern Corporation and Private Property*, 2 edition ed. (New Brunswick, N.J., U.S.A: Transaction Publishers, 1991).

[172] The International Institute for Sustainable Development (IISD) define corporate social responsibility (CSR) as promoting "business accountability to a wide range of stakeholders, besides shareholders and investors."

Fig. 3.9 Certification processes

with the data subject. The corrective controls are designed to limit the result of harm or the scope of harm that already existed. It usually provides the route of recourse for reimbursing the loss of harm. Directive controls are designed to ensure that a particular outcome can be achieved. It usually depends on a risk-management system that establishes a baseline for personal data protection. The detective controls are designed to identify occasions when undesirable outcomes have been realized. The effect is usually after the event of harm already occurred in the data subject, so they are only appropriated when it is possible to accept that loss or harm has already occurred.[173] The control step could be classified from "before the event" to "after the event." From this point of view, it is usually involved with assessment processes, such as the data protection assessment process and privacy impact assessment; Implementation processes, such as data protection by design; confirmation processes, such as personal data compliance audits; and certification processes (Fig. 3.9).

From national level, taken "Data Cross-border" context as an example, domestic-level information controls are today reinforced by norms promoted by states, which tries to shift governance away from multi-stakeholder or pluralist models toward more state-centric approaches. The concept of "Data Sovereignty" arose to protect the interest of data owners as well as the interest of each state. Both from internal control and external control perspective, it has a riot of advantages which been proposed by varieties of countries. With the evolvement data sovereignty, different types of control could be identified such as restriction the access to online resources or to control cyberspace domestically through laws, policies and digital infrastructure. From systemic point of view, different technical approaches could be identified in practical field referring as: "centralization approach," "regional approach," "decentralized approach." A European Strategy for Data stated that:

> In a society where individuals will generate ever- increasing amounts of data, the way in which the data are collected and used must place the interests of the individual first, in accordance with European values, fundamental rights and rules.[174]

Technological disruptions are mostly digital in nature, at the same time, a consistent technical risk we faced is that unaccountable algorithms "have taken center stage and now are used to make decisions for us, about us, or with us." It also generates fear that algorithms might allow those who use such techniques to wield power in ways society prohibits or should disfavor, but which society would not be able to detect. Domestic-level information controls are today reinforced by norms promoted by states try to shift governance away from multi-stakeholder or pluralist models toward more state-centric approaches. For nationals to regain the power of states in general and for the

---

[173] Hopkin, *supra* note 155 at 187.

[174] A European Strategy for data: See online: A European Strategy for data | Shaping Europe's digital future (europa.eu) (Visited at 5 April 5, 2023).

effective control of authoritarian states, concept "data sovereignty" is proposed associated with explosive growth of information technology. To give a general idea of data sovereignty, it could be defined as: "Managing information in a way that is consistent with laws, practices and customs of the national state in which it is located." Terms such as 'data sovereignty' are used to make digital information subject to the laws of the country in which such data is shared, processed and stored. Within different national privacy laws, for recognizing variability, "data sovereignty" could also be interpreted as "Information that would be illegal to provide in one location might be perfectly legal to disclose in other nations." From internal audit perspective, it has to have the ability to detect the "cross-border" activities; also, it required the abilities to identify what data has been provided overseas. It also required the ability to provide feasible solutions to control the cross-border activities.[175] For the concept of "to render an account," there are three levels should be recognized. First, it refers as the liability of the responsible person to report its actions on their own. Second, it means the "account" which gave to the related party could be adapted with the requirement of the account. Third, it means that if the responsible person failed to fulfill the requirement of the audience, sanctions will imply.

[Management Control System] As this book noted, it is not simply the case that the complexity of technological development cannot be controlled. Personal data is a broad concept, where almost every regulation about forming personal data stated the definition of personal data broadly as "identifiable." From another perspective, personal data could be a very detailed concept because it seems to be a context-based description, and where and how to regulate it seems to be a case-by-case problem. Nevertheless, as Fukuyama conceded, "no regulation regime is ever fully leakproof, and if one selects a sufficiently long timeframe, most technologies end up being developed eventually. However, this misses the point of social regulation in that no law is ever fully enforced. Every country makes murder a crime and attaches severe penalties to homicide, and yet murders occur nonetheless. The fact that they do have never been a reason for giving up on law or on attempts to enforce it."[176] In other words, to examine the effectiveness of personal data audits is to ask whether audit system intervention is effective. It is preferable to ask about the regulatory effectiveness in terms of a spectrum of effectiveness, rather than best or nothing. From an internal perspective, the effectiveness of audits could be influenced by several factors, such as audit scope, management response and professional judgment.[177] As this book noted, management played a large role in organizational governance and was more effective in applying regulations. For the internal audit of personal data, the goal of the audit has been extended to include, not only verifying

---

[175] *Ibid.*

[176] Carl Packman, "Our Posthuman Future: Consequences of the Biotechnology Revolution, by Francis Fukuyama. London: Profile Books, 2003." (2009) 21:2 Rethinking Marxism 317–323. See online: <https://doi.org/10.1080/08935690902940270> at 320 (Visited at 6 May 2023).

[177] Shamki Dhiaa, "Factors Influence Internal Audit Effectiveness" (2017) 10 International Journal of Business and Management at 143.

personal data compliance, but also assisting organizations in better accomplishing objectives of compliance by:

> Fetching a systemic and disciplined approach to improve and evaluate the control, risk management and the governance processes effectiveness.[178]

The definition of "management control" was first defined by Anthony as "the process by which managers ensure that resources are obtained and used effectively and efficiently in the accomplishment of the organization's objectives."[179] This definition did not entail the function of monitoring and operational control, so the definition of the Management Control System expanded this idea as "processes for influencing behavior."[180] As this book noted, in addition to the function of verification, personal data audits also serve as a management system for compliance purposes. From this point of view, the audit system could also be viewed as a management control system (hereafter MCS). Formal controls included rules, standard operating procedures and budgeting systems, which are usually visible components that are easy to observe. It could be classified as feedforward control (ex-anti control), administrative controls (standard operating procedures and rules), personnel controls (human resource management policies) and behavioral controls (the ongoing monitoring of activities and decisions).[181] Informal controls referred to as not consciously designed included the unwritten policies of the organization and the culture of the organization. From an organizational perspective, audit systems are preferred to focus on reducing uncertainty and emphasizing personal data problem solving. For compliance purposes, based on contingency studies reviewed by many researchers, the effectiveness of audit systems calls for assessing the different elements and how different elements corporate with each other.[182] These key variables and elements included "internal personal data process context, external personal data process context, personal data process management, management tools, organization structure, personal data protection strategy, etc."[183] While there are always critical evaluations, Christophe Lazaro noted: "control over personal data? True

[178] *Ibid* at 144.

[179] Robert N Anthony, *Planning and control systems; a framework for analysis* (Boston: Division of Research, Graduate School of Business Administration, Harvard University, 1965) at 13

[180] Eric G Flamholtz, T K Das & Anne S Tsui, "Toward an integrative framework of organizational control" (1985) 10:1 Accounting, Organizations and Society 35–50. See online: <https://www.sciencedirect.com/science/article/pii/0361368285900303> at 36 (Visited at 12 September, 2023).

[181] Kim Langfield-Smith, "Management control systems and strategy: A critical review" (1997) 22:2 Accounting, Organizations and Society 207–232.See online: <https://www.sciencedirect.com/science/article/pii/S0361368295000402> at 208 (Visited at 13 September, 2023).

[182] *Ibid* at 38.

[183] Robert H Chenhall, "Management control systems design within its organizational context: findings from contingency-based research and directions for the future" (2003) 28:2 Accounting, Organizations and Society 127–168. See online: <https://www.sciencedirect.com/science/article/pii/S0361368201000277> at 157 (Visited at 19 March, 2023).

remedy or fairy tale? "[184] Whereas the notion of control became the compass to manifest the effectiveness of personal data management. As a matter of fact, control has often been advocated as the key solution to the problems raised by personal data protection.[185] The notion of control became omnipresence in the regulation of personal data protection. From the perspective of the management of audit systems for personal data protection, the challenge of explaining the notion of control has two points of view. The first is a systemic explanation related to the notion of surveillance, which can be exercised by organizations to monitor and regulate the processing of personal data.[186] The second meaning of control comes from the right of the data subject, which means that individuals have the right to control their personal information. In other words, control serves as an agency for self-determination over personal information.[187] It entails the role of choice and individual self-determination over different values. Additionally, it supported the passive rights of data subjects, such as nondisclosure and data minimization. From a technical point of view, the notion of control from an audit point of view can be classified into two main criteria: the subject of control, which means who is in charge of processing personal data, and the object of control, which means how the personal data process could be in charge.[188] From the management perspective, audits served as management agents in the abstract data lifecycle model (hereafter ADLM) to ensure that compliance covered the data processing lifecycle.[189] From a contingency-based approach, the ADLM would be a specified context where personal data compliance could be proven under a specific context.[190] Data modelers are involved in the initial stage and establish the context for developing logical and physical prototypes for the application. Data subjects are the origination where personal data were collected. Data controllers are actors who specify the purpose for processing personal data. Data processors are the agents that process personal data under the direction of the data processor. Third parties are actors other than data subjects[191] (Fig. 3.10).

---

[184] *Control over Personal Data: True Remedy or Fairy Tale?*, SSRN Scholarly Paper, by Christophe Lazaro & Daniel Le Métayer, papers.ssrn.com, SSRN Scholarly Paper ID 2689223 (Rochester, NY: Social Science Research Network, 2015).

[185] Scott Peppet, "Unraveling Privacy: The Personal Prospectus and the Threat of a Full-Disclosure Future" (2011) Northwestern University Law Review.See online: <https://scholar.law.colorado.edu/articles/177> at 14 (Visited at 19 March, 2023).

[186] The idea of control societies originated from G. Deleuze idea: Johnson & Regan, *supra* note 102 in Chap. 1 at 613.

[187] Lazaro & Le Métayer, *supra* note 189 at 5.

[188] *Ibid* at 21.

[189] Ernest Teniente & Matthias Weidlich, *Business Process Management Workshops: BPM 2017 International Workshops, Barcelona, Spain, September 10–11, 2017, Revised Papers* (Springer, 2018) at 685.

[190] Chenhall, "Management control systems design within its organizational context", *supra* note 188 at 157. Contingency-based research has approached the study of MCS assuming that managers act with an intent to adapt their organizations to changes incontingencies in order to attain fit and enhanced performance.

[191] Teniente & Weidlich, *supra* note 194 at 687.

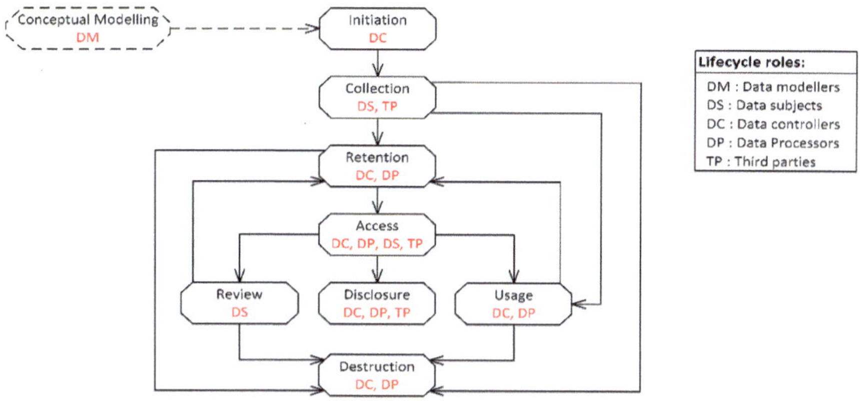

Fig. 3.10 The Abstract Personal Data Lifecycle (APDL) Model (*By Andrew Simpson, University of Oxford*)

In other words, PbD and PIAs are mandated within the regulation of the GDPR so that the audit system has to be compatible with such a process and in every stage. It was well understood that personal data without effective data management models may lead to data protection violations.[192] As Majed Alshammari noted:

> Each stage is an abstraction of a set of logically related data-processing activities. This classification is based on ……The nature and order of processing activities, and the role type of involved actors and their possible responsibilities.[193]

From an audit point of view, the input and output of the ADLM must be properly removed for clear verification (Table 3.3). Practically, big tech firms are not valuing personal data; rather, data subjects and data subject metrics are valued through tracking and recording of data subject engagement. As a result, the whole personal data lifecycle must be covered by an audit process. All data protection threats must be considered in the state-of-audit process to protect data subjects in a meaningful way. The audit system served as a personal data management system (hereafterPDMS) to cover the complete data lifecycle and list data protection threats that must be circumvented from a management perspective to achieve "cover" as a result.[194] However, the

---

[192] Sandra Senft & Frederick Gallegos, *Information Technology Control and Audit*, 3d ed. (New York: Auerbach Publications, 2008) at 13.

[193] Teniente & Weidlich, *supra* note 194 at 685.

[194] Nicolas Anciaux et al., "Personal Data Management Systems: The security and functionality standpoint" (2019) 80 Information Systems 13–35.

See online: <https://www.sciencedirect.com/science/article/pii/S0306437918304022> at 17 (Visited at 25 March, 2023).

Also see Kean Birch, DT Cochrane & Callum Ward, "Data as asset? The measurement, governance, and valuation of digital personal data by Big Tech" (2021) 8:1 Big Data & Society 20,539,517,211,017,308. See online: <https://doi.org/10.1177/20539517211017308> at 12 (Visited at 25 March, 2023).

Table 3.3 Stages, Associated Activities and Dependency of the APDL Model (*Ibid* at 688)

#	Stage	Activities	Input	Output
0	Conceptual Modelling	Specification, Conceptualization, Representation	Domain knowledge	A conceptual model
1	Initiation	Specification	A conceptual model, Privacy policies and procedures	A processing plan, A privacy notice
2	Collection	Specification, Collection or Acquisition	A processing plan, A set of data values	A set of collected data values
3	Retention	Specification, Storage, Archiving, Backup	A processing plan, A set of collected data values	A set of stored data values
4	Access	Specification, Retrieval	A processing plan, A set of data items	A set of retrieved data values
5	Review	Review, Rectification	A processing plan, A set of retrieved data values	A set of rectified data values
6	Usage	Specification, Manipulation, Presentation, Use	A processing plan, A set of retrieved data values	A set of manipulated data values
7	Disclosure	Preparation, Dissemination or Transmission or Make available	A processing plan, A set of retrieved data values	A set of disclosed data values
8	Destruction	Erasure or Disposal or Destruction or Anonymisation	A processing plan, Retention policies, Destruction policies, A set of data values	A set of destroyed data values

technical obstacle it may encounter is that, based on different stages, different solutions are called to tackle different stages of the lifecycle of the personal data in the audit process. Consider the cloud-based context as an example, where most existing solutions are directly inherited from those considered in the context of the corporate cloud. A typically distributed computation infrastructure strongly differs from a fully decentralized infrastructure of PDMS (ownership, legal agreements deployed hardware and software, etc.). As a result, PDMS must be integrated by default security measures to overcome the inherent weaknesses of PDMS (Fig. 3.11).

Another perspective is that unifying these solutions does not lead to a secure personal cloud architecture. As Nicolas noted:

> Building union of the proposals would undeniably face irreconcilable architectural choices. Indeed, it is observed that the existing personal data cloud solution covers a rather wide spectrum of architectural choices, but this leads to different, and sometimes contradictory, trust models and security measures. More precisely, each class of solutions is a specific subset of functionalities while considering a specific threat model.[195]

[195] *Ibid* at 19.

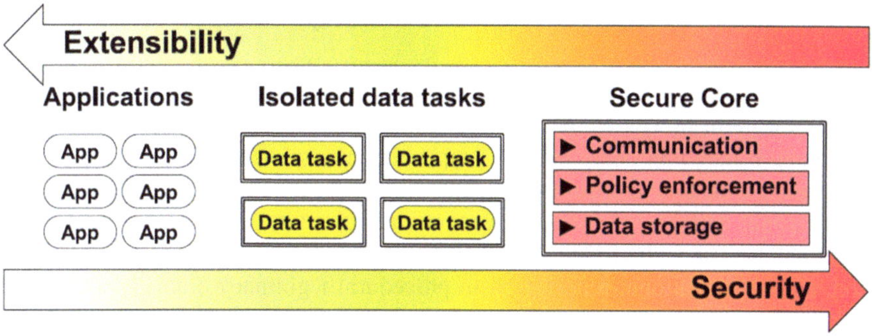

Fig. 3.11 PDMS Security Architecture (Ibid at 17)

In conclusion, effective risk management extends beyond mere mitigation of harm; it encapsulates the ethos of opportunity and enterprise, aligning with organizational values while fostering a culture of accountability and self-improvement. As organizations navigate the complex landscape of risk, particularly in the realm of personal data protection, it becomes imperative to adopt a sophisticated approach that encompasses hazard, opportunity, and control risks. This necessitates a systemic framework, such as the PACED principles, tailored to the organization's risk profile and business activities. Furthermore, the evolution of risk control, as evidenced by frameworks like COSO, underscores the importance of internal audits in enhancing operational effectiveness and ensuring compliance. From a broader perspective, the concept of "data sovereignty" emerges as a critical aspect, shaping governance models and reinforcing national-level information controls. In an era dominated by technological disruptions and concerns over algorithmic accountability, the notion of rendering an account becomes paramount, encompassing the obligation to report actions, adapt accountability to stakeholders' requirements, and face sanctions for non-compliance. Thus, by embracing a holistic approach to risk management and control, organizations can navigate uncertainties, protect personal data, and uphold integrity in an ever-evolving landscape of risks and opportunities.

3.3 Interpret Audit from Function of Legal Control

For this part, this book will discuss the control function of audit from legal perspective. For procedural arrangement, this part will exam the legal ground for conduct compliance audit and internal & external procedural arrangement for legal control. For substantial part, this book will exam the legitimacy of the audit work, mainly refers to validity of audit evidence and to the duty of care of auditors.

3.3.1 Legal Control from Procedure Perspective

The complex nature of business interactions within large enterprises poses challenges for audit processes, particularly in verifying data processing and personal information handling compliance. Compliance audits, mandated by national laws and regulations, aim to ensure alignment with legal requirements. However, ensuring personal data compliance involves intricate processes, often spanning various business operations. Internally, audit structures entail data mapping, risk identification, and organizational redesign, with procedural legitimacy crucially addressing stakeholders' rights. External audits serve as vital oversight mechanisms, particularly for personal data protection, requiring adherence to legal frameworks and external regulatory requirements. The effectiveness of external controls is paramount, necessitating clear, technology-neutral requirements and transparency from audit bodies. Additionally, the independence and powers of external audit authorities play a crucial role in shaping audit effectiveness and ensuring regulatory compliance. Ultimately, the evolving landscape of personal data protection regulation underscores the importance of robust audit mechanisms in safeguarding individuals' rights and organizational control.

3.3.1.1 Internal Procedure Arrangement

[Complex of audit] A large enterprise's business is complex, and there are many interactions between businesses, including internal and external, whether these business systems have enough evidence to support the restoration of data processing, and whether there is enough evidence to prove that the personal information collected is based on different context. So the current audit work of enterprises is a state of insufficient evidence, complex audit work and large audit investment. Compliance audit generally refers to a kind of supervision activities conducted by auditing institutions and auditors according to national laws, regulations and financial systems to determine whether the production and management activities of the audited entity and its related information are in compliance. As early as 1992, the Audit Office mentioned "compliance audit" in its "Opinions on Compliance Audit of Loans to Financial Institutions."[196] Later, the General Office of the Audit Office issued the "Chinese-English Audit Glossary 218" on January 18, 2004, which standardized the English translation of audit as "compliance audit."[197] From the perspective of personal information compliance work, compliance audit is a complex work, especially the compliance audit of personal delicate handling process needs to involve almost all business processes within the enterprise. This is a huge conflict

[196] Chunhui Wang, Eight highlights of the Draft Law on the Protection of Personal Information (Second Review Draft). See online: https://www.cnii.com.cn/gxxww/rmydb/202106/t20210604_283543.html (December 19, 2022).

[197] Ibid.

with the need for auditing, and how to move from the current state of disorder and inadequacy to a state of ready and continuous auditing is the difficulty of the current personal information protection compliance auditing work. The internal audit structure could be identified as data mapping, risk identification, organizational redesign and the internal control stage. Different stages constitute the internal audit process, and the process goes toward documentation, procedural arrangement and professional judgment.

[Internal Arrangement] Since audit process is usually viewed as roughly sequential in nature, differences in the extent and/or nature of evidence collected would result in different audit process planning. Broadly speaking, regulators are liable to be called to account in two fundamental directions; the first is about whether the objective or purpose associated with the regulatory target is appropriated. The second is about whether the regulators are setting about their regulatory objectives in the right kind of way.[198] However, for an organization to confirm their objectives of internal personal data auditing through procedural arrangement is complicated. In other words, in addition to the substantive position they need to justify, such as electronic records, the processes that they have employed to set the standards are questionable. When discussing procedural legitimacy, this book noted that proceduralism is As a matter of fact a congregation of the rights of different stakeholders. As Denis Galligan noted:

> Legitimacy is gained, not so much by the content of the outcomes, but from the fact that those who decide are elected by the people.[199]

Before external auditors claim that the standard set for internal audit is appropriate, internal auditors must justify that they are doing the right thing related to the commitment of different stakeholders. As this book noted, there are several stakeholders who could be identified for internal audits for personal data protection. Data subjects, which are referred to as data owners, have the right to execute their rights under the contract (privacy policy) between the data processor and data owner and under the oversight of data protection laws give data subjects the right to be forgotten.[200] Data controllers and data processors have the right to process the data of data subjects with the limitations of the regulations of data processing. Regulators (including self-regulators) have the right to verify whether data controllers and data processors protect the rights of data subjects and fulfill their obligations of processing personal data.

For internal audits for personal data protection, the internal auditors must ensure that the audit process arrangement can be signed up by different stakeholders inside the organization under the requirement of external auditors. "Signed up" does not mean that different stakeholders agree upon their different interests; it entailed that

---

[198] Brownsword, *supra* note 101 in Chap. 1 at 9.

[199] Denis Galligan, 'Citizens' Rights and Participation in the Regulation of Biotechnology' in Francesco Francioni (ed) *Biotechnologies and International Human Rights* (Oxford: Hart, 2007) at 335.

[200] Article 17 of GDPR: right to be erasure.

the procedure guaranteed the right and obligation of each subject could be fulfilled upon the requirement of data protection laws and standards. In other words, sometimes the tension between the interests of organizations and the rights of stakeholders exists with which procedural arrangement has to deal. That is the reason why the audit process became increasingly structured, which reflected the increasing demand for legitimate and transparent forms of standardized practice for management control purposes. On the other hand, the process must continually adjust to balance formal, defendable, economic and manageable structures for the audit process with the autonomy of auditor judgment.[201] However, these structures may not be congenial for the structure of the audit process within internal audits for compliance purposes. Thirty years ago, Dirsmith and Haskins suggested that the structure-judgment distinction is a more fundamental one between

> Mechanism which named an aspiration for an integrative formal approach to audit which holds out the promise of an algorithmic knowledge base that the "organism" assumed that the whole is always greater than the parts, and that the specificity of knowledge places limits on the mechanistic word view.[202]

Personal data protection audits, not only focus on compliance, monitoring, or examining the performance of the organization for personal data protection, but also on improving the capability of corporate governance on personal data, which is linked to risk management and helps managers understand how to prevent data breach accidents. As Hermanson and Rittenberg noted:

> Governance processes deal with the procedures utilized by the representatives of the organization's stakeholders to provide oversight of risk and control processes administered by management. The monitoring of organizational risks and the assurance that controls adequately mitigate these risks both contribute directly to the achievement of organizational goals and the preservation of organizational value. Those performing governance activities are accountable to the organization's stakeholders for effective stewardship.[203]

On the one hand, the external audit, which reflected on the legal basis for personal data, could not be a business that differed from the financial audit.[204] Because "Coast" and "Quality" could be a suppressed dilemma which pushed in different directions. Auditors are forced to resolve this dilemma through time budgeting and reporting processes that cannot be accepted for compliance purposes. The current governance environment increasingly emphasizes the relationship between internal

---

[201] Michael K Power, "Auditing and the production of legitimacy" (2003) 28:4 Accounting, Organizations and Society. See online: <https://www.sciencedirect.com/science/article/pii/S0361368201000472> at 382 (Visited at 23 Feburary, 2023).

[202] *Ibid* at 385.

[203] Hany Elbardan & Ahmed O Kholeif, *Enterprise Resource Planning, Corporate Governance and Internal Auditing: An Institutional Perspective* (Springer, 2017) at 21.

[204] Power, *supra* note 211 at 382. Auditing has always been a business. However, during the 1980s and 1990s the audit approaches of the large firms changed and evolved as the economics of auditing became more sensitive.

and external auditors.[205] The gap between external and internal audits is As a matter of fact another challenge that personal data audits must address. The procedure arrangement included the standardization transfer from external audit to internal audit, internal audit sourcing arrangements, external regulatory requirements, internal auditor competencies and the size of the internal audit team. The external body must deal with objectivity, technical competence, professional care and communication when deciding whether the process between external and internal is appropriate.[206] As a team-based activity comprising ongoing interactions, auditing is a comprehensive practice with important processual components.[207] Critical about the ritualistic of auditing is to argue that:

> It is a collective activity to bring order to a misinterpreted world; it must also be understood as an activity with significance beyond the manifest rational function attributed to it in official documents.[208]

For personal data protection, the credibility of the compliance statement is both essential for internal and external bodies. Substantive compliance and normative compliance are both essential for personal data protection audits. As Claus Holm noted:

> Organizations seek to establish congruence between the social values associated with or implied by their activities and the norms of acceptable behavior in the larger social system in which they are a part. Insofar as these two value systems are congruent, we can speak of organizational legitimacy. When an actual or potential disparity exists between the two value systems, there will exist a threat to organizational legitimacy.[209]

In practice, for instance, in Poland, 119 offices have been provided external audits of the GDPR implementation, and 58 offices have been provided external inspections of the GDPR implementation.[210] While the reality is that the highest difficulties in Polish offices were "internal/external audits, measurability and control of processes."[211] Again, the procedural arrangement, including data mapping, audit

---

[205] Andrew Ellul, "The Role of Risk Management in Corporate Governance" (2015) 7:1 Annual Review of Financial Economics 279–299. See online: <https://doi.org/10.1146/annurev-financial-111414-125820> at 731 (Visited at 11 June, 2023).

[206] Elbardan & Kholeif, *supra* note 213 at 66.

[207] Charles W Bame-Aldred et al., "A Summary of Research on External Auditor Reliance on the Internal Audit Function" (2012) 32:Supplement Auditing: A Journal of Practice & Theory 251–286. See online: <https://doi.org/10.2308/ajpt-50342> at 262 (Visited at 11 June, 2023).

[208] Power, *supra* note 211 at 385.

[209] Claus Holm & Mahbub Zaman, "Regulating audit quality: Restoring trust and legitimacy" (2012) 36:1 Accounting Forum (Restructuring, reform and regulation: Transformation possibilities after the crisis). See online: <https://www.sciencedirect.com/science/article/pii/S015599821100069X> at 58 (Visited at 12 June, 2023).

[210] Dominika Lisiak-Felicka, Maciej Szmit & Jolanta Vaiciuniene, "The General Data Protection Regulation 3 Years After Implementation: A Comparison between Local Government Administration in Poland and the Republic of Lithuania" (2022) XXV:1 European Research Studies Journal 382–394. See online: <https://ersj.eu> at 390 (Visited at 12 June, 2023).

[211] *Ibid.*

scope confirmation, purpose determination, lawful basis, storage period, and compliance statement is highly context-based. The control objective included the verification and validation process of processing personal data; the identification of responsibilities; transparency; accountability; security; etc. All these procedures applied to the set of audit procedures, methods and techniques. In the specific context of the audit, the audit objective pursued is to determine the degree of compliance of audit processing with regard to the required auditing criteria or requirements, which may arise from regulatory provisions, internal policies and rules of the data controller, and other plans defined within the organization. The requirements are dispatched to control objectives, which constitutes a statement of goals pursued by the implementation of different controls. As noted by the relevant ISO, the intention of relevant control procedures is to modify risk, such as preventive, detective or corrective.[212] As a matter of fact, there are several principles and methods regarding audit procedures applicable reference could be acquired. For instance, the general principles in ISO 19011,[213] the most specific aspects of software development in standards such as ISO//IEC 15504 SPICE,[214] methodologies such as METRICAV3,[215] standards such as CMMI or other reference frameworks such as COBIT and SOGP.[216] From the point of view of protecting personal data, it is important to highlight that the audit approach always comes from the perspective of using emerging technologies whose risks to the rights and freedoms of data subjects will have to be assessed. As Article 24 of the GDPR set forth, the obligation to "implement appropriate technical and organizational measures to ensure and to be able to demonstrate that processing is performed in accordance with this regulation."[217]

3.3.1.2 External Procedure Arrangement

[Legitimacy of Audit] The current revolution in technology has led to the concern that the process of personal data is not always ethically or legally acceptable. The goal of the regulatory system is to find and correct these undesirable situations and has also served as a starting point for reconsidering legitimacy, not only to the regulatory target, but also to the regulation itself. It helps in understanding regulatory

---

212 ISO 27000: Available at: https://www.27000.org/ (Visited at June 30, 2022).

213 Guidelines for auditing management systems ISO 19011;2018 See online: https://www.iso.org/standard/70017.html (Visited at June 30, 2022).

214 ISO/IEC 15504–1:2004 Information technology- process assessment- Part 1: Concepts and vocabulary. See online: https://www.iso.org/standard/38932.html (Visited at June 30, 2022).

215 Metrica V3 See online: https://administracionelectronica.gob.es/pae_Home/pae_Documentacion/pae_Metodolog/pae_Metrica_v3.html?idioma=en (Visited at June 30, 2022) [Translated].

216 The capability maturity model integration, Control objectives for information and related technologies (COBIT), Standard of good practice for information security 2020. See online: https://www.isaca.org/resources/cobit (Visited at June 30, 2022).

217 Article 24 of GDPR.

positions and practices. As mentioned, audits serve as regulatory function for protecting personal data and can be interpreted as "regulatory system" in which different components interact with each other. The audit is not a naturally coordinated series of technical steps; it is a social enterprise relying on deeply embedded perspectives.[218] However, the scandal of large audit firms in the financial sector disappointed and questioned the outcome of the audit, even the logic of the audit system. As Power, Carpenter and Dirsmith noted, audits within the accounting field are far from being self-evident, and the legitimacy of audits is being challenged.[219] Noted by Power as:

> The fact is that official guidance plays little role in everyday audit work, but rather it legitimizes work in the event of dispute with clients.[220]

For personal data protection audit, it is essential to check the legitimacy of such audit system as the start point. Taken China compliance audit of personal data protection as an example, it stated as Article 1 of attachment for the announcement as:

> This content is formulated in accordance with the "Personal Information Protection Law of the People's Republic of China" and other laws, administrative regulations and national standards, and provides reference for conducting personal information protection compliance audits.[221]

By which means it stated the legitimacy and legal ground for conduct compliance audit in according with relevant laws and regulations. Along with the attachment, the Article 1 of the announcement also indicated the purpose of compliance audit as:

> Guide and standardize personal information protection compliance audit activities, improve the compliance level of personal information processing activities, and protect personal information rights and interests, these measures are formulated in accordance with the 'Personal Information Protection Law of the People's Republic of China', administrative regulations, and relevant state regulations[222]

Another example, in the realm of personal data protection of United Kingdom, the effective legislation referred as Data Protection Act 2018 (hereafter DPA), which primarily addresses "data protection audits" in Articles 129 and Article 146.[223]

---

[218] Mark W Dirsmith & Mark E Haskins, "Inherent risk assessment and audit firm technology: A contrast in world theories" (1991) 16:1 Accounting, Organizations and Society 61–90. See online: <https://www.sciencedirect.com/science/article/pii/036136829190033B> at 64 (Visited at 10 June, 2023).

[219] Brian Carpenter & Mark Dirsmith, "Sampling and the abstraction of knowledge in the auditing profession: An extended institutional theory perspective" (1993) 18:1 Accounting, Organizations and Society 41–63. See online: <https://www.sciencedirect.com/science/article/pii/036136829390024Z> at 44 (Visited at 11 June, 2023).

[220] Power, *supra* note 211 at 383.

[221] Radical 1 of GDPR

[222] Article 1 of Announcement of compliance audit of personal data protection. See online: http://www.cac.gov.cn/2023-08/03/c_1692628348448092.htm (Visited at 5 August, 2023).

[223] An overview of the Data Protection Act 2018, Information Commissioner's Office, See online: https://ico.org.uk/media/2614158/ico-introduction-to-the-data-protection-bill.pdf at 26 (Visited at 15 February 15, 2024).

Article 129 outlines the "voluntary audit", wherein the commissioner possesses the authority to conduct assessments, contingent upon obtaining the consent of the controller or processor, to ascertain whether they adhere to best practices in personal data processing.[224] The assessment results should be communicated to the data controller or processor. Article 146 delineates the "mandatory audit" mechanism, wherein the commissioner may, through written notice (assessment notice), require the controller or processor to permit an assessment to determine their compliance with data protection regulations.[225] The ICO notes that, among the two aforementioned audit methods, they primarily conduct voluntary audits based on the provisions of Article 129 of the Data Protection Act. Audit activities are principally managed by ICO's Assurance Department.

From legal perspective of personal data, the definition of "control" can be interpreted from the perspectives of the owners and processors of personal data.[226] Regulators have endeavored to increase individual control over personal data as one of the most crucial solutions for tackling emergent technologies. Control over personal data is often conceived as "the claim of individuals to determine for themselves when, how, and to what extent data about them are communicated to others."[227] "Data protection as a control" theory, which was proposed by A. Westin, has been endorsed by a broad range of scholars.[228] It emphasizes the discretion of individuals over their data. For instance, the protection of personal data, stated in the EU Charter of Fundamental Rights, is defined as follows: "Everyone has the right to the protection of personal data concerning him or her. Such data must be processed fairly for specified purposes and on the basis of the consent of the person concerned or some other legitimate basis laid down by law. Everyone has the right to access data that have been collected concerning him or her and the right to have it rectified."[229] In other words, the right to process personal data is established on the basis of individual consent or consent by law, while the right to process personal data, constrained by the right to the protection of personal data, is established on the basis of the user's right to access and rectify these data as well as set a rule with a legitimate and specific purpose. In this regard, "control" can be described as an information management process through self-management. Also, it is subject to the idea of "privacy as an agency," which refers to "self-determination over information about oneself and the self-management of privacy."[230] Personal data self-

---

[224] Article 129 of DPA.

[225] Article 146 of DPA.

[226] Fuchs, *supra* note 80. In the field of privacy and data protection, the challenge of grasping the notion of control is reinforced by the fact that two totally different meanings are frequently ascribed to the concept of control.

[227] Westin, *supra* note 81. Also see: Lazaro & Métayer, "The control over personal data", *supra* note 81.

[228] Westin, *supra* note 81.

[229] *Ibid* at Article 8.

[230] Lazaro & Métayer, "The control over personal data", *supra* note 81 at 5. "The second way to consider the notion of control is in an individual/subjective manner and relates to the multiple ways

management is based on an individual's willingness to collect or use his/her personal information.[231] Although acknowledgement and consent from data subjects are one of the fundamental origins of grounds for processing personal information, we are still faced with cognitive problems, wherein people are reluctant to read privacy policies, or it is difficult for ordinary people to determine what is the "necessary and adequate" information for various purposes.[232] The purpose of consent is to ensure a certain degree of control concerning the personal information of the user, but practically, it has become a discretionary tool entitling Internet companies to circulate personal information; whether or not this processing action is justified hinges quite simply and exclusively on whether these companies have obtained user consent.[233] From a technical point of view in the digital world, most actions of control are carried out through IT devices, and if not all, then most interpretations of control assume that "the subject must be able to act, in one way or another, to exercise their rights such as rights to operate, read, modify or delete a file and the right to get access to a directory list."[234] Therefore, the different meanings of control in computer science can be classified as "the subject of control" (who is in charge of the control) and "the object of the control" (what the subject controls) in the personal data protection context.[235] The subject of control echoes individuals who own the right to decide how to process their data. Objects of control can be classified as active rights, such as consent, modification, and delegation. Negative rights refer to the principles of nondisclosure and data minimization. From the perspective of processors, the significance of control implies a "right to decide how to use the personal data of others."[236]

The personal data protection framework has "shifted to imposing information stewardship obligations on data controllers, who act as custodians of personal data"

---

in which individuals interact with each other and communicate personal information: the ways in which they participate in the self-construction of their digital identities. In this sense, control as an agency refers to self-determination over information about oneself and the self-management of privacy."

[231] The idea is that it is possible or desirable for every individual to monitor and manage a shifting collection of privacy settings of which they may only be dimly aware.

[232] Sabine Trepte et al., "Do People Know About Privacy and Data Protection Strategies? Towards the 'Online Privacy Literacy Scale' (OPLIS)" in Serge Gutwirth, Ronald Leenes & Paul de Hert, eds, *Reforming Eur Data Prot Law* Law, Governance and Technology Series (Dordrecht: Springer Netherlands, 2015) at 333.

[233] Gautrais, *supra* note 39 in Chap. 1 at 178 (Visiteda at May 16, 2019).

[234] Lazaro & Métayer, "The control over personal data", *supra* note 81 at 20.

[235] *Ibid* at 21.

[236] Goldberg, "Guide to the General Data Protection Regulation (GDPR)", (1 November 2018) See online: <https://ico.org.uk/for-organisations/guide-to-the-general-data-protection-regulation-gdpr/> (Visited on April 17, 2020). Additionally, see Mireille Hildebrandt & Bert-Jaap Koops, "The Challenges of Ambient Law and Legal Protection in the Profiling Era" (2010) 73:3 The Modern Law Review 428–460, online: <https://onlinelibrary.wiley.com/doi/abs/10.1111/j.1468-2230.2010.00806.x>.

over the last two decades.[237] Taking the GDPR as an example, "controller" is defined as

> The natural or legal person, public authority, agency or other body which…determines the purpose and means of processing data.[238]

And the controller is considered with the concept of a "processor," who "processes personal data on behalf of the controller."[239] In Canada, the concept of "controller" has not been explicitly expressed in relevant Canadian privacy statutes; instead, it is typically substituted by the concept of "organization" more broadly.[240] Generally, a controller always refers to the body that has the right to process personal data. As Orla argues:

> The right to data protection provides individuals with more rights over more types of data than the right to privacy.[241]

It suggests that the enhanced control over personal data provided by the right to data protection serves two purposes: first, it proactively promotes individual personality rights, which are threatened by personal data processing, and second, it reduces the power and information asymmetries between individuals and those who process their data.[242] Therefore, we can identify the right of personal data as having two layers. The bottom layer is the right to protect personal data based on the consent of the user or by law, and the top layer is the right to process personal data constrained by the right to protect personal data. For the purpose of personal data protection regulations such as the GDPR, the definition of "control" involves social, legal and technical backgrounds. It should also be recognized that internal control extends beyond just financial matters. However, there are many different tools that can be defined in this way, such as "trust marks, certifications, seals, and accreditation." All these processes exist only where there is a "verifiable assertion"; in other words, the objective assessment carried out by third parties is indispensable when these verification processes are involved. From this point of view, it is difficult to distinguish between the audits from these processes.

[**Effectiveness of external control**] External controls played an important role in explaining the effectiveness of the audit system in the personal data protection

---

[237] *Hero or Villain: The Data Controller in Privacy Law and Technologies*, SSRN Scholarly Paper, by Claudia Diaz, Omer Tene & Seda F Guerses, papers.ssrn.com, SSRN Scholarly Paper ID 2321480 (Rochester, NY: Social Science Research Network, 2013) at 3.

[238] GDPR at Article 4 (7).

[239] Ibid.

[240] Kadash Adam, *The International Comparative Legal Guide to: Data protection 2018* (Global Legal Group Ltd) at 55.

[241] Orla Lynskey, "Deconstructing data protection: The added-value of a right to data protection int the EU legal order" (2014) 63:3 International & Comparative Law Quarterly 569–597. See online: <https://www.cambridge.org/core/journals/international-and-comparative-law-quarterly/article/deconstructing-data-protection-the-addedvalue-of-a-right-to-data-protection-in-the-eu-legal-order/95BD4CCF4670466FD4F6EBAD7DDB4E76> at 588 (Visited at 12 June, 2023).

[242] *Ibid.*

regime. From the principal-agent type of explanation, external auditors played an essential role in responding to the suspectable internal audit process to external stakeholders, as well as the public, and became an important external control method for persona data protection.[243] Serving as an oversight method, the effectiveness of external audits is crucial for executable internal audit management. Compared with internal audits, external audits cover more issues related to the external market, laws and regulations.[244] Risk management internally relies on internal procedures, such as Privacy Impact Assessment (hereafter PIA) from an engineering perspective, whereas from an audit perspective, internal management procedures need to be verified from external audits to ensure that internal execution is aligned with legal requirements. For an audit, the external requirement, in other words, must be executable. As a matter of fact, a development process usually moves through different models. Model-driven design always supports engineers in analyzing and designing the system by the direction of external audits for compliance purposes. In other words, the framework of an external audit must be sufficient in a way that internal auditors and external auditors can follow. As Matthew noted:

> Organizations seek to establish congruence between the social values associated with or implied by their activities and the norms of acceptable behavior in the larger social system in which they are a part. Insofar as these two value systems are congruent, we can speak of organizational legitimacy.[245]

Within regulation on personal data protection compliance audits in China, Article 54 of personal information protection law stated that:

> Personal information processors shall regularly conduct compliance audits on their compliance with laws and administrative regulations in handling personal information.[246]

To explain how the audit worked, the Chinese regulatory body "Cyberspace Administration of China" published the "Draft of regulation on personal data protection compliance audits." It clearly identified the audit objective and the audit content.[247] For instance, the definition of audit states that:

> Personal information protection compliance audit refers to audit activities conducted for the purpose of examining whether the personal information processing activities of the audited subject comply with relevant laws and regulations of China.[248]

To guarantee audit quality is first priority for external auditors. As for a premise, external auditor has to grant relevant authority accessing to relevant documents. For instance, as Article 8 of the announcement stated:

---

243 Brewer et al., "External Control and Red Tape", *supra* note 78 at 357.

244 Anand & S. L., *supra* note 79 at 2887.

245 Holm & Zaman, "Regulating audit quality", *supra* note 219 at 53.

246 Personal Information Protection Law of People's republic of China. Article 54, See online: https://baike.baidu.com/item/个人信息保护法/8343360?fr=aladdin (Visited at 22 June, 2022).

247 Draft of regulation on personal data protection compliance audit: audit objective

248 Article 8 of Announcement of compliance audit of personal data protection. See online: http://www.cac.gov.cn/2023-08/03/c_1692628348448092.htm (Visited at August 5, 2023).

> Where a personal information processor entrusts a professional institution to conduct a personal information protection compliance audit in accordance with the requirements of the department performing personal information protection duties, it shall ensure that the professional institution can normally exercise the following authority:
> (1) Requiring the provision of or assisting in reviewing relevant documents or materials;
> (2) Entering places related to personal information processing activities;
> (3) Observing the personal information processing activities taking place in the premises;
> (4) Investigating relevant business activities and the information systems they rely on;
> (5) Inspecting and testing equipment and facilities related to personal information processing activities;
> (6) Obtaining and consulting data or information related to personal information processing activities;
> (7) Interviewing personnel related to personal information processing activities;
> (8) Conducting investigations, questioning and collecting evidence on relevant issues;
> (9) Other authority necessary to carry out compliance audit work.[249]

Compared with jurisdiction of China, The focal point of the audit stated by ICO from United Kingdom is to ascertain whether the data controller or processor has implemented policies and procedures for managing the processing of personal data, and whether said processing adheres to these policies and procedures.[250] Prior to commencing the audit, the ICO will engage in discussions with the data controller or processor to determine the scope to be covered. This scope may encompass any data protection issues or risks relevant to the data controller or processor, which could be identified based on ICO intelligence or the organization's own concerns. Additionally, it may encompass any data protection issues or risks that could impact its specific industry or organization more broadly.[251] The ICO will provide recommendations aimed at assisting organizations in mitigating non-compliance risks and reducing potential harm to individuals, as well as the likelihood of regulatory action being taken against data controllers or processors for breaches of data protection laws. Following the completion of the audit, the report will include a rating for each area covered, observations and findings focusing on weaknesses and maximum risks, or identified areas of particularly good practice, and recommendations for priority rating to address weaknesses and risks. Furthermore, they will provide an executive summary of the report's findings. The executive summary of the final report will be published on the ICO website.[252]

To ensure an effective external control, external auditors need to have access to the internal perspective of the audit trail to check and norm relevant data processing activities. Also, the external executable audit requirements are also crucial for the effective management of internal audits. On the one hand, it avoids regulatory

[249] Article 8 of Announcement of compliance audit of personal data protection. See online: http://www.cac.gov.cn/2023-08/03/c_1692628348448092.htm (Visited at 5August, 2023).

[250] Bart Custers et al., "A comparison of data protection legislation and policies across the EU" (2018) 34:2 Computer Law & Security Review at 237.

[251] Ibid at 239

[252] Torre Matteo La et al., "Protecting a new Achilles heel: the role of auditors within the practice of data protection" (2019) 36:2 Managerial Auditing Journal at 221.

overreach, where internal audits may operate in complex areas with many variables of risk. On the other hand, it avoided regulatory capture where law became less effective for the unregulated regime.[253] Additionally, it could avoid unintended consequences where "regulatory inventions, not only fail to achieve the desired effect, they generate undesired and unintended negative consequences."[254] In the starting point for personal data regulation, the five questions compatible with ICT regulation are as follows:

> (1) that what holds offline should also hold online; (2) that regulation should be 'technology neutral'; (3) that self-regulation should be the preferred regulatory option; (4) that regulation should be undertaken at an international level; and (5) that, where we have the technology, code-based approaches should be adopted by regulators.[255]

For effective external audit, the fact that an executable audit requirement needs to be internal-audit friendly, requirements need to be clear, technology neutral and interpreted for code-based regulation. The external audit must be fully connected to the technology where it can interpret and apply the law as declared of the legislation, or it can seek to reconnect the law to the internal audit by adopting a management approach. Internal audits cannot be left behind at any phase of the regulatory cycle. From an external audit of the personal data perspective, data protection regimes are designed for "large visible 'elephants' rather than highly mobile 'mice' that scurry hither and thither. In addition, the regulatory jungle is a shifting scene, and what we see today might be gone by tomorrow, constantly challenging the accuracy and focus of the regulatory gaze."[256] Another variable issue related to the transparency of the external body. For instance, Article 51 of GDPR required Member states to establish independent public authorities for monitoring the application of this regulation.[257] The independence, which means that the personal data protection authorities could not be supervised by other state bodies. As Pawet noted:

> Against a background of independence from the authorities of the Member States, probably the biggest practical implication of the ban on being bound by instructions will be that personal data protection authorities cannot be subordinated or even supervised by other state bodies. In other words, they cannot be linked to other management or supervisory ties.[258]

While recital 118 of GDPR also stated that:

[253] Brown sword, *supra* note 49 in Chap. 1 at 142.

[254] *Ibid* at 143.

[255] *Ibid* at 150.

[256] *Ibid* at 164.

[257] Article 51 of GDPR: ach supervisory authority shall contribute to the consistent application of this Regulation throughout the Union. For that purpose, the supervisory authorities shall cooperate with each other and the Commission in accordance with Chapter VII.

[258] Pawel Hajduk, "The Powers of the Supervisory Body in the GDPR as a Basis for Shaping the Practices of Personal Data Processing" (2021) 45 Rev. Eur & Comp L 57–76. See online: <https://heinonline.org/HOL/P?h=hein.journals/recol45&i=51> at 62 (Visited at 19 September 2022).

> The independence of supervisory authorities should not mean that they cannot be subject to mechanisms of control or monitoring in terms of expenditure or judicial review.[259]

Article 58 (1) of GDPR indicating the external authorities have following powers:

> (i) to require the controller and the processor to provide all information necessary for the supervisory authority to carry out its tasks; (ii) to conduct investigations in the form of data protection audits; (iii) to review the certifications granted under the Regulation; (iv)to notify the controller or processor of a suspected breach of the Regulation; (v) obtaining from the controller and the processor access to all personal data and all information necessary for the supervisory authority to carry out its tasks; (vi) obtaining access to all premises of the controller.[260]

Although compliance audits differ from financial audits, which have the nature of commercial activities, external audit bodies are not equally subject to the disclosure requirements applicable to them. The public may be concerned about the ability of the external audit body to apply and adapt the audit process to a changing personal data context about the harmonization of external regulatory requirements with internal audit requirements. Also, the powers of the external audit body constituted a basis for shaping effectiveness of audit. As a matter of fact, the external audit bodies have powers to carry out duties assigned to them, and this is ensured by independence of this body.[261]

In conclusion, the intricacies of modern business operations, coupled with evolving regulatory landscapes, underscore the critical role of audits in ensuring compliance, particularly concerning personal data protection. The complex nature of audit processes, both internally and externally, demands meticulous attention to detail and adherence to legal frameworks. Internally, audit structures must navigate the intricacies of stakeholder rights and procedural legitimacy, while external audits serve as vital oversight mechanisms, ensuring alignment with legal requirements and regulatory standards. The effectiveness of audits hinges on clear, technology-neutral requirements, transparency from audit bodies, and the independence and powers of external audit authorities. Ultimately, robust audit mechanisms are essential not only for safeguarding individuals' rights but also for upholding organizational accountability in an increasingly data-driven world.

[259] Recital 118 of GDPR.

[260] Article 58 (1) of GDPR.

[261] Article 52(1)of GDPR: each supervisory authority, shall, in carrying out its tasks and exercising its powers under this regulation, act with complete independence.

3.3.2 *Legal Control from Substantial Perspective*

For personal data protection audits, this book also questioned its legitimacy, which may give insights into smarter ways of achieving protection goals.[262] For this part, this book found that for an effective legal control of audit, audit evidence and objective and fairness is crucial for a true and fair statement of outcome. While for data, many of the evidence are in form of electronic which calls for legal admissibility and validation.

3.3.2.1 Evidence of Documentation for Legal Control

[Documentation] To fulfill the compliance requirements, the documentation process is the fundamental segment for internal audits. A distinction between audit in financial regime and for compliance is one of the objectives for financial auditing, which could be described as "fraud detection". While for compliance audit, it points in the direction of "examination."[263] Additionally, the distinction represents a new stage in the relationship between internal audit and external audit: management responsibilities for personal data protection need to be articulated with documentation processes. The documentation made the organization "knowable" and "auditable" in return. Within the documentation process, the power transfers from the bottom to the administrative center for an organization, where it continually balances the formal, defendable, economic and manageable structure for the audit process.[264] From a practical perspective, it is always critical that the staff overfocus on documentation, in addition to real risk control, which is referred to as the "two audits."[265] Documentation must be legitimate before it becomes effective. Otherwise, the audit process would convert into "certification of the unknowable, which requires ritual procedures to transfer indeterminacy into institutionalized order."[266]

Article 30 of the GDPR requires record keeping. All the provisions and requirements are clear when it referred to documentation. It required that each data controller and processor maintain a record of processing activities under its responsibility.[267] Additionally, relevant articles of ritical13, 82 and 89 entailed the maintenance and

---

[262] Brownsword, *supra* note 101 in Chap. 1 at 32.

[263] Power, *supra* note 211 at 382. This idea originated from the essay where Carpenter and Dirsmith also argued that the trend of financial audit tends to become an examination rather fraud detection.

[264] *Ibid.*

[265] Michael J Fischer, "'Real-izing' the benefits of new technologies as a source of audit evidence: An interpretive field study" (1996) 21:2–3 Account Organ Soc at 232.

[266] Brian T Pentland, "Getting comfortable with the numbers: Auditing and the micro-production of macro-order" (1993) 18:7 Account Organ Soc 605–620 at 608.

[267] Article 30(1)(a) states it should contain the name and contact details of the controller and, where applicable, the joint controller(s), the controller's representative and the data protection officer. This information is intended to enable an unambiguous identification of the controller(s) and whoever else is responsible under the GDPR. The notion of 'contact details' is not limited to a simple email address. It must contain all the elements (physical address, telephone number, contact person).

availability of the records. In accordance with Article 30 (1)(e),[268] the controller also needs to provide the information regarding the transfers of personal data to a third party in the case of the applicability of Article 49(1) of GDPR,[269] the documentation of suitable safeguards. Articles 30(1)(f) and (g) required that the controllers clarify the envisaged time limits for erasure of different categories of data and, where possible,[270] provide a general description of the technical and organizational security measures referred to Article 32 of the GDPR.[271] Additionally, these records of processing activities shall be in writing, including in electronic form, and kept up to date.[272] This enables controllers to provide DPAs with the records when requested under Article 30(4) GDPR and to comply with the principles of accountability and transparency.[273] In other words, the whole process of processing personal data must

[268] Article 30(1)(b) requires the controller to provide a description of the purposes of the processing. It is noteworthy that this does not extend to a description of the legal basis for the processing operations. However, this gap should be filled by interpreting the text in line with the principles of fair processing. Under the principle of accountability, according to which the controller must be able to demonstrate compliance with the GDPR, it must have a "*firm and reasoned notion about the legal basis of processing before it starts any operation, and this notion should be verifiable by means of its records. Thus, for the keeping of records to be meaningful, it will be necessary for the controller to be able to demonstrate on which legal basis it relies in its processing*".

[269] Article 30(1)(d) prescribes that controller should describe the categories of recipients to whom personal data have been or will be disclosed. The wording of the provision suggests that only the categories of addressees must be indicated, such as "*suppliers*", "*accountants*", "*marketing consultants*", or "*legal advisors*". However, this ambiguity does not seem advisable, as other provisions of the GDPR require the controller to keep track of individual recipients. For example, Article 15(1)(c) GDPR and Article 19 GDPR require the disclosure of "*recipients or categories of recipients*" and specific recipients "*if the data subject requests it*", respectively. As such, it would go against its aim of increasing accountability to not specify the recipients in the record of processing activities

[270] Article 30(1)(c) GDPR establishes that the record of processing activities shall describe the categories of data subjects and the categories of personal data. Examples of categories of data subjects are "*website visitors*", "*clinic patients*", "*employees*". Categories of personal data may be "*website clicks*", "*diagnosis*", "*holiday leave*", as well as "*union affiliations*". Scholars have highlighted that each category of personal data should be tied to the category of data subject it belongs to. For example, the record of processing activities should clearly show that the two categories "*holiday leave*" and "*union affiliations*" are processed regarding the "*employees*" category.

[271] Article 30 GDPR requires controllers and processors to maintain a record of processing activities (Article 4(2) GDPR). This obligation represents the expression of several data processing principles. On the one hand, it promotes accountability by allowing the controller to keep track of its processing and amend it where necessary. On the other hand, it increases the overall transparency of the processing and makes it easier for data subjects to exercise their rights. In practice, the record of processing activities is nothing more than an updated written account of the main elements of the processing.

[272] Article 30(1)(f) and (g) GDPR, respectively require controllers to clarify the envisaged time limits for erasure of different categories of data and, where possible, provide general description of the technical and organizational security measures referred to in Art 32.

[273] "Bundesdatenschutzgesetz: Das BDSG als übersichtliche Seite", See online: <https://dsgvo-gesetz.de/bdsg/>. Additionally, see: https://gdprhub.eu/Article_30_GDPR (Visited at June 30, 2022).

be traceable and transparent. To track changes to the entries, the changes should be maintained for at least 1 year.[274] Addressing this complicated situation, companies need to adopt automation tools for recording processing activity, as well as fulfilling data protection responsibility, while an essential question has been proposed for these electronic records: are these electronic records trustworthy? How would this record survive in court? How could these records be interpreted? The legitimacy of such records may be challenged through investigation or litigation.

[Electronic Records] This book first examined the legal admissibility of such electronic records. The legal status of electronic records impacts records management programs, such as data compliance platforms. Organizations seek "dependable systems" such as "blockchains" to ensure documentary veracity and validity.[275] Regulations, such as GDPR and PIPL, as well as LGPD, that introduced accountability principles also called for written records. From judicial consideration, the documented facts provided support for enforcing the principle of accountability. As Michael Buckland noted:

> Modern society seems to have decided that you can make people honest by requiring documentation, or at least, that you can make them more accountable.[276]

While trail traditions of "here-say"lead to distrust of second-hand information, such as written documents.[277] With the development of electronic records and digital technologies, judicial thinking was cast on the nature of such records and their admissibility as evidence. As Piasecki noted:

> In security and ambivalence about the reliability of electronic records and their inherent truth has caused an uneasiness about their value as evidence.[278]

Early debate remained in the field whether electronic records remain tied to paper or continue to emerge as a documentary medium, which moves away from the roots of paper documentation and may develop protocols and characteristics alien to paper records.[279] This idea originated from three basic rules of evidence of common law: "the best evidence rules," which requires that an original record be submitted as evidence whenever possible, and the authentication rule, which requires that either direct or circumstantial evidence be presented that a record submitted as evidence of a fact at issue is what it purports to be. Additionally, the "hearsay" rule

---

[274] DSK, Datenschutzkonferenz, 'Hinweise zum Verzeichnis von Verarbeitungstätigkeiten', Art. 30 DS-GVO, February 2018 at 3.

[275] Sara J Piasecki, "Legal Admissibility of Electronic Records as Evidence and Implications for Records Management" (1995) 58:1 The American Archivist 54–64.See online: <https://www.jstor.org/stable/40293888> at 54 (Visited at 15 March, 2022).

[276] Michael Buckland, "On the Nature of Records Management Theory" (1994) 57:2 Am Arch 346–351at 348. Additionally, see: Records Management in its intellectual context

[277] Piasecki, *supra* note 283 at 55.

[278] *Ibid* at 56.

[279] Vincent Gautrais, "Article 5 of Loi concernant le cadre juridique des technologies de l'information", See:www.lccjti.ca/article-5 (Visited at June 6, 2022).

entailed that the documents offered as evidence are hearsay as the material made outside a court of law.[280]

With the emergence of technology, there are hardly any areas of civil litigation that escape these writings, testimonies and material elements in the form of emails or screenshots, documents, etc.[281] Within some jurisdictions, courts upheld those electronic records created through imaging or scanning, and they are just as legally binding as paper documents if these electronic records are regarded as evidence. For instance, within the U.S., the Federal rules of evidence provided clear rules of guidance on the electronic records. The rule 1003 stated that:

> A duplicate is admissible to the same extent as the original unless a genuine question is raised about the original's authenticity or the circumstances make it unfair to admit the duplicated.[282]

In other words, digital records created by a responsible service provider using a rigorous and well-documented process would likely be admissible.[283] With Canadian legislation, the uniform electronic evidence act (hereafterUEEA) representative of federal, provincial as well as territorial governments of Canada, and various law reforms agencies.[284] The UEEA shifted the authentication and best evidence rules from the to the "integrity" of the system.[285] As Luciana Duranti noted:

> The fundamental concerns of the law of evidence with any type of evidence, including electronic records, are relevance, admissibility, and weight.[286]

In Quebec, for instance, the Act respecting the legal framework for information technology stated that:

> They represent functional equivalence of the documents and their legal value, regardless of the document media, as well as the interchangeability of the media and the technologies that carry them.[287]

Additionally, the law stated that:

---

[280] Heather MacNeil, Trusting records: legal, historical and diplomatic perspectives (Dordrecht, 2000) at 3. Additionally, see: Luciana Duranti, Corinne Rogers & Anthony Sheppard, "Electronic Records and the Law of Evidence in Canada: The Uniform Electronic Evidence Act Twelve Years Later" (2010) 70 Archivaria at 97.

[281] Vincent Gautrais, "La preuve technologique". See online: <https://www.gautrais.com/publications/la-preuve-technologique/>.

[282] Federal Rules of Evidence, Rule 1003: See online: https://www.rulesofevidence.org/article-x/rule-1003/ (Visited at 16 June, 2022).

[283] Exploring admissibility of electronic records and electronic signatures. See: https://www.stria.com/wp-content/uploads/2018/08/Signatures-and-eRecords.pdf (Visited at 6 June, 2022).

[284] The Uniform Electronic Evidence Act: See: https://ulcc-chlc.ca/ULCC/media/EN-Uniform-Acts/Uniform-Electronic-Evidence-Act_2.pdf (6 June, 2022).

[285] Duranti, Rogers & Sheppard, "Electronic Records and the Law of Evidence in Canada", *supra* note 290.

[286] *Ibid* at 119.

[287] Act respecting the legal framework for information technology See: https://www.canlii.org/fr/qc/legis/lois/rlrq-c-c-1.1/derniere/rlrq-c-c-1.1.html (Visited at 6 June, 2022).

> For the purpose of this law, any database whose structuring elements allow the creation of documents by delimiting and structuring their information entered therein is assimilated into a document, with the definition given by law that information inscribed on a medium constitutes a document.[288]

By which means whether the medium could be paper-based or electronic-based would not impede the records constituted as documents. Additionally, the law stated that

> The legal value of a document, particularly its capacity to produce legal effects and its admissibility as evidence, is neither increased nor diminished solely because of the medium or technology chosen.[289]

While the integrity of the document could not be ensured may be admissible as "testimonial evidence" or "real evidence" as article 2865 of civil code of Quebec regulated.[290] In other words, electronic records created by hesitating providers or created without a well-documented process are more likely to be challenged as admissible and legally binding. The Act stated that:

> The integrity of a document is ensured if it is possible to verify that the information it contains has not been altered and has been maintained in its entirety and that the medium used provides stability and the required serenity to the information. The integrity of a document must be maintained throughout its lifecycle, from creation, during transfer, consultation and transmission, during retention and until archiving or destruction.[291]

The law asked for verification of the integrity of the document if it is possible, while the law put this duty in a negative way, which means that:

> It is not necessary to prove…its integrity, unless the person contesting the admission of the documents establishes, upon a preponderance of evidence, that the integrity of the documents has been affected. (Presumption of Integrity)[292]

However, the nature of electronic records challenges traditional rules of evidence and procedure and requires their restructuring. The law admitted the legal value of the electronic records unless someone challenges the integrity of the documents. The act also served as an interpretative tool to apply "old" law to new situations.[293] However, the law also asked for new requirements for record-keeping systems for reliability, integrity, compliance, and comprehensiveness to create and maintain records that maintain integrity during the lifecycle of data. Within the Jurisdiction of China, electronic evidence, also known as electronic data, is one of the eight

[288] Ibid.

[289] Ibid at Division two, Clause five.

[290] Ibid at Division two, Clause five.

[291] Ibid at Division two, Clause six. Additionally, See online: www.lccjti.ca/article-6 (Visited at 6 June, 2022).

[292] Ibid at Division two, Clause seven. The clause is consistent with the regulation of UEEA: The presumptions of integrity are rebuttable by the opposing party. They require an opposing litigant who wishes to dispute admissibility of an electronic record to make an objection of substance by offering "evidence to the contrary," and not to make a serious issue out of an insubstantial or technical objection that the electronic record is not the best evidence.

[293] Vincent Gautrais, "Article 9", www.lccjti.ca/article-9 (Visited at June 9, 2022).

forms clearly stipulated in Chinese major procedural laws: civil, criminal and administrative procedures.[294] As one of the eight major forms of evidence in litigation, electronic evidence should also have the usual attributes of evidence, namely, objectivity, which exists independently and objectively without being changed by subjective will and relevance, and there is an objective connection between the evidence and the facts to be proven and lawful. The collection and use of evidence must comply with legal procedures.[295] As noted by the "explanations of the Supreme People's Court on Evidence in Civil Litigation" issued in December 2019, which was made to provide guidance for the fair and efficient use of electronic data evidence.[296] The explanation ruled that:

> When courts investigate and collect electronic data, it shall require the person under investigation to provide the original medium.[297]

The original medium generally referred to the computer equipment or storage medium that saved the electronic data. However, if it is impossible to provide the original medium, copies can be identified as proof. The court had the right to ask about its source and production process in the investigative process.[298] Article 93 of the explanation stimulated the authenticity review of electronic data. This article focused on the medium of the electronic records, which has a strong technical feature. For example, it asked to verify whether the medium (i.e., software, hardware) of the computer system from electronic data that is generated, store, and transmitted is complete and reliable. The provision imposed a heavy burden of proof on the party and the need to provide electronic evidence. In other words, it is adamantine to prove the authenticity that courts may require to provide the whole computer system for verification purposes. As for the result, the explanation gave five situations in which electronic evidence can be presumed to be true: (1) Electronic data submitted or kept by the parties to their disadvantage, (2) Provided or confirmed by a neutral third-party platform that records and saves electronic data. (3) Formed in normal business activities. (4) kept in the way of file management, and (5) kept,

---

[294] Specifically, Paragraph 5 of Article 63 of the Civil Procedure Law of the People's Republic of China stipulates that the type of evidence includes electronic data. Paragraph 4 of Article 33 of the Administrative Procedure Law of the People's Republic of China stipulates that evidence includes electronic data. Article 50, paragraph 2, Item 8 of the Criminal Procedure Law of the People's Republic of China stipulates that evidence includes electronic data.

[295] Lehao: The Theoretical Basis, Practical Exploration and Institutional Improvement of the Application of Electronic Case Files by the People's Courts, Archives Science Study, 2022 Vol.36 at 43.

[296] The explanations of the Supreme People's Court on Evidence in Civil Litigation, Supreme Court of People's republic of China. December 2019. See online: https://www.court.gov.cn/zixun-xiangqing-212721.html (20 June 2022).

[297] Supreme Court of People's republic of China, "The explanations of the Supreme People's Court on Evidence in Civil Litigation". See online: https://www.court.gov.cn/zixun-xiangqing-212721.html (20 June 2022).

[298] [Translate by Author]: Ibid at Article 23, paragraph 2.

transmitted and extracted in the way agreed upon by the parties.[299] Within European jurisdiction, electronic evidence is defined as:

> Any evidence derived from data contained in or produced by any device, the functioning of which depends on a software program or data stored on or transmitted over a computer system or network.[300]

Metadata referred to electronic information about other electronic data, which may reveal the identification, or history of the evidence, as well as relevant data and times. Electronic evidence should be evaluated in the same way as other types of evidence regarding its admissibility, authenticity, accuracy and integrity. The treatment of electronic evidence should not be disadvantageous to the parties or give unfair advantage to one of them.[301]

From an audit perspective, the lack of internal validation of electronic records rendered their internal audit about external audits more suspect, especially for data processors, who are keenly aware of their legal requirements and the obligations of their records, such as the GDPR. Additionally, they need to establish the legality and admissibility of the documents into evidence in their care. Electronic records, such as personal data protection, are stipulated in different jurisdictions based on different legal traditions originating from both common law and civil law, while the basic understanding of the electronic records for personal data audits is as follows: first, the evidence made by the data processors or controllers themselves is not easily accepted by courts or regulatory agencies unless they can prove the integrity and legal value of such records. However, it is the GDPR that required that the processing records be documented for a period for regulatory checking. Therefore, processors were required to take certain actions to ensure that such records could be recorded correctly, such as implementing a records management system, using third-party documentation platforms, or using depended mediums, such as blockchain. Second, the method of recording for audit purposes called for standardization in which, not only the courts, but also regulatory agencies could admit for GDPR compliance audits, and it called for standardization agencies to publish related standards and protocols for data processors, as well as controllers to follow. Audits shall be managed by organizations, while for records of data processing, a standardization process needs to be established for lawfulness exposition. This type of record shall be admitted by the regulatory body or admitted by the court through standardization procedures. This idea entailed two layers of understanding the concept: one should understand the concept of standard narrowly (the standard that an agent or agency of government authorized to set the stage in a specified field) and the concept of the standard broadly (as encompassing whatever measures "regulators" take to set the stage in the desired way, like ISO). Another stress that a personal data

---

[299] Ibid.

[300] Council of Europe, *Electronic Evidence in Civil and Administrative Proceedings* (2019) at 7. Regulation No910/2014 of European Parliament and of the council. See online: https://eur-lex.europa.eu/legal-content/EN/TXT/PDF/?uri=CELEX:32014R0910 (Visited at 2 June 2022).

[301] *Ibid.*

protection audit may encounter is with the technology medium that the audit process must consider. The legitimacy of technology where internal audits are employed may also be challenged by regulators.

3.3.2.2 The Judgment of Auditor for Legal Control

[Judgment of Auditor] Independent auditors are essential for formulating opinions about the fairness of their compliance statements. As Edward noted:

> Auditors exercise professional judgment in determining the type and extent of information to collect and in assessing the implications of this information.[302]

An individual professional judgment plays an extremely crucial role in auditing. From another perspective, it also calls for verification of the validity of auditor judgments by distinguishing correctly from incorrect judgments. The fundamental questions for the legitimacy of judgment arose from two perspectives: "the independent position" and "unimpeachable validation criteria." The position of the auditors regarding a series of data breaches received lots of attention because of the accountability principle of data protection.[303] From the data protection perspective, the elements that the audit tried to structure are as follows:

> The context and external forces influencing understanding and aims of data protection practices; the ends and activities of data protection, reflecting its teleological orientation; the actors and participants engaged in this practice; and the role of auditors within data protection's effective structure.[304]

Data protection activities aimed to ensure a reasonable degree of security and that related risks are adequately managed. The cross-sectional function between data security and cybersecurity for data protection purposes is accountability with which auditors are held responsible for. The role of auditors must consider laws or regulations that have direct or indirect effects on compliance statements. Additionally, auditors must respond to further external pressure stemming from the demand of society for privacy and data protection. Distinguished by Noel O'Sullivan from a financial auditor which mission is to:

> Transmit a positive signal to users regarding the accuracy of management disclosures in financial statements.[305]

---

[302] Edward J Joyce, "Expert Judgment in Audit Program Planning" (1976) 14 Journal of Accounting Research 29–60. See online: <https://www.jstor.org/stable/2490445> at 29 (Visited at 17 July, 2023).

[303] Matteo La Torre, John Dumay & Michele Antonio Rea, "Breaching intellectual capital: critical reflections on Big Data security" (2018) 26:3 Meditari Accountancy Research 463–482. See online: <https://doi.org/10.1108/MEDAR-06-2017-0154> at 464 (Visited at 17 July, 2023).

[304] Theodore R Schatzki, "On Organizations as they Happen" (2006) 27:12 Organization Studies 1863–1873. See online: <https://doi.org/10.1177/0170840606071942> at 1863 (Visited at 17 July, 2023).

[305] Noel O'Sullivan, "Auditors' Liability: Its Role in the Corporate Governance Debate" (1993) 23:sup1 Accounting and Business Research 412–420. See online: <https://doi.org/10.1080/00014788.1993.9729908> at 415 (Visited at 18 July, 2023).

The current scope of audit is unremitted by regulation, and the process of the audit consists of planning, execution, concluding and reporting on audit.[306] The changes in roles for auditors could be examined from three perspectives: practical understanding, the end of activities and rules.[307] From practical understanding, data protection requirements impacts all the stages of the audit process, which enabled auditors to change in response. As systems increase in size and complexity, auditors must adopt a risk assessment strategy for the audit, and external auditors must participate in audit work internally from the start of the audit process. In this way, the role of internal auditors and external auditors is blurred in some way.[308] From this point of view, the role of auditors is not limited to:

> Recognizing and assessing legal permission and corporate access policies to data but extend to give signals about the effectiveness of internal data protection and security systems.[309]

From ends of activities perspective, auditors ruled by professional ethical standards have always been aware of the privacy, confidentiality and independence issues surrounding the data. Auditors must prove that when they engage in audit activities, confidentiality can be maintained for the audit, and proper grants are given so that legal authorization to access certain data can be obtained. From the perspective of rules, the basic principles and procedures that direct the auditors on how to perform an audit are known as audit standards. Within the context of personal data protection, the role of audit changed from scrutinizing the facts to a more analytical role, and this will necessitate a change to audit standards.[310] As Moroney noted:

> The format of audit reports is currently set out in ISA 701, and the standard recently introduced the requirement for the auditor to report on KAMs. are those matters that the auditors regarded as most significant in the performance of the audit.[311]

Due to socio-technological changes, new KAMs will be required that provide guidance on new and emerging issues resulting from the need for data protection. For the qualification of the auditor, the law also gave a clear instruction as:

> Personal information processors carry out personal information protection compliance audits on their own, which may be carried out by the organization's internal agencies or

[306] Torre Matteo La et al., "Protecting a new Achilles heel: the role of auditors within the practice of data protection" (2019) 36:2 Managerial Auditing Journal 218–239. See online: <https://doi.org/10.1108/MAJ-03-2018-1836> at 229 (Visited at 19 July, 2023).

[307] *Ibid* at 230.

[308] Deniz Appelbaum, Alexander Kogan & Miklos A Vasarhelyi, "Big data and analytics in the modern audit engagement: Research needs" (2017) 36:4 Auditing 1–27.Seeonline: <https://researchwith.montclair.edu/en/publications/big-data-and-analytics-in-the-modern-audit-engagement-research-ne> at 19 (Visited at 20 July, 2023).

[309] La et al., "Protecting a new Achilles heel", *supra* note 262 at 231.

[310] David L Coss et al., "Big Data in Auditing: A Value-Focused Approach to Cybersecurity Management" (2019) 15:2 Journal of Information System Security 77–100. See online: <https://www.jissec.org/Contents/V15/N2/V15N2-Coss.html> at 96 (Visited at 24 July, 2023).

[311] Raymond N Johnson et al., *Auditing: A Practical Approach with Data Analytics* (John Wiley & Sons, 2019) at 193.

> entrusted professional institutions in accordance with the requirements of these measures according to the actual situation.[312]

For the competency of the external auditor, the announcement set the following conditions to guarantee the independence as:

> Professional institutions that perform personal information protection compliance audits shall maintain independence and objectivity, and shall not conduct more than three consecutive personal information protection compliance audits for the same audit object.[313]

Also, Article 14 stated as:

> When engaging in personal information protection compliance auditing activities, professional institutions shall be honest and upright, and make professional judgments on compliance auditing in a fair and objective manner. Professional institutions shall not subcontract and entrust third parties to conduct personal information protection compliance audits.[314]

Although the regulation left a room for internal audit instead of a mandatory external audit, the announcement also set conditions for an mandatory external audit as:

> Departments performing personal information protection duties may require personal information processors to entrust professional institutions to conduct compliance audits of their personal information processing activities if they discover that there are relatively high risks in personal information processing activities or personal information security incidents occur during the performance of their duties.[315]

In conclusion, the judgment of auditors for legal control plays a pivotal role in ensuring compliance with data protection regulations and maintaining accountability in personal information processing activities. Auditors exercise professional judgment in collecting and assessing information, with a focus on maintaining independence and objectivity. The evolving landscape of data protection necessitates auditors to adapt their roles and responsibilities, including adopting risk assessment strategies and considering new and emerging issues. Regulatory measures, such as those outlined in Article 14, aim to uphold the integrity and competence of auditors while ensuring fair and objective compliance auditing. While internal audits may be permissible, conditions for mandatory external audits are also established to address high-risk scenarios or security incidents. Ultimately, auditors serve as crucial guardians of data protection, ensuring that organizations adhere to legal standards and safeguard individuals' privacy rights.

---

[312] Article 8 of Announcement of compliance audit of personal data protection. See online: http://www.cac.gov.cn/2023-08/03/c_1692628348448092.htm (Visited at August 5, 2023).

[313] Article 8 of Announcement of compliance audit of personal data protection. See online: http://www.cac.gov.cn/2023-08/03/c_1692628348448092.htm (Visited at August 5, 2023).

[314] Article 14 of Announcement of compliance audit of personal data protection. See online: http://www.cac.gov.cn/2023-08/03/c_1692628348448092.htm (VIsited at August 5, 2023).

[315] Article 6 of Announcement of compliance audit of personal data protection. See online: http://www.cac.gov.cn/2023-08/03/c_1692628348448092.htm (Visited at August 5, 2023).

Chapter 4
Summary

This book undertakes the challenge of untangling the enigma of audit by deconstructing its definition by functional approach. A recurring theme underlying audits is the demand it surfaces in environments characterized by lack of trust and by calling for accountability and transparency. Audits materialize when resources are entrusted, yet trust remains elusive and necessitates restoration. The catalyst for audits emerges as external agents—auditors—who intervene to rectify inherent trust deficits. The underlying conundrum lies in effectively assessing risk within various application contexts for personal data protection. It's crucial to delineate that "audit" should not be indiscriminately interchanged with terms like "verification," "validation," "certification," or "assessment". The "control revolution" underscores the transformative impact of technology on organizations. Audits encounter management and legal challenges in their role as regulatory entities for personal data protection. The audit system connects the function of management control and legal control internally and externally. The goal of audit extends to assisting organizations in better achieving compliance objectives, necessitating comprehensive audit coverage across the data lifecycle, and play a crucial role in audit effectiveness, especially through external auditors' role in responding to internal audit processes for external stakeholders and the public

H. Wu, C. Zhang, *Audit the Audit*, https://doi.org/10.1007/978-981-95-2473-0_4

Bibliography

Books

1. Acosta, Maribel, Cudré-Mauroux, Philippe, Maleshkova, Maria, et al., *Semantic Systems. The Power of AI and Knowledge Graphs: 15th International Conference, SEMANTiCS 2019* (Karlsruhe, Germany, Proceedings. Springer Nature, 2019).
2. Adam, Kadash, *The International Comparative Legal Guide to: Data protection* (global Legal Group Ltd).
3. American Accounting Association & Committee on Basic Auditing Concepts, *A statement of basic auditing concepts* (Sarasota: American Accounting Association, 1973).
4. Anthony, Robert N., *Planning and control systems; a framework for analysis* (Boston: Harvard University, 1965)
5. Auerbach, Jerold S., *Justice Without Law?: Non-Legal Dispute Settlement in American History*, (Oxford: Oxford Univ Press, 1983)
6. Belson, Jeffrey, *Certification Marks* (Sweet & Maxwell, 2002)
7. Bennett, Colin J., *PLUS 8830: implementing privacy codes of practice* (Etobicoke, Ont: Canadian Standards Association, 1995).
8. Berle, Adolf, & Means, Gardiner, *The Modern Corporation and Private Property* (New Brunswick: Transaction Publishers, 1991).
9. Bertalanffy, Ludwig von, *General System Theory* (New York: George Braziller Publishers, 2000)
10. Blair, Margaret M., *Ownership and Control: Rethinking Corporate Governance for the Twenty-First Century,* (Washington, D.C.: Brookings Institution Press, 1995).
11. Brownsword, Roger, *Rights, Regulation and the Technological Revolution,* (Oxford: Oxford University Press, 2011).
12. Burch, John G., *Systems Analysis, Design and Implementation*, 2nd ed (Boston, MA: Boyd & Fraser Pub Co, 1992)
13. C de Hoghton, *The Company: Law, Structure and Reform in Eleven Countries,* (London: George Allen & Unwin, 1970).
14. Carey, John L., *Rise of the Accounting Profession,* (City: Boston, American Institute of Certified Public Accountants, 1970).
15. Carissa, Hanratty, *Legal Risk to be a DPO* (City: Italy, IAPP, 2017)
16. Cavoukian, Ann, *Privacy By Design: Take the Challenge* (City: Montreal, Ann Cavoukian, 2009).
17. Cole, Eric, *Network Security Bible* (Indianapolis: Wiley, 2009).

H. Wu, C. Zhang, *Audit the Audit*, https://doi.org/10.1007/978-981-95-2473-0

18. Collins Dictionaries, *Collins English Dictionary and Thesaurus Boxed Set: All the words you need, every day* (Collins, 2019).
19. Conroy, Michael E., *Branded!: How the "Certification Revolution" is Transforming Global Corporations* (Gabriola, B.C: New Society Publishers, 2007)
20. Dennis, Ian, *Auditing Theory,* (Routledge, 2015)
21. Desai, Deven R., Lianos, Ioannis, & Waller, Spencer Weber, *Brands, competition law and IP* (Cambridge University Press: Cambridge University Press, 2015)
22. Dicksee, Lawrence Robert, & Rowland, Stanley William, *Auditing: A Practical Manual for Auditors,* (Gee, 1933)
23. Elbardan, Hany & Kholeif, Ahmed O., *Enterprise Resource Planning, Corporate Governance and Internal Auditing: An Institutional Perspective* (Springer, 2017).
24. Farrar, John H., *Farrar's Company law*, 3rd ed (London: Butterworths, 1991).
25. Federico, Giacomo Di, *The EU Charter of Fundamental Rights: From Declaration to Binding Instrument* (Springer Science & Business Media, 2010).
26. Flint, David, *Philosophy and principles of auditing: an introduction,* (Macmillan Education, 1988).
27. Fuller, Lon L., *The Morality of Law*, (City: Yale University Press, 1969)
28. Gaffiot, Felix, *Dictionary Latin-Francais* (Paris, 1934).
29. Garner, Bryan A., *Black's Law Dictionary* (St. Paul, MN: West Group, 2004).
30. Gautrais, Vincent, *Droit du commerce electronicque* (Montreal: Editions Themis, 2002).
31. Giddens, Anthony, *The Consequences of Modernity* (Stanford: Stanford University Press, 1991).
32. Goldberg, Ian, *Privacy Enhancing Technologies for the Internet III: Ten Years Later.*
33. Goldreich, Oded, *Foundations of Cryptography: A Primer,* (Boston: Now Pub, 2005).
34. Goyder, George, *The responsible company,* (Oxford: Blackwell, 1961).
35. Gratton, Eloïse, *Understanding Personal Information: Managing Privacy Risks* (Ontario: Markham, 2013)
36. Gratton, Eloïse, *Understanding Personal Information: Managing Privacy Risks,* (Markham, 2013).
37. Gray, Iain, & Manson, Stuart, *The Audit Process: Principles, Practice and Cases,* 5th ed (Andover: Cengage Learning EMEA, 2011)
38. Haes, Steven De, & Grembergen, Wim Van, *Enterprise Governance of Information Technology: Achieving Alignment and Value in Digital Organizations,* (Springer International Publishing, 2020)
39. Hardin, Russell, *Trust and trustworthiness, Trust and trustworthiness* (New York, NY, US: Russell Sage Foundation, 2002)
40. Havighurst, Harold Canfield, *The Nature of Private Contract,* (Toronto: F.B. Rothman, 1981)
41. Hayes, Rick, *Principles of Auditing*, 3rd ed (Harlow: Trans-Atlantic Publications Inc, 2014).
42. Hildebrandt, Mireille, *Smart Technologies and the End(s) of Law: Novel Entanglements of Law and Technology* (Cheltenham: Edward Elgar Pub, 2016).
43. Hodges, Christopher, *Organizational Accountability in Data Protection Enforcement* (British: CIPL, 2021).
44. Hood, C., & Jones, D. K. C., *Accident And Design: Contemporary Debates On Risk Management* (London: Routledge, 1996).
45. Hopkin, Paul, *Fundamentals of Risk Management: Understanding, Evaluating and Implementing Effective Risk Management* (New York: Kogan Page, 2018).
46. Horák, Martin, Stupka, Václav, & Husák, Martin, *GDPR Compliance in Cybersecurity Software: A Case Study of DPIA in Information Sharing Platform*, (New York, NY, USA: Association for Computing Machinery, 2019)
47. IDM, *Cambridge Advanced Learner's Dictionary with CD-ROM* (Cambridge: Cambridge University Press, 2013).
48. In, Lee, *Electronic Business: Concepts, Methodologies, Tools, and Applications: Concepts, Methodologies, Tools, and Applications* (IGI Global, 2008).

49. Jay, Rosemary, *Data Protection Law & Practice* (London: Sweet & Maxwell, 2012).
50. Jay, Rosemary, *Guide to the General Data Protection Regulation: A Companion to Data Protection Law and Practice* (London: Sweet & Maxwell, 2017)
51. Johnson, Deborah G., & Regan, Priscilla M., *Transparency and Surveillance as Sociotechnical Accountability: A House of Mirrors* (New York: Routledge, 2014)
52. Johnson, Raymond N., Wiley, Laura Davis, Moroney, Robyn, et al., *Auditing: A Practical Approach with Data Analytics* (John Wiley & Sons, 2019)
53. Kindleberger, Charles P., & Aliber, Robert Z., *Manias, Panics and Crashes: A History of Financial Crises* (Palgrave Macmillan, 2011).
54. Koontz, Harold, & Weihrich, Heinz, *Management* (New York: McGraw-Hill Inc., 1988)
55. Kuner, Christopher, Bygrave, Lee, Docksey, Christopher, et al., *The EU General Data Protection Regulation (GDPR): A Commentary*, (Oxford, New York: Oxford University Press, 2020).
56. Lambert, Paul, *The Data Protection Officer : Profession, Rules, and Role,* (City: Auerbach Publications, 2016).
57. Lee, T. A., & Parker, R. H., *Evolution of Corporate Financial Reporting* (City: Routledge, 2014).
58. Lee, T. A., *Company auditing* (Wokingham: Van Nostrand Reinhold, 1986).
59. Lewis-Beck, Michael, Bryman, Alan E., & Liao, Tim Futing, *The SAGE Encyclopedia of Social Science Research Methods* (City: SAGE Publications, 2003).
60. Littleton, A. C., *Accounting evolution to 1900* (New York: American Institute Pub. Co., Inc., 1933).
61. Lopucki, Lynn M., & Warren, Elizabeth, *Secured Credit: A Systems Approach*, (New York: Kluwer Law Intl, 2011).
62. Lyon, Bruce Dale, *Constitutional and Legal History of Medieval England* (New York: Norton, 1980).
63. MacNeil, Heather, *Trusting records: legal, historical and diplomatic perspectives* (Dordrecht: Publisher, 2000).
64. Mautz, Robert Kuhn, & Sharaf, Hussein Amer, *The Philosophy of Auditing* (American Accounting Association, 1961)
65. Mayer-Schonberger, Viktor, & Cukier, Kenneth, *Big Data: A Revolution That Will Transform How We Live, Work, and Think* (Boston: Eamon Dolan/Mariner Books, 2014).
66. McConnell, Steve, *Code Complete* (Redmond, Wash: Microsoft Press, 2004).
67. McGraw, Gary R., *Software Security: Building Security* (Upper Saddle River: Addison-Wesley Professional, 2006).
68. Moeller, Robert R., *IT Audit, Control, and Security*, 1 ed (Wiley, 2010).
69. National Institute of Standards and Technology, *NISTIR 8053 De-Identification of Personal Information: NiSTIR 8053* (CreateSpace Independent Publishing Platform, 2015).
70. Niglia, Leone, *Pluralism and European Private Law,* (Oxford: Hart Publishing, 2013).
71. *Oxford Dictionary of English* (New York, NY: Oxford University Press, 2010)
72. Pasquale, Frank, The Black Box Society*: The Secret Algorithms That Control Money and Information* (Cambridge: Harvard University Press, 2016).
73. Pass, C. L., Lowes, B., & Davies, L., *Collins Dictionary of Economics* (Glasgow: Harper Collins Pub Ltd, 1991).
74. Post, James E., Preston, Lee E., & Sauter-Sachs, Sybille, *Redefining the Corporation: Stakeholder Management and Organizational Wealth,* (Stanford: Stanford University Press, 2002).
75. Power, Michael, *Organized Uncertainty: Designing a World of Risk Management*, (Oxford, New York: Oxford University Press, 2007).
76. Power, Michael, *The Audit Society: Rituals of Verification* (Oxford: Oxford University Press, 1999).

77. Raji, Inioluwa Deborah, & Buolamwini, Joy, *Actionable Auditing: Investigating the Impact of Publicly Naming Biased Performance Results of Commercial AI Products* , (Honolulu,: Association for Computing Machinery, 2019).
78. Raz, Joseph, *The authority of law: Essays on law and morality* (Oxford: Oxford University Press, 1979).
79. Regan, Priscilla M., & Johnson, Deborah G., "Privacy and Trust in Socio-technical Systems of Accountability", in Ilten, Carla, Kroener, Inga, Neyland, Daniel, et al., eds., *Managing Privacy through Accountability* (London: Palgrave Macmillan, 2012).
80. Rittenberg, Larry E., *The Outsourcing Dilemma: What's Best for Internal Auditing,* (New York: Institute of Internal Auditors Research Foundation, 1997)
81. Romano, Roberta, *The Genius of American Corporate Law,* (New York, American Enterprise Institute, 1993).
82. Rosnay, Joël de, *The macroscope: A new world scientific system* (New York: Harper & Row, 1979)
83. Rott, Peter, *Certification – Trust, Accountability, Liability* (Singapore, Springer, 2019).
84. Royal Society Study Group, *Risk: Analysis, Perception and Management* (London: The Royal Society, 1992).
85. Schedler, Andreas, Diamond, Larry, & Plattner, Marc F., *The Self Restraining State: Power and Accountability in New Democracies* (Boulder, Colo.: Lynne Rienner Pub, 1999).
86. Senft, Sandra, & Gallegos, Frederick, *Information Technology Control and Audit* (New York: Auerbach Publications, 2008).
87. Shearing, Clifford D., & Stenning, Phillip C., *Private Policing* (Boston: SAGE Publications, 1987)
88. Sikka, P., *Philosophy and principles of auditing: An introduction* (Basingstoke: Macmillan, 1988).
89. Souyris, Jean, Wiels, Virginie, Delmas, David, et al., *Formal Verification of Avionics Software Products* (Berlin: Springer, 2009).
90. Steele, Anthony, *Audit Risk and Audit Evidence: The Bayesian Approach to Statistical Auditing* (London: Academic, 1992).
91. Stein, Peter, *Legal Evolution: The Story of an Idea* (Cambridge: Cambridge University Press, 2009).
92. Stevens, Mark, *The Big Eight* (New York: Scribner, 1984).
93. Trade and Cross-Border Data Flows, by Francesca Casalini & Javier López González, OECD iLibrary (Paris: OECD, 2019).
94. Trudel, Pierre., *Privacy Protection on the Internet: Risk Management and Networked Normativity* (The Netherlands: Springer, 2009)
95. Webster, Noah, *New International dictionary of the English language* (Springfield: Merriam, 1949).
96. West, Brian P., *Professionalism and Accounting Rules* (Routledge, 2003).
97. Whittington, R., & Pany, K., *Principles of Auditing & Other Assurance Services* (New York, NY: McGraw-Hill Education, 2015)
98. Wright, David & de Hert, Paul, *Privacy Impact Assessment, Law, Governance and Technology Series* (The Netherlands: Springer, 2012).
99. Wright, David, & Hert, Paul De, *Enforcing Privacy: Regulatory, Legal and Technological Approaches* (Springer, 2016).
100. Greenleaf, Graham, *Asian Data Privacy Laws: Trade & Human Rights Perspectives* (Oxford: OUP, 2014)

Secondary Materials: Articles

101. Administracion Electronica, “Metrica V3” online: https://administracionelectronica.gob.es/pae_Home/pae_Documentacion/pae_Metodolog/pae_Metrica_v3.html?idioma=en
102. Alhadeff, Joseph, Alsenoy, Brendan Van, & Dumortier, Jos, “The Accountability Principle in Data Protection Regulation: Origin, Development and Future Directions” in Guagnin, Daniel, Hempel, Leon, and Ilten, Carla, eds., *Manage Privacy Account* (London: Palgrave Macmillan UK, 2012).
103. Ambrose, Stephen F. Jr. & Gelb, Joseph W. “Consumer Privacy Regulation and Litigation Survey” (2001) 57:3 Bus. Law. 1231 at 1241.
104. Anand, Karthik, & Suremya, S. L., “External and Internal Rules of Corporate Governance” (2021) 4 Int. J. L. Manag. Hum. 2887–2902 at 2887.
105. Anciaux, Nicolas, Bonnet, Philippe, Bouganim, Luc, et al., “Personal Data Management Systems: The security and functionality standpoint” (2019) 80 Inf. Syst. 13–35 at 17.
106. Andrews, Leighton, “Public administration, public leadership and the construction of public value in the age of the algorithm and ‘big data’” (2019) 97:2 Public Adm. 296.
107. ANSI Webstore, "Standard Specification For Audit And Disclosure Logs For Use In Health Information Systems" online: ANSI Webstore <https://webstore.ansi.org/Standards/ASTM/ASTME214718?gclid=CjwKCAjwmrn5BRB2EiwAZgL9osWSjNToFm_HyVeABvxCQyp3HJDPSKj5efW-35KQZt2yXiDjWlemHRoCvqoQAvD_BwE>
108. Appelbaum, Deniz, Kogan, Alexander, & Vasarhelyi, Miklos A., “Big data and analytics in the modern audit engagement: Research needs” (2017) 36:4 Aud. 1–27 at 26.
109. Bame-Aldred, Charles W., Brandon, Duane M., Messier Jr, William F., et al., “A Summary of Research on External Auditor Reliance on the Internal Audit Function” (2012) 32 Supp. Aud. J. Pract. Theory 251–286 at 262.
110. Bartos, Vaclav, Zadnik, Martin, Habib, Sheikh Mahbub, et al., “Network entity characterization and attack prediction” (2019) 97 Future Gen. Comput. Syst. 674-686.
111. Bateman, Robert, “Conducting a GDPR Data Audit” online: Terms Feed <https://www.termsfeed.com/blog/gdpr-data-audit>
112. Bayne, David C., “The Definition of Corporate Control” (1964) 9:4 St. Louis Uni. L. J. 445–463
113. Becker, Regina, Alper, Pinar, Grouès, Valentin, et al., “DAISY: A Data Information System for accountability under the General Data Protection Regulation” (2019) 8:12 GigaScience, giz140.
114. Bennett, Colin J., “The Accountability Approach to Privacy and Data Protection: Assumptions and Caveats” in Guagnin, Daniel, Hempel, Leon, & Ilten, Carla, eds., *Manage Privacy Account* (London: Palgrave Macmillan UK, 2012)
115. Berman, Paul Schiff, “Global Legal Pluralism” (2007) SSRN Scholarly Paper 985340.
116. Bhardwaj, Anant, Bhattacherjee, Souvik, Chavan, Amit, et al., “DataHub: Collaborative Data Science & Dataset Version Management at Scale” (2014) ArXiv14090798.
117. Birch, Kean, Cochrane, D. T., & Ward, Callum, “Data as asset? The measurement, governance, and valuation of digital personal data by Big Tech” (2021) 8:1 Big Data Soc. 20539517211017308
118. Bonnici, Jeanne Pia Mifsud, Tudorica, Melania, & Cannataci, Joseph A., “The European Legal Framework on Electronic Evidence: Complex and in Need of Reform” (2018) Handl. Exch. Elect. Evid. Eur. 189–235 at 192.
119. Bovens, Mark, “Analysing and Assessing Accountability: A Conceptual Framework” (2007) 13:4 Eur Law J 447.
120. Branch, Amanda, "Misleading Privacy Claims Results in $9 Million Dollar Penalty for Facebook" online: Bereskin & Parr <https://www.bereskinparr.com/doc/misleading-privacy-claims-results-in-9-million-dollar-penalty-for-facebook?utm_source=Mondaq&utm_medium=syndication&utm_campaign=LinkedIn-integration>

121. Brewer, Gene A., Walker, Richard M., Bozeman, Barry, et al., “External Control and Red Tape: The Mediating Effects of Client and Organizational Feedback” (2012) 15:3 Int. Public Manag. J. 288–314 at 357.
122. Broeders, Dennis, Schrijvers, Erik, Sloot, Bart van der, et al., “Big data and security policies: Towards a framework for regulating the phases of analytics and use of Big Data” (2017) 33:3 Comput Law Secur Rev 309 at 318.
123. Bryson, Joanna J., Diamantis, Mihailis E., & Grant, Thomas D., “Of, for, and by the people: the legal lacuna of synthetic persons” (2017) 25:3 Artif. Intell. Law 273–291.
124. Buckland, Michael, “On the Nature of Records Management Theory” (1994) 57:2 Am. Arch. 346–351.
125. Burgunder, Lee B., “An Economic Approach to Trademark Genericism” (1985) 23 Am. Bus. L. J. 391–416 at 875.
126. Burrell, Jenna, “How the machine ‘thinks’: Understanding opacity in machine learning algorithms” (2016) 3 Big Data Soc. 2053951715622512.
127. Carpenter, Brian, & Dirsmith, Mark, “Sampling and the abstraction of knowledge in the auditing profession: An extended institutional theory perspective” (1993) 18:1 Acc. Org. Soc. 41–63.
128. Casey, Bryan, Farhangi, Ashkon, & Vogl, Roland, “Rethinking Explainable Machines: The GDPR’s ‘Right to Explanation’ Debate and the Rise of Algorithmic Audits in Enterprise” (2018) SSRN Scholarly Paper 3143325.
129. Cate, Fred H., & Mayer-Schönberger, Viktor, “Notice and consent in a world of Big Data,” (2013) 3 Intl. Data Priv. L. 67
130. Cecily Raiborn et al., “The Internal Audit Function: A Prerequisite for Good Governance” (2017) 28:2 J. Corp. Acc. Fin. 10–21.
131. Center for Internet & Human Rights of European University Viadrina, “The Ethics of Algorithms: from radical content to self-driving cars”, online: Center for Internet & Human Rights <https://cihr.eu/wp-content/uploads>.(Visited on April 16, 2019).
132. Chenhall, Robert H., “Management control systems design within its organizational context: findings from contingency-based research and directions for the future” (2003) 28:2 Acc. Org. Soc. 127–168 at 152–157.
133. Cherney, Max A., "Luckin Coffee to resume trading Wednesday after being halted for more than a month" online: Market Watch <https://www.marketwatch.com/story/luckin-coffee-to-resume-trading-wednesday-as-company-receives-delisting-notice-2020-05-19>
134. Chon, Margaret, “Marks and more(s): certification in global value chains” online: Elgar Online <https://www.elgaronline.com/view/edcoll/9781781953907/9781781953907.00013.xml>
135. Christian Fuchs, “Towards an alternative concept of privacy” (2011) 9:4 J. Inf. Commun. Ethics Soc. 220–237.
136. Colaert, Veerle, “Systematisation as a Response to Regulatory Expansion in the Financial Sector” online: SSRN <https://www.academia.edu/31897087/RegTech_as_a_response_to_regulatory_expansion_in_the_financial_sector>.
137. Computer, “Software Engineering Body of Knowledge (SWEBOK) | IEEE Computer Society”, online: <https://www.computer.org/education/bodies-of-knowledge/software-engineering> at STD-610.
138. Connolly, Chris, “Trustmark Schemes Struggle to Protect Privacy.” Online: Galexia <http://www.galexia.com/public/research/assets/trustmarks_struggle_20080926>
139. Contreras, Jorge L., “Trademarks, Certification Marks and Technical Standards” (2018) SSRN Scholarly Paper ID 3209855.
140. Coss, David L., Smith, Kane, Foster, Jackson, et al., “Big Data in Auditing: A Value-Focused Approach to Cybersecurity Management” (2019) 15:2 J Inf. Syst. Secur. 77–100.
141. Cruz-Correia, Ricardo, Boldt, Isabel, Lapão, Luís, et al., “Analysis of the quality of hospital information systems Audit Trails” (2013) 13 BMC Med. Inf. Decis. Mak. 84
142. Cusumano, Michael A., & Smith, Stanley A., “Beyond the waterfall : software development at Microsoft” online: <https://dspace.mit.edu/handle/1721.1/2593>

143. Darby, Michael, & Karni, Edi, “Free Competition and the Optimal Amount of Fraud” (1973) 16 J. L. Econ. 67–88 at 67.
144. Data Protection Working Party, "Opinion3/2010 on the principle of accountability," online: Data Protection Working Party, Article 29. https://www.dataprotection.ro/servlet/ViewDocument?id=654
145. Datta, Amit, Tschantz, Michael Carl, & Datta, Anupam, “Automated Experiments on Ad Privacy Settings: A Tale of Opacity, Choice, and Discrimination” (2015) ArXiv14086491 Cs.
146. de Carvalho, Renata M., Prete, Camillo Del, Martin, Yod Samuel, et al., “Protecting Citizens' Personal Data and Privacy: Joint Effort from GDPR EU Cluster Research Projects” (2020) 1:4 SN Comput. Sci. 217.
147. Debessay, Araya, “Auditing and Assurance Services (Book)” (2003) 18:1 Issues Acc. Educ 107.
148. Desai, Deven R., & Kroll, Joshua R., “Trust But Verify: A Guide to Algorithms and the Law” (2017) 31 Harv. J. L. & Tech. 1.
149. Dhiaa, Shamki, “Factors Influence Internal Audit Effectiveness” (2017) 10 Int. J. Bus. Manag. 143.
150. Diaz, Claudia, Tene, Omer, & Guerses, Seda F., “Hero or Villain: The Data Controller in Privacy Law and Technologies,” (2013) SSRN Scholarly Paper ID 2321480
151. Dirsmith, Mark W., & Haskins, Mark E., “Inherent risk assessment and audit firm technology: A contrast in world theories” (1991) 16:1 Acc. Org. Soc. 61–90 at 64.
152. Duranti, Luciana, Rogers, Corinne, & Sheppard, Anthony, “Electronic Records and the Law of Evidence in Canada: The Uniform Electronic Evidence Act Twelve Years Later” (2010) 70 Archivaria 97.
153. EC Data Protection Working Party, “Legitimate Interests” online: <https://ec.europa.eu/justice/article-29/press-material/public-consultation/notion-legitimate-interests/files/20141126_overview_relating_to_consultation_on_opinion_legitimate_interest_.pdf>.
154. EC Europa, “Guidelines on Automated individual decision-making and profiling for the purposes of regulation 2016/679” online: EC Europa https://ec.europa.eu/newsroom/article29/item-detail.cfm?item_id=612053.
155. ECSG, "APEC data privacy pathfinder projects implementation work plan" 2008/SOM1/ECSG/024, online: ECSG <https://www.apec.org/about-us/about-apec/fact-sheets/apec-privacy-framework>
156. Ekstrand, Victoria Smith, “Lessig, Lawrence. The Law of the Horse: What Cyberlaw Might Teach (1999) 113 Harv. L. Rev. 501.
157. Electronic Commerce Steering Group (ECSG), "APEC Privacy Framework," online: ECSG <http://mddb.apec.org/Documents/2016/SOM/CSOM/16_csom_012app17.pdf>
158. Ellul, Andrew, “The Role of Risk Management in Corporate Governance” (2015) 7:1 Ann. Rev. Fin. Econ. 279–299 at 731.
159. EuroPrise, “Home” online: EuroPrise <https://www.euprivacyseal.com/EPS-en/Home>
160. Ezzamel, Mahmoud, “Accounting, Control and Accountability: Preliminary Evidence From Ancient Egypt” (1997) 8:6 Crit. Perspect. Account. 563.
161. Fama, Eugene F., “Agency Problems and the Theory of the Firm” (1980) 88 J. Polit. Econ. 288–307.
162. Federal Trade Commission (FTC), “TRUSTe Settles FTC Charges it Deceived Consumers Through Its Privacy Seal Program” online: FTC https://www.ftc.gov/news-events/press-releases/2014/11/truste-settles-ftc-charges-it-deceived-consumers-through-its
163. Federal Trade Commission, “In the Matter of True Ultimate Standards Everywhere, Inc., a corporation. Agreement containing consent order” online: FTC <https://www.ftc.gov/news-events/press-releases/2015/03/ftc-approves-final-order-truste-privacy-case>
164. Financial Reporting Council, “Standards and Guidance” online: FRC <https://www.frc.org.uk/auditors/audit-assurance/standards-and-guidance>
165. Fischer, Michael J., “‘Real-izing’ the benefits of new technologies as a source of audit evidence: An interpretive field study” (1996) 21:2–3 Acc. Org. Soc. 219–242.

166. Flamholtz, Eric G., Das, T. K. & Tsui, Anne S., "Toward an integrative framework of organizational control" (1985) 10:1 Acc. Org. Soc. 35–50.
167. Flemming, Ruud, "Corporate Governance und Interne Revision" (2001) 75 Schweiz Treuhander 521–534
168. FTC News, "FTC Imposes $5 Billion Penalty and Sweeping New Privacy Restrictions on Facebook", online: FTC News <https://www.ftc.gov/news-events/press-releases/2019/07/ftc-imposes-5-billion-penalty-sweeping-new-privacy-restrictions>
169. Fuchs, Christian, "Towards an alternative concept of privacy" (2011) 9:4 J. Inf. Commun. Ethics Soc. 220–237.
170. Gautrais, Vincent, "COVI: dommage!" online: Gautrais <https://www.gautrais.com/blogue/2020/06/05/covi-pourquoi-pas/>
171. Gautrais, Vincent, & Gingras, Patrick, "La preuve des documents technologiques" online: LESCPI <https://www.lescpi.ca/articles/v22/volume-22-numero-2/la-preuve-des-documents-technologiques/>.
172. Gautrais, Vincent, "Circulation des renseignements personnels et web 2.0", online: Gautrais https://www.gautrais.com/publications/circulation-des-renseignements-personnels-et-web-2-0/
173. Gautrais, Vincent, "La preuve technologique" online: Gautrais <https://www.gautrais.com/publications/la-preuve-technologique/> .
174. Gautrais, Vincent, "Neutralité technologique: Rédaction et interprétation des lois face aux changements technologiques" (2012) Ed Themis.
175. Gautrais, Vincent, "Normativité et droit du technique", online: <https://www.gautrais.com/publications/normativite-et-droit-du-technique/>.
176. Gellert, Raphaël, "Understanding the notion of risk in the General Data Protection Regulation" (2018) 34:2 Comput. L. Secur. Rev. 279–288 at 283.
177. Gellman, Robert, "The Deidentification Dilemma: A Legislative and Contractual Proposal" (2010) 21 Fordham Intell. Prop. Media & Ent. LJ (2010).
178. Gils, Diane van, Visscher, Christian de, & Sarens, Gerrit, "Le développement de l'audit interne dans le secteur public belge" (2012) 18:3 Télescope Rev D'analyse Comparée En Adm Publique 73–107.
179. Gong, Mengchun, Wang, Shuang, Wang, Lezi, et al., "Evaluation of Privacy Risks of Patients' Data in China: Case Study" (2020) 8:2 JMIR Med. Info. e13046.
180. Gordon, Robert W., "Critical Legal Histories Critical Legal Studies Symposium" (1984) 36: Issues 1 & 2 Stanf. L. Rev. 57–126
181. Grabosky, Peter N., "Using Non-Governmental Resources to Foster Regulatory Compliance" (1995) 8:4 Governance 527–550.
182. Gramling, A., A., "Research Opportunities in Internal Auditing" (2003) Inst. Intern. Audit Res. Found. 2.
183. Gratton, Eloïse, "If Personal Information is Privacy's Gatekeeper, then Risk of Harm is the Key: A Proposed Method for Determining What Counts as Personal Information" (2013) SSRN Scholarly Paper 2334938.
184. Greene, Frederick D., Petrocine, Alfonse R., & FitzPatrick, Richard C., "Holding Accountants Accountable: The Liability of Accountants to Third Parties" (2003) 15:1 Empl. Respons. Rights J. 23–29.
185. Greenleaf, Graham, "Accountability Without Liability: 'To Whom' and 'With What Consequences'?" (2019) SSRN Scholarly Paper 3384427
186. Guagnin, Daniel, Hempel, Leon, & Ilten, Carla, eds., *Manage Privacy Account* (London: Palgrave Macmillan UK, 2012)
187. Guidotti, Riccardo, Monreale, Anna, Ruggieri, Salvatore, et al., "A survey of methods for explaining black box models." (2018) 51 ACM Comput. Surv. 1-42.
188. Hansen, Morris H., "Some History and Reminiscences on Survey Sampling" (1987) 2 Stat. Sci. 180–190.

189. Harner, Michelle M., "Barriers to Effective Risk Management Securities Regulation and the Global Economic Crisis: What Does the Future Hold" (2010) 40:4 Seton Hall L. Rev. 1323–1366 at 1326.
190. Harrod, R. F., "The Theory of Monopolistic Competition. by Edward Chamberlin" (1933) 43 Econ. J. 661–666 at 213–215.
191. Hay, David, "Internal Control: How it Evolved in Four English-speaking Countries" (1993) 20:1 Acc. Hist J. 79.
192. Hellner, Jan, "The New Swedish Tort Liability Act" (1974) 22 Am. J. Comp. L. 1–16.
193. Heurix, Johannes, Zimmermann, Peter, Neubauer, Thomas, et al., "A taxonomy for privacy enhancing technologies" (2015) 53 Comput. Secur. 1–17 at 2.
194. Hildebrandt, Mireille, & Koops, Bert-Jaap, "The Challenges of Ambient Law and Legal Protection in the Profiling Era" (2010) 73 Mod. L. Rev. 428–460.
195. Hildebrandt, Mireille, "The Dawn of a Critical Transparency Right for the Profiling Era" online: BePress <https://works.bepress.com/mireille_hildebrandt/40/>.
196. Hoare, C. A. R., "An axiomatic basis for computer programming" (1969) 12:10 Commun. ACM 576–580 at 576.
197. Holm, Claus, & Zaman, Mahbub, "Regulating audit quality: Restoring trust and legitimacy" (2012) 36:1 Acc. Forum 51–61 at 58.
198. Hoskin, Keith, "The 'awful idea of accountability': inscribing people into the measurement of objects" in Rolland Munro & Jan Mouritsen, eds., *Accountability: Power, ethos and the technologies of managing* (City: Publisher, 1996).
199. Hynes Farrar, John, "Corporate Governance and the Judges" (2003) SSRN Scholarly Paper ID 2146394.
200. IAPP, "Corporate" online: IAPP <https://iapp.org/join/corporate/>
201. IAPP: "Certifications, Seals and Marks under the GDPR and Their Roles as Accountability Tools and Cross-Border Data Transfer Mechanisms" online: IAPP. https://iapp.org/media/pdf/resource_center/cipl_gdpr_certifications_discussion_paper_12_april_2017.pdf,
202. ICO, "Legitimate interests" online: ICO <https://ico.org.uk/for-organisations/guide-to-data-protection/guide-to-the-general-data-protection-regulation-gdpr/lawful-basis-for-processing/legitimate-interests/>.
203. ICO, "Guide to the General Data Protection Regulation (GDPR)", online: ICO <https://ico.org.uk/for-organisations/guide-to-the-general-data-protection-regulation-gdpr/>.
204. Informatica, "data mapping" online: Informatica <https://www.informatica.com/resources/articles/data-mapping.html>
205. Informatica, "What is data mapping?" online: Informatica <https://www.informatica.com/resources/articles/data-mapping.html>
206. International Commissioner's Office (ICO), "Guide to the General Data Protection Regulation (GDPR)", online: ICO <https://ico.org.uk/for-organisations/guide-to-the-general-data-protection-regulation-gdpr/>.
207. International Organization for Standardization (ISO), "ISO/IEC 27001 Information security management" online: ISO <https://www.iso.org/isoiec-27001-information-security.html>
208. International Organization for Standardization, "Conformity assessment-requirements for bodies certifying products, processes and services" online: ISO http://www.iso.org/iso/catalogue_detail.htm?csnumber=46568
209. Investopedia, "Accounting Standards Committee" online: Investopaedeia <https://www.investopedia.com/terms/a/accounting-standards-committee/asc.asp>
210. ISACA, *COBIT*, online: ISACA https://www.isaca.org/resources/cobit.
211. ISO, "Definition of Risk" online: ISO <https://www.iso.org/standard/43170.html>
212. ISO, "Guidelines for auditing management systems ISO 19011" online: ISO <https://www.iso.org/standard/70017.html>
213. ISO, "ISO 27000" online: ISO <https://www.27000.org/>
214. ISO, "ISO 31000 Risk Management" online: ISO https://www.iso.org/iso-31000-risk-management.html

215. ISO, “ISO/IEC 15504-1:2004 Information technology- process assessment-Part 1: Concepts and vocabulary” online: ISO <https://www.iso.org/standard/38932.html>
216. ITSC, “Risk assessment, classification and mitigation” online: ITSC <https://itsc.hkust.edu.hk/it-policies-guidelines/risk-assessment-classification-and-mitigation>
217. Jayasinghe, Upul, Lee, Gyu Myoung, Um, Tai-Won, et al., “Machine Learning Based Trust Computational Model for IoT Services” (2019) 4:1 IEEE Trans. Sust. Comput. 39–52.
218. Jenn, Riley, “Understanding Metadata” online: <https://www.niso.org/publications/understanding-metadata>
219. Joyce, Edward J., “Expert Judgment in Audit Program Planning” (1976) 14 J. Acc. Res. 29–60 at 29.
220. Kaminski, Margot E., “Binary Governance: Lessons from the GDPR’s Approach to Algorithmic Accountability” (2019) SSRN Scholarly Paper 3351404.
221. Kaminski, Margot E., “The Right to Explanation, Explained” (2018) SSRN Scholarly Paper 3196985.
222. Keasey, Kevin, & Wright, Mike, “Issues In Corporate Accountability and Governance: An Editorial” (1993) 23:91 Account Bus Res 291 at 291.
223. Kent, William, *Data and Reality: A Timeless Perspective on Perceiving and Managing Information in Our Imprecise World*, (Westfield: Technics Publications, LLC, 2012)
224. Kim, Pauline, “Auditing Algorithms for Discrimination” (2017) 166 Univ. Pa. L. Rev. 166
225. Klinke, A., & Renn, O., “Prometheus unbound - challenges of risk evaluation, risk classification, and risk management” online: OSTI <https://www.osti.gov/etdeweb/biblio/20039357>
226. Kratzke, William P., “Normative Economic Analysis of Trademark Law, SSRN Scholarly Paper” 1991 SSRN Scholarly Paper ID 1702386
227. Krogstad, Jack L., Ridley, Anthony J., & Rittenberg, Larry E. "Where we're going." (1999) 56 Int. Aud. 27-27.
228. Kurth, Hunton Andrews, "French Highest Administrative Court Upholds 50 Million Euro Fine against Google for Alleged GDPR Violations" online: Hunton Andrews Kurth <https://www.huntonprivacyblog.com/2020/06/23/french-highest-administrative-court-upholds-50-million-euro-fine-against-google-for-alleged-gdpr-violations/>
229. Lachaud, Eric, “Why the certification process defined in the General Data Protection Regulation cannot be successful” (2016) 32:6 Comput. L. Sec. Rev. 814–826, at 815.
230. Langfield-Smith, Kim, “Management control systems and strategy: A critical review” (1997) 22:2 Acc. Org. Soc. 207–232.
231. Lazaro, Christophe, & Métayer, Daniel Le, “Control over Personal Data: True Remedy or Fairy Tale?” (2015) SSRN Scholarly Paper 2689223.
232. LCCJTI, "GAUTRAIS V. and GINGRAS P., "Proof of technological documents" online: https://www.lccjti.ca/doctrine/gautrais-gingras/
233. LCCJTI, “Frequently Asked Questions” online: <https://www.lccjti.ca/faq/>
234. LCCJTI.ca, “Article 7” online: https://www.lccjti.ca/articles/article-7/
235. Lessig, Lawrence, “The Law of the Horse: What Cyberlaw Might Teach” (1999) 113:2 Harv Law Rev 501–549
236. Levinthal, Daniel A., & Fichman, Mark, “Dynamics of Interorganizational Attachments: Auditor-Client Relationships” (1988) 33 Adm. Sci. Q. 345–369.
237. Lisiak-Felicka, Dominika, Szmit, Maciej, & Vaiciuniene, Jolanta, “The General Data Protection Regulation 3 Years After Implementation: A Comparison between Local Government Administration in Poland and the Republic of Lithuania” (2022) XXV:1 Eur. Res. Stud. J. 382–394 at 390.
238. LoPucki, L., & Triantis, George G., “A Systems Approach to Comparing U.S. and Canadian Reorganization of Financially Distressed Companies”, online: </paper/A-Systems-Approach-to-Comparing-U.S.-and-Canadian-LoPucki-Triantis/b38cbc0e258ec0cf25ee852e3ca36d2c80843f13>.
239. LoPucki, Lynn M., “Systems Approach to Law” (1996) 82:3 Cornell L. Rev. 479–522.

240. Lowe, D., Geiger, Marshall, & Pany, Kurt, "The Effects of Internal Audit Outsourcing on Perceived External Auditor Independence" (1999) 18 Audit J. Pract. Theory 41–44
241. Lugaresi, Nicola, "Principles and Regulations about Online Privacy: 'Implementaion Divide' and Misunderstanding in the European Union", (2002) TPRC 2002 Working Paper 42
242. Lynskey, Orla, "Deconstructing Data Protection: The 'Added-Value' of a Right to Data Protection in the EU Legal Order" (2014) 63 Int. Comp. L. Q. 569–597.
243. Maillart, Thomas, Zhao, Mingyi, Grossklags, Jens, et al., "Given enough eyeballs, all bugs are shallow? Revisiting Eric Raymond with bug bounty programs" (2017) 3:2 J Cybersecurity 81–90.
244. Malkin, Bonnie, "Water pistol emoji replaces revolver as Apple enters gun violence debate" online: The Guardian <https://www.theguardian.com/technology/2016/aug/02/apple-replaces-gun-emoji-water-pistol-revolver-violence-debate>.
245. Management study guide, "Function of management" online: Management study guide <https://www.managementstudyguide.com/management_functions.htm>
246. Mantelero, Alessandro, "The Future of Consumer Data Protection in the E.U. Rethinking the "Notice and Consent" Paradigm in the New Era of Predictive Analytics" (2014) 30 Comp. L. & Sec. Rev. 643
247. Matteo La, Torre, Botes, Vida Lucia, Dumay, John, et al., "Protecting a new Achilles heel: the role of auditors within the practice of data protection" (2019) 36:2 Manag. Aud. J. 218–239 at 229.
248. Mazur, Joanna, "Right to Access Information As a Collective-Based Approach to the GDPR's Right to Explanation in European Law" (2018) SSRN Scholarly Paper 3356770.
249. Merchant, Kenneth, "The control function of management" (1992) 23 Sloan Manag. Rev. 43
250. Merry, Sally Engle, "Legal Pluralism" (1988) 22:5 L. Soc. Rev. 869–896
251. Michael, Conroy, "Can Advocacy-Led Certification Systems Transform Global Corporate Practices? Evidence and Some Theory" (2001) Pol. Econ. Res. Inst. 4.
252. Moore, Don A., Tetlock, Philip E., Tanlu, Lloyd, et al., "Conflicts of interest and the case of auditor independence: Moral seduction and strategic issue cycling" (2006) 31 Acad. Manag. Rev. 10–29
253. Moores, Trevor, "Do consumers understand the role of privacy seals in e-commerce?" (2005) 48 Commun. ACM 86–91.
254. Morse, Janice M., Barrett, Michael, Mayan, Maria, et al., "Verification Strategies for Establishing Reliability and Validity in Qualitative Research": (2016) 1 Int. J. Qual. Methods 13.
255. Moses, Lyria Bennett, "Agents of Change: How the Law Copes with Technological Change Special Issue: The Laws of Technology and the Technology of Law" (2011) 20 Griffith L. Rev. 763–794.
256. Mulgan, Richard, "'Accountability': An Ever-Expanding Concept?" (2000) 78:3 Public Adm. 555–573 at 560.
257. Nelson, Phillip, "Information and Consumer Behavior" (1970) 78 J. Pol. Econ. 311–329.
258. O'Malley, Pat, "Uncertain subjects: risks, liberalism and contract" (2000) 29:4 Econ. Soc. 460–484 at 460.
259. O'Sullivan, Noel, & Wong, Pauline, "Internal versus External Control: An Analysis of Board Composition and Ownership in UK Takeovers" (1998) 2:1 J Manag Gov 17–35.
260. O'Sullivan, Noel, "Auditors' Liability: Its Role in the Corporate Governance Debate" (1993) 23 Acc. Bus. Res. 412–420 at 415.
261. OECD, "Explanatory of Memorandum of OECD Guideline," online: OECD <https://www.oecd.org/internet/ieconomy/oecdguidelinesontheprotectionofprivacyandtransborderflowsofpersonaldata.htm#memorandum>
262. Ohm, Paul, "Broken Promises of Privacy: Responding to the Surprising Failure of Anonymization" (2009) SSRN Scholarly Paper 1450006
263. Orel, Andrej, & Bernik, Igor, "GDPR and Health Personal Data; Tricks and Traps of Compliance" (2018) 255 Stud. Health Tech. Inf. 155–159

264. Pacini, Cael, Martin, Mary Jill, & Hamilton, Lynda, "At the Interface of Law and Accounting: An Examination of a Trend Toward a Reduction in the Scope of Auditor Liability to Third Parties in the Common Law Countries" (2000) 37:2 Am. Bus. L. J. 171–236 at 178.
265. Packman, Carl, "Our Posthuman Future: Consequences of the Biotechnology Revolution, by Francis Fukuyama. London: Profile Books, 2003." (2009) 21:2 Rethink Marx 317–323.
266. Paul Belleville, "Systemic approach: Definition" online: Dico Agroecologie https://dicoagro-ecologie.fr/en/encyclopedia/systemic-approach/
267. Paul, George, & Baron, Jason, "Information Inflation: Can The Legal System Adapt?" (2007) 13:3 Richmond J. L. Tech. 10.
268. PDP4E Project, "Risk Management" online: PDP4E https://www.pdp4e-project.eu/risk-management/
269. Pentland, Brian T., "Getting comfortable with the numbers: Auditing and the micro-production of macro-order" (1993) 18:7 Acc. Org. Soc. 605–620 at 605–612.
270. Peppet, Scott, "Unraveling Privacy: The Personal Prospectus and the Threat of a Full-Disclosure Future" (2011) Northwest. Univ. L. Rev.
271. Peter, Urwin, "Valuing brands in the UK economy" online: Westminster Business Brands Group <https://westminsterresearch.westminster.ac.uk/item/918qv/valuing-brands-in-the-uk-economy>
272. Piasecki, Sara J., "Legal Admissibility of Electronic Records as Evidence and Implications for Records Management" (1995) 58:1 Am. Arch. 54–64
273. Pieters, Rik G. M., & Raaij, W. Fred Van, "Functions and management of affect: Applications to economic behavior" (1988) 9:2 J Econ. Psychol. 251–282
274. Piras, Luca, Al-Obeidallah, Mohammed Ghazi, Pavlidis, Michalis, et al., "DEFeND DSM: a data scope management service for model-based privacy by design GDPR compliance." online: RGU Repository <https://rgu-repository.worktribe.com/output/1003508/defend-dsm-a-data-scope-management-service-for-model-based-privacy-by-design-gdpr-compliance>
275. Plessis, Jean du, McConvill, James, & Bagaric, Mirko, "Principles of Contemporary Corporate Governance", online: Cambridge Core </core/books/principles-of-contemporary-corporate-governance/73681FC8D4569775FF90843982CD5200>
276. Plutora, "Verification vs. Validation", online: www.plutora.com.
277. Power, Michael K., "Auditing and the production of legitimacy" (2003) 28:4 Acc. Org. Soc. 379–394 at 382.
278. Power, Michael, "Making things auditable" (1996) 21:2 Acc. Org. Soc. 289–315 at 289.
279. Privado, "Best Practices for Data Mapping" online: Privado <https://www.privado.ai/post/gdpr-data-mapping#4>
280. Raab, Charles, "The Meaning of 'Accountability' in the Information Privacy Context" in Guagnin, D., Hempel, L., Ilten, C., et al. eds., *Managing Privacy through Accountability* (London: Palgrave Macmillan, 2012) 15.
281. Raiborn, Cecily, Butler, Janet B., Martin, Kasey, et al., "The Internal Audit Function: A Prerequisite for Good Governance" (2017) 28:2 J. Corp. Acc. Fin. 10–21.
282. Raji, Inioluwa Deborah, Smart, Andrew, White, Rebecca N., et al., "Closing the AI Accountability Gap: Defining an End-to-End Framework for Internal Algorithmic Auditing" (2020) ArXiv200100973 Cs at 4.
283. Reidenberg, Joel R., "Lex Informatica: The Formulation of Information Policy Rules through Technology" (1997) Tex. L. Rev. 553–594 at 553.
284. Reidenberg, Joel, "The Fundamental Role of Privacy and Confidence in the Network" (1995) 30 Wake For. Rev. 105
285. Rhee, Joseph, & Ross, Brian, "Terror Group Gets 'A' Rating From Better Business Bureau?" online: ABC News https://abcnews.go.com/Blotter/business-bureau-best-ratings-money-buy/story?id=12123843
286. Rice, Ronald E., & Borgman, Christine L., "The use of computer-monitored data in information science and communication research" (1983) 34:4 J Am Soc Inf Sci 247–256.

287. Robert Day, "UK Accounting Regulation: An Historical Perspective", online: </paper/UK-Accounting-Regulation%3A-An-Historical-Perspective-Day/cb21aae40a89fb8b6edd8a973498837d77b6a822>.
288. Robert, Baldwin, "Why Rules Don't Work" (1990) Mod. Law Rev. 331.
289. Roberts, John, "The possibilities of accountability" (1991) 16:4 Acc. Org. Soc. 355–368.
290. Rodrigues, Rowena, Barnard-Wills, David, De Hert, Paul, et al., "The future of privacy certification in Europe: an exploration of options under article 42 of the GDPR" (2016) 30 Int. Rev. L. Comput. Tech. 248-270.
291. Rodrigues, Rowena, Wright, David, & Wadhwa, Kush, "Developing a privacy seal scheme (that works)" (2013) 3 Int. Data Priv. L. 100–116.
292. Rose, Nikolas, & Miller, Peter, "Political Power beyond the State: Problematics of Government" (1992) 43:2 Br. J. Sociol. 173–205.
293. Rossiter, C., "How internal audit adds value to the governance process" online: Protiviti https://www.protiviti.com/US-en/insights
294. Sandvig, Christian, Hamilton, Kevin, Karahalios, Karrie, "Auditing Algorithms: Research Methods for Detecting Discrimination on Internet Platforms" (2014) 22 Data Disc. Convert Crit. Conc. Prod. Inq. 4349-4357.
295. Schatzki, Theodore R., "On Organizations as they Happen" (2006) 27:12 Org. Stud. 1863–1873.
296. Schedler, Andreas, "Conceptualizing Accountability" online: BePress <https://works.bepress.com/andreas_schedler/22/>.
297. Schwartz, Paul, "The EU-U.S. Privacy Collision: A Turn to Institutions and Procedures" (2013) Harv. L. Rev. 1966.
298. Search Compliance, "IT Controls" online: Search Compliance https://searchcompliance.techtarget.com/definition/IT-controls.
299. Shapiro, Susan P., "The Social Control of Impersonal Trust" (1987) 93:3 Am. J. Sociol. 623 at 649, 652.
300. Sloot, Bart van der, & Schendel, Sascha van, "Ten Questions for Future Regulation of Big Data: A Comparative and Empirical Legal Study" (2016) 7:2 JIPITEC 124.
301. Spira, Laura F., & Page, Michael, "Risk management: The reinvention of internal control and the changing role of internal audit" (2003) 16:4 Acc. Audit Acc. J. 640–661.
302. Stirling, Andy, "Science, precaution, and the politics of technological risk: converging implications in evolutionary and social scientific perspectives" (2008) 1128 Ann. NY Acad. Sci. 95–110.
303. Stone, Katherine, "Labor and the Corporate Structure: Changing Conceptions and Emerging Possibilities" (1988) 55:1 U. Chic. L. Rev. 146.
304. Stoneburner, Gary, Goguen, Alice, & Feringa, Alexis, "Risk Management Guide for Information Technology Systems" (2002) 800 NIST, Spec. Pub. 800-30.
305. Torre, Matteo La, Dumay, John, & Michele Antonio Rea, "Breaching intellectual capital: critical reflections on Big Data security" (2018) 26:3 Medit. Acc. Res. 463–482 at 464.
306. Trepte, Sabine, Teutsch, Doris, Masur, Philipp K., et al., "Do People Know About Privacy and Data Protection Strategies? Towards the 'Online Privacy Literacy Scale' (OPLIS)" in Gutwirth, Serge, Leenes, Ronald, & Hert, Paul de, eds., *Reforming European Data Protection Law* (Dordrecht: Springer Netherlands, 2015).
307. Trudel, Pierre, "Web 2.0 Regulation: A Risk Management Process" (2009) SSRN Scholarly Paper 1573980.
308. Tsohou, Aggeliki, Magkos, Manos, Mouratidis, Haralambos, et al., "Privacy, Security, Legal and Technology Acceptance Requirements for a GDPR Compliance Platform" (2020). Comput. Secur. 204–223.
309. Turing, A. M., "On Computable Numbers, with an Application to the Entscheidungsproblem" (1937) s2-42:1 Proc Lond Math Soc 230–265
310. Urhc, Erwin J., "The Law Code of Hammurabi" (1929) 15:7 Am. Bar Assoc. J. 437.

311. Viscusi, W Kip, "A Note on 'Lemons' Markets with Quality Certification" (1978) 9:1 Bell J. Econ. 277–279.
312. W3C, online: https://www.w3.org.
313. Wachter, Sandra, Mittelstadt, Brent, & Russell, Chris, "Counterfactual Explanations without Opening the Black Box: Automated Decisions and the GDPR" (2018) ArXiv171100399 Cs.
314. Walsh, James P., & Seward, James K., "On the Efficiency of Internal and External Corporate Control Mechanisms" (1990) 15 Acad. Manag. Rev. 421–458.
315. Warren, Elizabeth, "Bankruptcy Policymaking in an Imperfect World" (1993) 92:2 Mich. L. Rev. 336–387.
316. Watts, Ross L., & Zimmerman, Jerold L., "Positive Accounting Theory: A Ten Year Perspective" (1990) 65 Acc. Rev. 131–156.
317. Westin, Alan, "Privacy And Freedom" (1968) 25 Wash. Lee L. Rev. 166.
318. Whitford, William C., "A Critique of the Consumer Credit Collection System" (1979) 4 Wis. L. Rev. 1047–1144.
319. Wieringa, Maranke, *What to account for when accounting for algorithms: a systematic literature review on algorithmic accountability* (Barcelona, Spain: Association for Computing Machinery, 2020).
320. Wright, David, "The state of the art in privacy impact assessment" (2012) 28:1 Comput. L. Secur. Rev/ 54–61 at 57.
321. Xiaomi, "Introduction of Xiaomi" online: MI <https://www.mi.com/global/about/>
322. OECD, *Recommendation of the Council Concerning Guidelines Governing the Protection of Privacy and Trans-border Flows of Personal Data,* Doc. No. OECD/LEGAL/0422 (2016).
323. Chairman Sir Norman Lindop, *Report of the Committee on Data Protection: Presented to Parliament by the Secretary of State for the Home Department by Command of Her Majesty* (London: H.M.S.O., 1978) at 11-12, para. 2.12.
324. Federal Rules of Evidence, "Rule 1003" online: Rules of Evidence <https://www.rulesofevidence.org/article-x/rule-1003/>.
325. *Guide to the General Data Protection Regulation: Legitimate Interests.* UK Information Commissioner's Office 2018.
326. Council of Europe, Electronic Evidence in Civil and Administrative Proceedings, 2019.
327. American Accounting Association & Committee on Basic Auditing Concepts, A statement of basic auditing concepts, (Sarasota, Fla.: American Accounting Association, 1973.
328. Federal Trade Commission, In the Matter of True Ultimate Standards Everywhere, Inc., a corporation. Agreement containing consent order, 2015.
329. International Standardization Organization: Conformity Assessment: Requirements for Bodies Certifying Products, Processes and Services, EN-ISO/IEC 17065/2012.
330. International Standard Organization: ISO/IEC 31000, Risk Management.
331. Information Systems Audit and Control Association: COBIT5: Control Objectives for Information and Related Technology.
332. ASIA-Pacific Economic Cooperation, APEC Privacy Framework, 2005
333. Canadian Standards Association, Model Code for the Protection of Personal Information, 1996.
334. Guidelines of the Committee of Ministers of the Council of Europe on electronic evidence in civil and administrative proceedings, 2019.
335. Acosta, Maribel et al, eds, Semantic Systems. The Power of AI and Knowledge Graphs: 15th International Conference, SEMANTiCS 2019, Karlsruhe, Germany, September 9–12, 2019, Proceedings, Information Systems and Applications, incl Internet/Web, and HCI (Springer International Publishing, 2019)

Legislation & Jurisprudence

336. *Canadian Personal Information Protection and Electronic Document Act,* S. C. 2000, c. 5.
337. *General Data Protection Regulation,* 2016/679
338. *Personal Information Protection and Electronic Documents Act,* S.C. 2000, c. 5, Schedule 1.
339. *Personal Information Protection Law of the People's Republic of China, 2021*
340. *Data Security Law of the People's Republic of China, 2021*
341. *Bill 64, An Act to Modernize Legislative Provisions as Regards the Protection of Personal Information, National Assembly of Quebec, 2020*
342. *Uniform Electronic Evidence Act of Canada , 1998*
343. *Federal Rules of Evidence, United States of America, 2019.*
344. *Act to Establish a Legal Framework for Information Technology, CQLR, 2021.*
345. *Civil Code of Quebec, CQLR c CCQ,1991*
346. *Brazilian Data Protection Law, National Congress of Brazil,No.13,709, 2018*
347. *Civil Procedure law of People's Republic of China, NPC, 2022*
348. *The protection of individuals with regard to the processing of personal data and on the free movement of such data, Directive 95/46/EC, European Parliament 1995*
349. *Act to establish a legal framework for information technology. CQLR c C-1.1, 2001.*
350. *Bill C-12: An Act amend to the Personal Information Protection and Electronic Documents Act, 1st Sess 41 Parl., 2011*
351. *An Act Respecting the Protection of Personal Information in the Private Sector, RSQ A-2.1*
352. *European Parliament and Council Directive 2002/58/EC of 12 July 2002 concerning the processing of personal data and the protection of privacy in the electronic communications sector, EC, 2002.*
353. *Health Insurance Portability and Accountability Act, ,U.S.C, 1996.*
354. *Privacy Act of 1974, U.S.C, 2000.*
355. *California Consumer Privacy Act, Part 4 of California Civil Code.*
356. *Data Protection Act of United Kingdom, C.12, 2018.*
357. *Single Audit Act of United States, S.1510, 1984.*
358. *On specific requirements regarding statutory audit of public interest entities and repealing Commission Decision, 2005/909/EC, Regulation (EU) No 537/2014.*
359. *Relative à la protection des données personnel's , LOI n° 2018-493.*
360. *Alexander v Cambridge Credit Corp. Ltd.* (1987) 9 NSWL 310.
361. *Opinion 3/2010 on the Principle of Accountability* [2010] 00062/10/EN WP 173.
362. *Google Inc. v. Commission nationale de l'informatique et des libertés (CNIL),* case C-507/17
363. *CNIL v. Facebook, No SAN-2021-024, 2021*
364. *CNIL v. Amazon, No SAN-2020-012, 2020*
365. *Google LLC v. CNIL, Case C-507/17*
366. *Hamburg Commissioner for Data Protection and Freedom of Information v. H&M, 2020.*
367. *ICO v. British Airways, 2020,No. COM0783542*
368. *ICO v. Marriott, 2020, No. COM0804337*
369. *Bulgarian Citizen v. National Revenue Agency of Bulgaria, No. 2606/2021.*
370. *ARTHUR ANDERSEN LLP V. UNITED STATES (04-368) 544 U.S. 696 (2005)*
371. *BMG Canada v. John Doe, 2004, FC 488 (CanLII)*
372. Hangzhou Internet Court (2020), Zhejiang, China, Minchu No.10605
373. Hangzhou Internet Court (2020), Zhejiang, China Minchu No. 10993
374. Hangzhou Internet Court (2021), Zhejiang, China, Minchu No.5426
375. Hangzhou Internet Court (2022), Zhejiang, China, Minchu No. 4330
376. The Cyberspace Administration of China V. Didi Global Co.,Ltd, 2022.

Index

H. Wu, C. Zhang, *Audit the Audit*, https://doi.org/10.1007/978-981-95-2473-0

MIX
Papier aus verantwortungsvollen Quellen
Paper from responsible sources
FSC® C105338

If you have any concerns about our products,
you can contact us on
ProductSafety@springernature.com

In case Publisher is established outside the EU,
the EU authorized representative is:
Springer Nature Customer Service Center GmbH
Europaplatz 3, 69115 Heidelberg, Germany

Printed by Libri Plureos GmbH
in Hamburg, Germany